Perspectives
on Northern Northwest Coast Prehistory

Edited by
Jerome S. Cybulski

Mercury Series
Archaeological Survey of Canada
Paper 160

Published by
Canadian Museum of Civilization

NATIONAL LIBRARY CANADIAN CATALOGUING IN PUBLICATION DATA

Main entry under title:
Perspectives on northern northwest coast prehistory

(Mercury series, ISSN 0316-1854)
(Paper/Archaeological Survey of Canada,
ISSN 0317-2244; no. 160)
"The papers in this volume evolve from a 1996 symposium presented in Halifax, Nova Scotia..."
Introduction.
Includes a resumé in French.
Includes bibliographical references.
ISBN 0-660-17844-3

1. Northwest coast of North America — Antiquities — Congresses.
2. Antiquities, Prehistoric — Northwest coast of North America — Congresses.
3. Native peoples — Northwest coast of North America — Congresses.
4. Excavations (Archaeology) — Northwest coast of North America — Congresses.
I. Cybulski, Jerome S., 1942- .
II. Canadian Museum of Civilization.
III. Archaeological Survey of Canada.
IV. Series.
V. Series: Paper (Archaeological Survey of Canada); no. 160.

E78.N78P47 2001   971.1'01'00497   C2001-980006-1

 PRINTED IN CANADA

Published by
Canadian Museum of Civilization
100 Laurier Street
P.O. Box 3100, Station B
Hull, Quebec
J8X 4H2

Senior production officer: Deborah Brownrigg
Cover design: Roger Langlois Design

Front cover: Excavation in 1968 at the Gitaus site, GdTc-2, Kitselas Canyon, Skeena River (catalog CYB 615) photograph by Jerome Cybulski.

Inset: The warrior's cache excavated at the Boardwalke site, GbTo-31, Prince rupert Harbour (catalog CYB 582) photograph by Jerome Cybulski.

Both excavations were part of the museum's North Coast Prehistory Project directed by Dr. George MacDonald.

OBJECT OF THE MERCURY SERIES

The Mercury Series is designed to permit the rapid dissemination of information pertaining to the disciplines in which the Canadian Museum of Civilization is active. Considered an important reference by the scientific community, the Mercury Series comprises over three hundred specialized publications on Canada's history and prehistory.

Because of its specialized audience, the series consists largely of monographs published in the language of the author.

In the interest of making information available quickly, normal production procedures have been abbreviated. As a result, grammatical and typographical errors may occur. Your indulgence is requested.

Titles in the Mercury Series can be obtained by calling 1-800-555-5621;
by e-mail to <publications@civilization.ca>;
by Internet to
<http://www.cyberboutique.civilization.ca>;
or by writing to:

Mail Order Services
Canadian Museum of Civilization
100 Laurier Street
P.O. Box 3100, Station B
Hull, Quebec J8X 4H2

BUT DE LA COLLECTION MERCURE

La collection Mercure vise à diffuser rapidement le résultat de travaux dans les disciplines qui relèvent des sphères d'activités du Musée canadien des civilisations. Considérée comme un apport important dans la communauté scientifique, la collection Mercure présente plus de trois cents publications spécialisées portant sur l'héritage canadien préhistorique et historique.

Comme la collection s'adresse à un public spécialisé, celle-ci est constituée essentiellement de monographies publiées dans la langue des auteurs.

Pour assurer la prompte distribution des exemplaires imprimés, les étapes de l'édition ont été abrégées. En conséquence, certaines coquilles ou fautes de grammaire peuvent subsister : c'est pourquoi nous réclamons votre indulgence.

Vous pouvez vous procurer les titres parus dans la collection Mercure par téléphone, en appelant au 1 800 555-5621,
par courriel, en adressant votre demande à <publications@civilisations.ca>, par Internet, à <http://www.cyberboutique.civilisations.ca> ou par la poste, en écrivant au :

Service des commandes postales
Musée canadien des civilisations
100, rue Laurier
C.P. 3100, succursale B
Hull (Québec) J8X 4H2

ABSTRACT

Thirteen scientists provide insight into the archaeology of the north coast of British Columbia in celebration of field work begun by George F. MacDonald for the National Museum of Canada in 1966. A decade of field seasons saw excavation at 18 sites representing 5000 years of human occupation. Dr. MacDonald and the editor introduce the volume and provide an overview of fieldwork at Prince Rupert Harbour where most of the archaeology was done. Following chapters investigate paleoenvironmental influences on human settlement, theoretical concepts involved in northern Northwest Coast research, and the interplay of Aboriginal oral traditions and archaeological findings. Consideration is given to the biological relationships of ancient and historic human populations, preserved organics and their role in the identification of ethnicity, zooarchaeological remains and their bearing on subsistence and seasonality, the emergence and maintenance of ranked society, and protohistoric competition and trade. A final chapter treats the crucial issues of site preservation and increasing First Nations involvement.

RÉSUMÉ

Treize scientifiques se penchent sur l'archéologie du nord de la côte de la Colombie-Britannique en l'honneur des premières fouilles entreprises par George F. MacDonald pour le compte du Musée national du Canada, en 1966. Une décennie de fouilles a permis de mettre au jour 18 sites représentant 5000 ans d'occupation humaine. MM. MacDonald et Cybulski présentent l'ouvrage et donnent un aperçu des travaux archéologiques effectués à Prince Rupert Harbour, où a eu lieu la majeure partie des fouilles. Les chapitres subséquents étudient les contextes paléoenvironnementaux qui ont eu une incidence sur les établissements humains, les concepts théoriques en présence dans la recherche concernant le nord de la côte ouest ainsi que l'interaction entre les traditions orales amérindiennes et les découvertes archéologiques. On y traite des liens biologiques entre les populations humaines anciennes et historiques, des éléments organiques conservés et de leur rôle dans l'établissement de l'ethnicité, des restes zooarchéologiques et de leur rapport avec la subsistance et les cycles saisonniers, de l'émergence et du maintien d'une société hiérarchisée ainsi que de la concurrence et du commerce protohistoriques. Un dernier chapitre examine la question fondamentale de la préservation des sites et de l'implication croissante des Premières Nations.

CONTENTS

Defending the Mouth of the Skeena: Perspectives on Tsimshian Tlingit Relations 61

Susan Marsden

Human Biological Relationships for the Northern Northwest Coast 107

Jerome S. Cybulski

North Coast Prehistory - Reflections From Northwest Coast Wet Site Research 145

Dale R. Croes

Prospects and Opportunities for Archaeological Site Management in the Prince Rupert Harbour Area

Bjorn O. Simonsen

LIST OF CONTRIBUTORS

David J.W. Archer is an Anthropology/Sociology Instructor and Associate Academic Head at Northwest Community College, 130-1ˢᵗ Avenue, Prince Rupert, BC, Canada V8J 1A8.

Gary Coupland is an Associate Professor of Anthropology at the University of Toronto, Sidney Smith Hall, 100 St. George Street, Toronto, ON, Canada M5S 1A1.

Dale R. Croes is Professor of Anthropology at South Puget Sound Community College, Anthropology MS101, 2011 Mottman Road Southwest, Olympia, WA, U.S.A. 98512.

Jerome S. Cybulski is Curator of Physical Anthropology at the Archaeological Survey of Canada, Canadian Museum of Civilization, 100 Laurier Street, P.O. Box 3100, Station B, Hull, Quebec, Canada J8X 4H2.

Knut R. Fladmark is Professor of Archaeology at Simon Fraser University, 8888 University Drive, Burnaby, BC, Canada V5A 1S6.

George F. MacDonald is Chief Executive Officer of Museum Victoria and Director of the Melbourne Museum, GPO Box 666E, Melbourne 3001, VIC, Australia.

Susan Marsden is Registrar and Acting Director of the Museum of Northern British Columbia, 100 First Avenue, P.O. Box 669, Prince Rupert, BC, Canada V8J 3S1.

Andrew R.C. Martindale is an Assistant Professor in the Department of Anthropology, McMaster University, 1280 Main Street West, Hamilton, ON, Canada L8S 4L9.

Paul Prince is an Anthropology Instructor at Trent University, Peterborough, ON, Canada K9J 7B8.

Bjorn O. Simonsen is Principal of Bastion Group Heritage Consultants, 109 Kenneth Street, P.O. Box 670, Duncan, BC, Canada V9L 3Y1.

Frances L. Stewart is Honourary Research Associate in Anthropology at the University of New Brunswick, P. O. Box 4400, Fredericton, NB, Canada E3B 5A3.

Kathlyn M. Stewart is a Research Scientist with the Canadian Museum of Nature, P.O. Box 3443, Station B, Ottawa, ON, Canada K1P 6P4.

Patricia D. Sutherland is Curator of the Helluland Archaeology project at the Archaeological Survey of Canada, Canadian Museum of Civilization, 100 Laurier Street, P.O. Box 3100, Station B, Hull, Quebec, Canada J8X 4H2.

Introduction: The Prince Rupert Harbour Project

George F. MacDonald & Jerome S. Cybulski

ABSTRACT

The Prince Rupert Harbour Project began in 1966 as part of a larger effort building on work initiated immediately after World War I by Harlan I. Smith, Diamond Jenness and Marius Barbeau of the National Museum of Canada (Canadian Museum of Civilization). The excavation program was designed to add time depth to the incredibly rich ethnohistorical record then compiled. Village sites, resource-linked seasonal camps, and fortified sites were sampled, resulting in a 5000-year cultural sequence. Aims of the program were to (1) record the development of the distinctive settlement pattern and architectural features known at the period of historic contact; (2) study development of the distinctive material culture known at that time, particularly in wood and perishable materials; and (3) document the physical anthropology of the harbour in part to detect if intrusive populations had inhabited the area at any time over the last five millennia as suggested in the mythology.

RÉSUMÉ

Le projet de Prince Rupert Harbour débuta en 1966 en partie pour poursuivre l'initiative entreprise immédiatement après la première guerre mondiale par Harlan I. Smith, Diamond Jenness et Marius Barbeau du Musée national du Canada (Musée canadien des civilisations). Les fouilles visaient à placer dans un cadre temporel l'enregistrement ethnologique, incroyablement riche, déjà compilé. Les sites des anciens villages, camps saisonniers établis en fonction des ressources, et les sites fortifiés ont été échantillonnés et ont révélé une séquence culturelle longue de 5000 ans. Les objectifs du programme consistaient à (1) retracer l'évolution des modes d'établissement et des éléments architecturaux caractéristiques

In *Perspectives on Northern Northwest Coast Prehistory*, edited by Jerome S. Cybulski. Hull: Canadian Museum of Civilization, Archaeological Survey of Canada, Mercury Series Paper 160, pp. 1-23, © 2001.

connus à la période historique de contact; (2) à étudier l'épanouissement de la culture matérielle connue à cette époque, particulièrement les objets en bois et en matière périssable; et (3) à documenter l'anthropologie physique des gens du port partiellement pour détecter si, comme le suggère la mythologie, des populations intruses avaient habité la région à un moment donné au cours des cinq derniers millénaires.

INTRODUCTION

The papers in this volume evolve from a 1996 symposium presented in Halifax, Nova Scotia, at the twenty-ninth Annual Meeting of the Canadian Archaeological Association. The symposium, "Perspectives on Northern Northwest Coast Prehistory, 1966-1996," was organized by Patricia Sutherland and Jerome Cybulski to commemorate the thirtieth anniversary of George MacDonald's inception of National Museum of Canada archaeological work on the north coast of British Columbia. Prior to 1966, little archaeology had been done in the region. Through ten field seasons, 18 sites were excavated and many more identified through survey. Major excavations were focused at Prince Rupert Harbour, known to archaeologists since early in the twentieth century for the existence of large prehistoric shell middens (Smith 1909). Ten sites were investigated from 1966 to 1973 and an eleventh salvage-excavated in 1978 (MacDonald and Inglis 1981: Table 2). These eleven excavations constitute the "Prince Rupert Harbour Project."

This chapter of the volume provides an overview of the project. The papers on human biology by Jerome Cybulski, prehistoric subsistence by Kathlyn Stewart and Frances Stewart, and wet site research by Dale Croes focus on materials recovered at the time and weigh them in contemporary terms. The paper by Patricia Sutherland re-examines a significant theoretical framework for the Prince Rupert Harbour Project, the "North Coast interaction sphere," while Susan Marsden's discourse on Tsimshian-Tlingit relations examines related elements from the perspective of native oral tradition.

Other North Coast areas were investigated during the Prince Rupert Harbour Project, and additional or related fieldwork has been carried out in the region since 1973/1978. The papers by David Archer, by Gary Coupland, Andrew Martindale and Susan Marsden, and by Paul Prince reflect the continuing efforts. Knut Fladmark's treatise provides the environmental framework for northern Northwest Coast archaeology with emphasis on early habitation possibilities, and Bjorn Simonsen's contribution examines the crucial public issue of archaeological site management and the increasing involvement of First Nations. For supplementary research and other site information, the reader is referred to the synthesis of North Coast archaeology by Gary Coupland (1993) and two recent volumes on Northwest Coast archaeology as a whole. The books by R.G. Matson and Gary Coupland (1995) and by Kenneth Ames and Herbert Maschner (1999) give insight into current thought on the prehistory of the northern Northwest Coast including southeast Alaska, the Queen Charlotte Islands, and the Nass River and Skeena River regions. In the latter work, Kenneth Ames especially provides significant information on the Prince Rupert Harbour Project sites, drawing on his own experience as a field crew member and excavation supervisor during the early years and, later, his research on the artifacts discovered in the sites (see also Ames 1976 and works referenced elsewhere in this volume).

The contributors to the present volume were asked to update and expand their manuscripts as they saw fit given the time lapsed since the 1996 symposium and the inception of subsequent research. All complied and, therefore, each contribution here is a significant elaboration of the original presentation. Professor Madonna L. Moss of the University of Oregon served as a discussant in the symposium, providing valuable commentary. We regret that due to time constraints in the preparation of this volume, we were unable to incorporate her comments, this through no fault of her own. We thank all of the contributors for their hard work and Patricia Sutherland for her help with the early stages of the volume.

THE PRINCE RUPERT HARBOUR PROJECT

The Prince Rupert Harbour Project was an outgrowth of intensive anthropological work along the Skeena River instituted immediately after World War I by Harlan I. Smith, Diamond Jenness and Marius Barbeau of the National Museum of Canada (today's Canadian Museum of Civilization). The fieldwork included limited archaeological survey by Harlan Smith (1929), expanding on that he had done previously for the American Museum of Natural History (Smith 1909)[1]. However, the major portion of the Skeena River project was devoted to the study of ethnohistory (e.g., Barbeau 1929), a phase which blossomed in the 1920's but ceased during the Depression and Second World War. When appointed West

---

[1] In the 1960's, Katherine Capes, while in the employ of the National Museum of Canada, compiled a list of British Columbia archaeological sites described by Harlan Smith from his fieldwork, the information of native informants, and the work of other investigators. Up to 55 sites were reported for "Region I: Nass River to Skeena River: Tsimshian Territory" (Capes 1976).

Coast Archaeologist at the Canadian Museum of Civilization in the mid-1960's, one of George MacDonald's goals was to add time depth or archaeological perspective to the incredibly rich ethnohistoric record compiled earlier.

The extensive shell middens of Prince Rupert Harbour were tested to some extent by Philip Drucker in the 1930's (Drucker 1943). In the 1950's, James Baldwin, a local high school student, revisited those sites and, with Professor Charles Borden of the University of British Columbia, excavated at Co-op, GbTo-10. That site, for which a detailed report was prepared by Gay Calvert (1968), an early Prince Rupert Project crew member, was later identified to be part of Lachane (GbTo-33), a Project midden located at the south end of the city (MacDonald and Inglis 1981:43).

Fig. 1. Shell midden at Garden Island (GbTo-23) exposed by wave action in 1966. (Photo by G.F. MacDonald).

EXCAVATIONS

The 1966 excavation program of the National Museum of Canada began with a small survey and testing crew. Radiocarbon samples collected that year indicated the deepest sites were as much as 5000 years old (MacDonald 1969). A main focus of the research plan was to record the development of the distinctive settlement pattern and architectural features of precontact period communities in the context of the ranked social order of the peoples of the northern coast. A second aim was to document the development of their distinctive material culture, particularly in wood and perishable materials. A third aim of the project was to document the physical anthropology of the harbour populations, particularly to detect if intrusive populations had inhabited the area at any time over the last five millennia, as suggested in the mythology (MacDonald 1969).

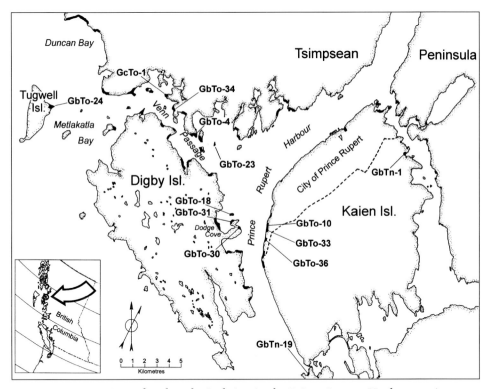

Fig. 2. Locations of archaeological sites in the Prince Rupert Harbour region discussed in the text. (Modified from a drawing by D.W. Laverie).

Excavations commenced in the summer of 1966 on Garden Island (GbTo-23) at the end of Venn Passage directly opposite the city of Prince Rupert. Heavy ferry traffic to and from Alaska had eroded the eastern face of the island providing for the study of long, deep shell midden exposures (Fig. 1). Burials were also eroding from the bank, requiring salvage work. With a crew of three, a vertical face was excavated which revealed a pattern typical of many of the sites in the harbour.

Occasional lithic artifacts were encountered at the base of the midden in sands overlying a marine clay. Between these basal sands and the midden proper was a black organic layer averaging 10 cm in thickness and containing only lithic remains. On top of the organic layer, the lowest shell deposits, ranging from 30 to 50 cm deep, were solely made up of highly fragmented pieces of *Mytilus edulis*. Above this were two to three metres of loose deposits of basket cockle, horse clam, other clam species, and a variety of other shellfish remains including barnacle and blue mussel.

Fig. 3. The Boardwalk site (GbTo-31) in 1968, looking east from Dodge Cove. (Photo by J.S. Cybulski).

Excavations were continued on Garden Island in 1967 and begun on Dodge Island (GbTo-18), a site less prone to stormbound conditions and closer to facilities at Norwegian Village in Dodge Cove, Digby Island (Fig. 2). GbTo-18 proved to have very disturbed deposits due to grading and excavations done early in the twentieth century for the construction of a wartime quarantine hospital for the Prince Rupert area and, later, use of the site for flower and vegetable gardens. Patricia Sutherland (1978) undertook analysis of the artifact collection from

Dodge Island while Jerome Cybulski undertook analysis of human burials recovered from this site along with those recovered from Garden Island and, later, other Prince Rupert Harbour sites (e.g., Cybulski, 1974, 1978, 1992; this volume).

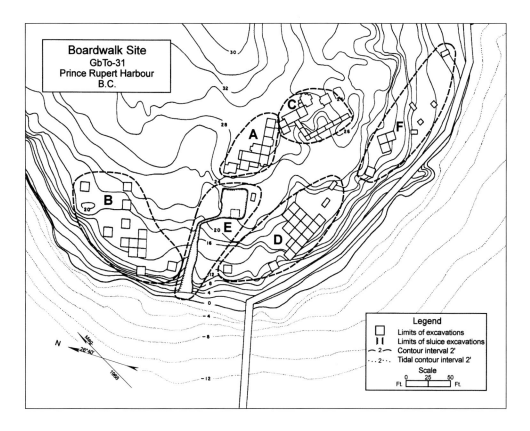

Fig. 4. Boardwalk site plan. (From a 1969 drawing by T. Kobayashi).

In 1968, excavations began at a more pristine, nearby midden deposit which became known as the Boardwalk site (GbTo-31). In contrast to the first two, this site had only minor disturbance on its margins where posts for a boardwalk had been sunk and a path had been cleared for a bridge to the hospital on Dodge Island. Over most of its three-acre surface, the topography of the last occupation of Boardwalk was intact, including a row of deep house depressions. The only significant problem with the excavation was a dense stand of hemlock and spruce trees whose roots formed a formidable protective network through the top half-metre of the site (Fig. 3).

The Boardwalk site was investigated over three consecutive field seasons. An initial trench line was excavated in alternating 10-foot squares from the high water line on the north side of a small stream bed, designated as Area B (Fig. 4). Another block of squares was excavated on the south side of the stream into a flat terrace (Area D). A third excavation to the southeast (Area C) included a five-foot-wide trench positioned to cut across three house depressions and adjacent ridges. Other squares were excavated into the mound of deposits at the rear and north of these house depressions (Areas A and C).

BURIALS

Close to 100 human burials were encountered on the site, most in the deep midden ridges behind the house depressions.[2] The excellent state of preservation of many of the skeletal remains and the impression of a whole cemetery initially suggested that this was a site abandoned a few centuries before native contact with Europeans. Subsequent radiocarbon dates indicated, however, that the latest graves were closer to 2000 years old.

Early on in the excavation of Boardwalk, it seemed clear that warfare played a significant role in the lives and deaths of the people buried there. Several separately found human skulls initially suggested this insofar as they implied trophy heads severed from slain enemies. The idea of warfare was reinforced by the discovery in the centre of one Area A excavation unit of a suspected warrior's cache of artifacts in the same pit as an articulated skull and mandible lacking other skeletal parts (MacDonald 1983). The cache (Fig. 5), originally thought to be much older but now dated to about 1800 years B.P. (Cybulski 1993), included copper-wrapped cedar sticks which could have been the remnants of rod armour similar to that worn by Tsimshian warriors 1500 years later (MacDonald and Cove 1987). Other elements in the cache probably represented weaponry for hand-to-hand combat. Evidence for the latter in the form of skeletal and dental fractures was frequent among the Prince Rupert Harbour midden burials (Cybulski 1999).

---

[2] A minimum of 120 individuals were ultimately determined as represented in the Boardwalk skeletal collection, including intact and partly intact burials and disturbed remains (Cybulski 1992:41-44).

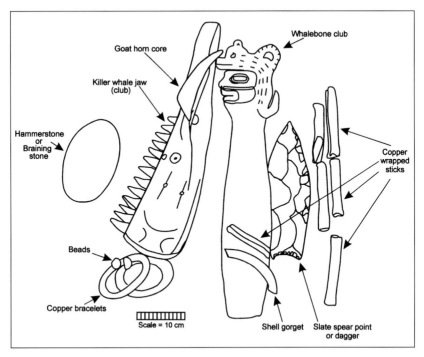

Fig. 5. Warrior's cache in Area A of the Boardwalk site. (From a 1968 field sketch by G.F. MacDonald).

Many of the Boardwalk burials, as well as those at other sites, appeared to have been placed in boxes. Aside from the tightly flexed attitudes of most skeletons, there was direct evidence in five cases in the form of preserved wood fragments. An additional, novel finding was that partial or complete whitish clay outlines accompanied eight other skeletons (Fig. 6). This may indicate a secondary use of food storage boxes for burial (Cybulski 1992:52-59). According to one source, the Tsimshian used clay to seal the seams of boxes used to store meat (Robinson and Wright 1962:41).

TRADE

There was ample evidence for long distance trade at the Boardwalk site, principally among items associated with human burials (Table 1). Copper from Alaska, dentalium shells from the southern Northwest Coast, sea otter teeth from Haida Gwaii, obsidian from the interior, and amber from Russia and possibly other sources indicate that trade was a significant factor in the economy of the residents of Prince Rupert Harbour from at least Period II times, ca. 3500 to 1500 B.P. As part of the project, a much more extensive picture of prehistoric trade in the area was compiled from ethnohistoric sources, particularly from the work of William Beynon, a Tsimshian scholar of Port Simpson (see Marsden, this volume, for references). His grandfather, Arthur Wellington Clah, born in 1835, not long after initial European - native contact on the coast, was the first literate Tsimshian historian. Based on their data, known trading trails and lists of trade goods were published as Plate 13 in Volume I of the *Historical Atlas of Canada* (MacDonald, Coupland and Archer 1987). More than 30 trails were mapped which connected Prince Rupert Harbour to regions as far away as Yukon Territory.

Fig. 6. Burial 525 in Unit G6, Area B, of the Boardwalk site. Note the partial box outline formed of white clay. The large rock may have been used to secure the lid of the box. Large rocks, boulders or slabs were associated with 49% of the Prince Rupert Harbour Project burials, to secure lids, to mark graves, or as cairns (Cybulski 1992:59-60). (Photo by J.S. Cybulski).

SURVEY AND FAUNAL REMAINS

During the first and second Boardwalk site field seasons and again in 1972, small scale excavation and testing was carried out at a shell midden on Parizeau Point (GbTo-30) where field crews had been lodged in an old doctor's residence associated with the quarantine hospital. Collagen-based radiocarbon dates of 2250 ± 75 years B.P. (S-2548) and 1460 ± 75 years B.P. (S-2549) bracketed 12 human burials represented among the collected materials. Non-human faunal remains and up to 400 artifacts were also collected but have not yet been studied in detail.

Table 1. Artifact associations with human burials of the Prince Rupert Harbour Project.

Burial	Sex	Age at death	Artifact descriptions and remarks
			Dodge Island site (zGbTo-18):
166	Male	20-24 yr.	Stone labret between folded right hand and distal left forearm
170	Male	25-29 yr.	Ground slate knife or dagger 20 cm long on chest in line with spinal column and pointing toward the head; skeleton flexed on back
179	??	6-9 mos.	Two pieces of split animal bone, possibly blanket pins
416	Male	45-49 yr.	"Lid of box inset with sea-otter teeth"
			Garden Island site (GbTo-23):
183	Male	30-39 yr.	Stone labret between femur shafts (skeleton incomplete); two bone points 0.30 m E of knees
			Boardwalk site (GbTo-31):
322	Male	17-20 yr.	Necklace of 250 shell disc beads, 25 dentalium shells, amber bead 1.5 cm long, and a copper-wrapped wood bead 1.4 cm long; cylinder-like cedar segment 5.6 cm long; ankle bracelet of dentalium shells; copper stains on posterior skull, manubrium, proximal end of left humerus, distal end of left radius, and left carpals
325	Male	12-16 yr.	Thin copper disc earring, 2.5 cm in diameter, on each side of skull; 38 amber beads 0.3 to 0.9 cm long; large amber bead 2.7 cm long; large pendant with band of fibres under one disc; three shell gorgets, one with scalloped edge; copper stains on temporals, left mandibular ramus, left clavicle and scapula, and third and fourth cervical vertebrae
350	Male	22-28 yr.	Shell gorget 7.5 cm long on torso; bone point 8.4 cm long next to posterior part of head
370a	Male	60-69 yr.	Stone labret near facial skeleton
371	??	7-8 yr.	Three bear canine teeth reported with left tibia, two at medial and one at lateral side of distal end, suggesting an ankle bracelet
375	Male	22-28 yr.	Three parts of two apparent trophy skulls
390	Male	22-28 yr.	Twenty-two amber beads 0.3 to 1.5 cm long reportedly scattered near the skull and thought to represent a necklace
399	Male	30-39 yr.	Bone dagger 15.2 cm long, cobble tool 10.5 by 6.5 cm, and 200 sea otter teeth reported with skeleton
410	Male	60-69 yr.	Carved stone bird ("raven") pendant between two right ribs; worked bone fragments on left ilium
412	Female	35-44 yr.	Red stain, possibly ochre, on lateral end of right clavicle

(**Table 1.** *continued*)

Burial	Sex	Age at death	Artifact descriptions and remarks
			(**Boardwalk site (GbTo-31) continued**)
521	Male	20-24 yr.	Four copper-wrapped cedar cylinders, each 6 cm long, large amber bead 1.7 cm long, and large amber pendant 2 cm long found near skull; copper stains on parts of facial skeleton, right upper limb, left clavicle, and sternum
525	Male	30-39 yr.	Stone labret at front of jaw; retouched chert flake; bone needle fragment; animal bone epiphysis; quartz flakes on rock covering skeleton; whitish clay outline of box
			Lachane site (GbTo-33):
489	Female	35-44 yr.	Fluted, bilaterally side-notched bone projectile point on sternum, possibly a pendant; skeleton fully extended on back
			Baldwin site (GbTo-36):
505	Male	35-44 yr.	Zoomorphic stone labret "between long bones and fingers—near mandible"
512	Male	35-44 yr.	Reportedly associated quartz flake, cobble chopper, another flake, and hammerstone
515	Male	30-39 yr.	Bone points placed in mouth and lodged in ear holes
516	Female	17-20 yr.	Ground slate mirror (described as "abrader/palette" in artifact catalogue) reported beneath rib cage

In addition to the inside coastal sites of Prince Rupert Harbour, limited work was carried on at the outer coast site of GbTp-1 in the Lucy Islands group of Chatham Sound. It was thought that faunal samples from this site might reflect different exploitation strategies between inner and outer harbour locations. Only limited data are available at this time. As part of the interest in research on faunal remains, a large comparative collection, ranging from hummingbirds to whales, was assembled as part of the Prince Rupert Harbour Project primarily through the efforts of Howard Savage and Frances Stewart (Stewart and Stewart, this volume).

Site location surveys continued throughout the course of the project, adding 20 sites to the lists assembled by Harlan Smith, Philip Drucker, and James Baldwin. Survey and testing has continued to the present day with the research of David Archer, one of the veterans from the earliest years of the project, whose fieldwork in the 1980's added 71 sites to the previous harbour inventory of 100 (Archer 1992). His systematic dating of surface deposits from many of those midden sites also indicated that a substantial number were abandoned in the first few centuries of the Christian era and never reoccupied. Other changes in settlement pattern bearing on the elucidation of social ranking in the archaeological record were also suggested by this work (Archer, this volume). The Boardwalk site appears to have been one example of a temporary population exodus from the area. It appears that the harbour was gradually reoccupied sometime before the era of native contact with Europeans until nine winter village tribes moved to the Hudson's Bay Company post built just north of Port Simpson in 1834. An opportunity for the Tsimshian to become intermediaries in the trade generated at the post and secure safety from marauding Queen Charlotte Islanders saw the Prince Rupert Harbour virtually abandoned again in the middle decades of the nineteenth century.

PRESERVED ORGANICS

In 1972, industrial development plans for the total destruction of a very important site adjacent to the Co-op fish plant launched a sizable rescue project on the south edge of Prince Rupert. Excavation of the Lachane, or Reservoir shell midden (GbTo-33) led to the discovery of an area of numerous artifacts made of preserved organic materials. Earlier excavations at the Ozette site on the Olympic Peninsula of Washington state had demonstrated the existence of wet site environments at Pacific coastal shell middens (Daugherty 1973; Gleeson and Grosso 1976). In fact, the coincidence of large scale man-made site deposition at these locations was bound to block drainage of the fresh water streams that were primary factors for the establishment of village sites.

During the 1969 excavations at the Boardwalk site, water saturated deposits were noted in Area E and excavated with the aid of high power water hoses capable of washing away the thick organic deposits in such trapped stream beds. House planks and a variety of wooden artifacts were uncovered, providing experience with the techniques of hydraulic excavation that proved useful on a larger scale at Lachane in 1973.

Richard Inglis, another early veteran of the Prince Rupert Harbour Project, took charge of the Lachane site excavations (Inglis 1974). Much of the field effort was initially devoted to salvaging evidence from the shell deposits but sampling with hydraulics in the stream bed which bisected the site (Area C) proved increasingly rewarding. The operation there resulted in an outstanding collection of unique artifacts spanning almost a millennium of site use (Inglis 1976). More than 400 objects of wood and fibre were recovered along with even larger numbers of worked wood fragments and partially processed raw materials including spruce root bundles ready for the weaver. All of the artifacts underwent extensive treatment in polyethylene glycol at the Canadian Conservation Institute in Ottawa but, unfortunately, required several years to consolidate. By the time they were returned to the National Museum's Archaeological Survey of Canada division for analysis, staff were committed to other research projects. Hence, except for the basketry which has been studied by Dale Croes (1989), no thorough research assessment has yet been made of the wooden artifacts which provide one of the most complete single site samples yet found on the coast of British Columbia.

As demonstrated elsewhere in this volume, the analysis of the basketry has so far provided the best evidence for continuity of the Tsimshian speaking peoples on the northern coast of British Columbia. Dale Croes has analyzed over seventy basket remains and compared them with extensive museum collections of Tlingit and Haida basketry. The latter two language groups make their baskets from spruce roots and begin with circular bases. Tsimshian baskets on the other hand use flat splints of cedar bark and even round baskets are built with a square checkered base. Rim treatments are equally distinct between the Haida and Tlingit baskets on the one hand and the Tsimshian on the other. Generally, Tsimshian basket rims are much more elaborate than those of either the Tlingit or Haida. The Tsimshian prefer open work and crenulated rims. As Dale Croes has demonstrated, and others elsewhere on the coast, the major language communities coincide with traditional basket weaving patterns. In fact, baskets can yield numbers of attributes similar to those of the rim sherds of pottery and might profitably be used for seriation studies if large enough samples could be obtained for statistical validity.

While the wooden objects of Lachane have not been thoroughly described, a summary provided by Richard Inglis (1976) included the following inventory. There were woodworking tools such as elbow adze handles, straight shafted chisel handles in a range of sizes, and about 80 wedges, many with their cedar root collars still intact. Finished wooden products included parts of wooden planks and posts as well as a number of bent boxes up to about a three-litre size and carved wooden bowls, some still in the early stages of manufacture. One of the surprising features of the heavier wood-working was the smooth and broad cross grain cuts that would seem impossible to have accomplished with mussel shell adze blades. They were not also made with stone tools unless the blades were very thin ones made of jade.

Hunting equipment in the Lachane site included parts of bows and arrow shafts as well as clubs and harpoon shafts. Strangely, there were no parts of halibut hooks which were very common in historic Tsimshian communities. Women's utensils, in addition to the basketry, included impressive digging sticks with large knobs and (or) flanges on top and ranging down in size to small root digging sticks. There were a large number of curved sticks up to a metre in length with rounded points at either end which were probably drying sticks for fish and other meat. Some very large wooden labrets were found which once held shell inlays. Surprisingly, there was little decorated wood from the Lachane site in comparison with the Ozette collection. However, the Ozette village was a thriving community which had been effectively stopped in time by a mud slide, whereas all of the Lachane material appears to have been discarded or lost in the stream bed.

A few exceptions to the above include an intriguing zoomorphic handle that was once mortised with two square pegs to the lid of a container (illustrated in Inglis 1976:178). It is noteworthy that the mortise and tenon technique extends back on this basis more than a millennium on the North Coast; peat surrounding the handle was radiocarbon dated at 1630 ± 100 years B.P. (S-808; ibid.). Kerfing of joints for making steamed cedar boxes is also represented in one or more examples as are lap joints that were once bound together, as with spruce root, or pegged with hardwood dowels.

Cedar and birch bark were also recovered from Lachane and included several examples of cedar bark trays with rims reinforced with spruce root withers. The bark had been folded at the ends to form the walls of the container giving credence to Bill Holm's speculation that the slope-sided wooden food trays of the North Coast were copies in wood of earlier trays and boxes made of folded bark and associated with peoples of the Interior (Holm 1983:72). Virtually identical ethnographic examples are in the collections of the Canadian Museum of Civilization from Dene groups in British Columbia and the Yukon as well as from the Kwakiutl.

Wooden paddles with pointed blades and crutch handles were represented in the sample but no canoe parts could be identified. It is a shame to note that possibly as much as two-thirds of the Lachane wet site deposit still remained when the developer's bulldozers moved in for the coup de grâce for the site. Wooden artifacts without provenience were collected from the bulldozed ridges for several weeks after the archaeological crew was evicted. It was a unique deposit that would have justified several years more excavation and would surely have yielded a much more complete picture of early wood and fibre material culture in the region.

It is highly probable, however, that there are many more wet sites yet to be excavated at Prince Rupert Harbour. Many old stream beds on village sites have been completely covered over with later midden deposits as was the case at the Musqueam Northeast site (DhRt-4) in Vancouver (Borden 1976). One such locality in the harbour that appears to have all of the indicators of a very large wet site is at the western end of Roberson Point, Venn Passage, where a stream had been dammed by accumulated midden deposits (site GbTo-4). It is now an embayment of skunk cabbage and other moisture loving plants. A survey specifically to locate wet site deposits is in order for the harbour. Current microsampling techniques afforded by the AMS method would allow artifacts to be accurately dated with little appreciable damage to the piece, of special importance when the pieces are elaborately decorated ones.

HOUSES

In 1971 and 1972, Richard Inglis (1971, 1972, 1973) excavated early historic period house structures at two sites in Venn Passage. They were the K'nu site (GcTo-1), opposite the historic central village of Metlakatla, and Kitandach (GbTo-34), to the southeast. The house feature at K'nu measured 50' x 45', and included ten large posts, the two largest at 3.5' in diameter. The house at Kitandach measured 45' x 45', and included eight posts varying from 2.5' to 3' in diameter (Inglis 1973). It was undoubtedly the house of the head chief of the Gitando tribe who, in the 1800's at least, was chief Skagwait. The house was marked by a clear large central depression in which the timbers which served to create a retaining wall around the fire pit were still mostly intact as was much of the floor planking around the fireplace (Fig. 7). A remarkable feature of the house was the presence of double posts holding up two massive timbers which supported the roof. Ethnohistorical accounts suggest that one of the double posts on each side may have been older carved posts relocated from Metlakatla.

Reverend William Duncan lead the Tsimshian from Fort Simpson back to Metlakatla in 1862 largely to Christianize them but also to save them from the smallpox which was ravaging the coast and had reached Fort Simpson in May of that year (Usher 1974; Boyd 1999:193-199). As part of the recolonization effort, Duncan noted in his diary that all of the old village sites near Metlakatla were cleared of vegetation and that the house pits were leveled to create vegetable gardens. Undoubtedly, this process included tearing down old house remains that were abandoned there decades earlier and using the boards and other debris to fill the house pits.

Fig. 7. Excavation of historic period house at Kitandach (GbTo-34) in 1971. (Photo by R.I. Inglis).

ART

The evidence for artistic development in the Prince Rupert Harbour begins with geometric decorations on possible brow bands, drinking tubes that may have been associated with puberty rituals, and some women's utensils. Equally early in the Prince Rupert II phase were examples of zoomorphic art inscribed on silt stone concretions. They may relate to Shamanic practices intended to encourage the annual return of fish and game. The use of joint marks and suggestions of internal organs on the incised figures are also very early features which have a separate history in Siberian traditions (e.g., Arutiunov and Fitzhugh 1988).

Totemic art, in the sense of the use of crest animals, birds or fish, only manifests itself in the last 1500 years. It is logical that it correlates with social ranking as emblems of clan affiliation and solidarity. One exception could be a raven pendant with Burial 410 at the Boardwalk site which was collagen dated at 2575 ± 125 (S-1432). However, students of comparative mythology have speculated that the Raven cycle may date back to the first millennium in the Bering Straits area, and not be part of the lineage crest system.

A final correlate may be drawn from David Archer's observation (personal communication to G.F. MacDonald 1997) that sites dating before A.D. 100 do not have significant petroglyphs associated with them although later sites do. The most significant petroglyphs appear to be located at prime locations in the passage of schools of salmon, where shaman could intercede in the passage of the fish via rituals like the first salmon ceremonies described by Boas (1916) for the first canyon of the Skeena at Kitselas. At this petroglyph site, the shaman is predominantly an x-ray skeletal style in communication with bear spirits in which their internal organs are also emphasized (Walker 1979).

Recent archaeology in Southeast Alaska and Haida Gwaii have begun to produce a new source of evidence on the development of the distinctive art style of the north coast. This time the evidence comes from dry cave sites which were used either for temporary camps or for burial purposes. Burial caves and remote shamans' grave houses on the north coast have yielded many museum specimens that exhibit a very archaic style. A box recovered from a burial cave in Southeast Alaska has recently been dated at about 700 years B.P. (Irish 2000). There are several dozen similar boxes or box fragments on the storage shelves of North American museums which will probably provide a bridge into the prehistoric phase of North Coast art styles. A burial box was excavated at the Gust Island rock shelter in Skidegate Inlet on Haida Gwaii which might provide a test for this supposition (MacDonald 1973).[3] Many dry caves exist on the West Coast of Haida Gwaii and Prince of Wales Island that will contribute to a further documentation of the development of northern Northwest Coast art over the next few decades.

It is clear to students of the ethnographic material culture of North Coast peoples that many private and institutional collections contain boxes, bowls, spoons and other decorated items which are more than two centuries old. Their preservation is a function of their care by owners who protect them as heirlooms and sometimes as trophies of war hidden away in chests for occasional display purposes. The first pieces collected by Israel W. Powell, the first Indian Commissioner of British Columbia, or by the geologist, George Mercer Dawson, among the Haida, are prime examples now in the collections of the American Museum of Natural History and the McCord Museum respectively.

---

[3] Editor's note: The Gust Island burial assemblage, together with all other burial remains from Haida Gwaii in the collections of the Canadian Museum of Civilization, are being repatriated to the Islands in August 2000 through an agreement between the museum and the Haida.

It is very likely that extraordinary preservation environments, both wet and dry, will yield sufficient samples of material preserved over the past two millennia to document the development of an art style which has already been acknowledged by the world heritage and art community as of outstanding significance to the history of humankind. It is a challenge in terms of both recovery and preservation technologies, as well as funding requirements, to ensure that this is done in a way comparable to all the other great artistic achievements of humankind.

CONCLUDING REMARKS

Elsewhere in this volume, Susan Marsden draws on information in the *adawx* of the Tsimshian and *at.oow* of the Tlingit, correlating the information with the archaeological record from Prince Rupert Harbour. These data, including the skeletal and artifactual evidence for warfare in the region, and the shifts in settlement patterning in the first few centuries A.D. point to marked changes in the region. It appears that Tlingit displaced the Tsimshian temporarily. It also appears to coincide with the falling off of burials in the middens and the possible alternative of cremation to dispose of the dead. Fortifications around the ranked villages may also typify this development as appears to be the case at K'nu village which has a very prominent protective ridge (with a possible gate) encircling the house area on its forested side.

George MacDonald revisited the K'nu site in 1995 with Art Sterrit, then chief of the North Coast Tribal Council and was very impressed by the continuous high ridge of shell at the rear of the K'nu site. The ridge averages three metres in height above either the midden on one side of it or the forest floor on the other. This steep sided ridge is continuous for several hundred metres from the northern to the southern shoreline behind the site with the exception of a single opening on a trail between the house area and the northern shoreline. This might be interpreted as the location of a timber gate of the type described in the war epics of the Tsimshian for fort sites (MacDonald and Cove 1987).

It is intriguing that there is to date no evidence of occupation of the Prince Rupert Harbour by the Tlingit after they apparently forced the Tsimshian to abandon it early in the Christian era. The ethnographic record suggests that the Tsimshian withdrew a short distance up the Skeena and used inner passages as trade routes, but they continued to travel, albeit with caution, to the mouth of the Nass for spring eulachon fishing. Perhaps the Tlingit even tolerated the Nass expeditions in order to benefit from the seasonal trade that occurred there.

The Tlingit are recorded as occupying villages on the outer islands of the Coast south of the Nass, particularly Dundas and Porcher Islands. The *adawx* traditions relate (Susan Marsden, this volume) that the Tlingit warrior or, at least, the successor to his name, Gage, was absorbed into the Tsimshian at the time the harbour was re-occupied. It is tempting to speculate if this may have influenced the settlement pattern of the subsequent villages towards more differentiated house sizes. The episode of intense military conflict between the Tlingit and Tsimshian may have broken the previous egalitarian mould of the Tsimshian settlements, concentrating power into the hands of a few war chiefs. It is just such chiefs that are recorded in the *adawx* which relate to these events.

REFERENCES CITED

Ames, K.M. (1976). The Bone Tool Assemblage from the Garden Island Site, Prince Rupert Harbor, British Columbia: An Analysis of Assemblage Variation Through Time. Ph.D. Dissertation, Department of Anthropology, Washington State University, Pullman.

Ames, K.M., and H.D.G. Maschner (1999). *Peoples of the Northwest Coast; Their Archaeology and Prehistory.* Thames and Hudson, London.

Arutiunov, S.A., and W.W. Fitzhugh (1988). Prehistory of Siberia and the Bering Sea. In *Crossroads of Continents: Cultures of Siberia and Alaska*, edited by W.W. Fitzhugh and A. Crowell, Smithsonian Institution Press, Washington, pp. 117-129.

Barbeau, M. (1929). Totem Poles of the Gitksan, Upper Skeena River, British Columbia. *National Museum of Canada Bulletin* 61.

Borden, C.E. (1976). A water-saturated site on the southern mainland coast of British Columbia. In *The Excavation of Water-saturated Archaeological Sites (Wet Sites) on the Northwest Coast of North America*, edited by D.R. Croes, Archaeological Survey of Canada Mercury Series Paper 50, Canadian Museum of Civilization, Hull, pp. 233-260.

Boyd, R.T. (1999). *The Coming of the Spirit of Pestilence: Introduced Infectious Diseases and Population Decline Among Northwest Coast Indians, 1774-1874.* UBC Press, Vancouver.

Calvert, S.G. (1968). The Co-Op Site: A Prehistoric Midden Site on the Northern Northwest Coast of British Columbia. Unpublished manuscript (Ms. 175), Information Management Services (Archaeological Records), Canadian Museum of Civilization, Hull.

Capes, K. (1976). A Compilation of Harlan Smith's West Coast Site Records. Unpublished manuscript, Resource Information Centre, Heritage Conservation Branch, Government of British Columbia, Victoria.

Croes, D.R. (1989b). Lachane basketry and cordage: A technological, functional and comparative study. *Canadian Journal of Archaeology* 13:165-205.

Cybulski, J.S. (1974). Tooth wear and material culture: precontact patterns in the Tsimshian area, British Columbia. *Syesis* 7:31-35.

Cybulski, J.S. (1978). Modified human bones and skulls from Prince Rupert Harbour, British Columbia. *Canadian Journal of Archaeology* 2:15-32.

Cybulski, J.S. (1992). *A Greenville Burial Ground: Human Remains and Mortuary Elements in British Columbia Coast Prehistory*. Archaeological Survey of Canada Mercury Series Paper 146. Canadian Museum of Civilization, Hull.

Cybulski, J.S. (1993). Notes on the Cache in Area A of the Boardwalk Site (GbTo 31). Unpublished manuscript, Information Management Services (Archaeological Records), Canadian Museum of Civilization, Hull.

Cybulski, J.S. (1999). Trauma and warfare at Prince Rupert Harbour. *The Midden* 31 (2):5-7.

Daugherty, R.D. (1973). The Ozette Project. Banquet Address, Annual Meeting of the Canadian Archaeological Association, Burnaby.

Drucker, P. (1943). Archeological survey on the northern Northwest Coast. *Bureau of American Ethnology Bulletin* 133 (Anthropological Papers No. 20): 1-142.

Gleeson, P., and G. Grosso (1976). Ozette site. In *The Excavation of Water-Saturated Archaeological Sites (Wet Sites) on the Northwest Coast of North America*, edited by D.R. Croes, Archaeological Survey of Canada Mercury Series Paper 50, Canadian Museum of Civilization, Hull, pp. 13-44.

Hill, B., and R. Hill (1975). *Indian Petroglyphs of the Pacific Northwest*. University of Washington Press, Seattle.

Holm, B. (1974). Structure and design. In *Boxes and Bowls: Decorated Containers by Nineteenth Century Haida, Tlingit, Bella Bella, and Tsimshian Indian Artists*, edited by W.C. Sturtevant, Smithsonian Institution Press, Washington, pp. 20-32.

Holm, B. (1983). *The Box of Daylight; Northwest Coast Indian Art*. University of Washington Press, Seattle & London.

Inglis, R.I. (1971). Preliminary Report: Archaeological Research in Prince Rupert Harbour, 1971. Unpublished manuscript (Ms. No. 1119), Information Management Services (Archaeological Records), Canadian Museum of Civilization, Hull.

Inglis, R.I. (1973). The Problems of Historical Research in the Prince Rupert Area; A Definition of the Protohistoric and Historic Periods. Unpublished manuscript (Ms. No. 1120), Information Management Services (Archaeological Records), Canadian Museum of Civilization, Hull.

Inglis, R.I. (1974). Contract salvage 1973: a preliminary report on the salvage excavations of two shell middens in the Prince Rupert Harbour, B.C. GbTo-33/36. In *Archaeological Salvage Projects 1973*, edited by W.J. Byrne, Archaeological Survey of Canada Mercury Series Paper 26, Canadian Museum of Civilization, Hull, pp. 64-73.

Irish, J.D. (2000). Decapitation and Cremation: A Southeast Alaskan Burial Practice Reserved for Native Warriors Killed in Battle. *American Journal of Physical Anthropology* Supplement 30:187-188 (Abstract of poster presented at 69th Annual Meeting of the American Association of Physical Anthropologists, San Antonio).

MacDonald, G.F. (1969). Preliminary culture sequence from the Coast Tsimshian area, British Columbia. *Northwest Anthropological Research Notes* 3 (2):240-254.

MacDonald, G.F. (1973). Haida Burial Practices: Three Archaeological Examples. In *Archaeological Survey of Canada Mercury Series Paper 9*, Canadian Museum of Civilization, Hull, pp. 1-59.

MacDonald, G.F., G. Coupland, and D.J.W. Archer (1987). The Coast Tsimshian, ca. 1750. In *The Historical Atlas of Canada, Vol. 1: From the Beginning to 1800*, edited by R.C. Harris (G.J. Matthews, Cartographer/Designer), University of Toronto Press, Toronto, pp. 32-33.

MacDonald, G.F., and J. Cove, eds. (1987). *Tsimshian Narratives: Volume 2, Trade and Warfare*. Canadian Museum of Civilization, Hull.

MacDonald, G.F., and R.I. Inglis (1981). An overview of the North Coast Prehistory Project (1966-1980). *BC Studies* 48:37-63.

Matson, R.G., and G. Coupland (1995). *The Prehistory of the Northwest Coast*. Academic Press, San Diego and London.

Robinson, W., and W. Wright (1962). *Men of Medeek*. Northern Sentinel Press Ltd., Kitimat.

Smith, H.I. (1909). Archaeological remains on the coast of northern British Columbia and southern Alaska. *American Anthropologist, n.s.* 11:595-600.

Smith, H.I. (1929). Kitchen-middens of the Pacific coast of Canada. *National Museum of Canada Bulletin* 56:42-46.

Smith, H.I. (1936). The man petroglyph near Prince Rupert, or The Man Who Fell from Heaven. In *Essays in Anthropology Presented to A. L. Kroeber in Celebration of His Sixtieth Birthday, June 11, 1936*, edited by R.H. Lowie, University of California Press, Berkeley, pp. 309-312.

Sutherland, P.D. (1978). Dodge Island: A Prehistoric Coast Tsimshian Settlement Site in Prince Rupert Harbour, British Columbia. Unpublished manuscript (Ms. 1345), Information Management Services (Archaeological Records), Canadian Museum of Civilization, Hull.

Usher, J. (1974). *William Duncan of Metlakatla: A Victorian Missionary in British Columbia*. National Museum of Man Publications in History No. 5. Canadian Museum of Civilization (National Museums of Canada), Hull.

Walker, D. (1979). Petroglyphs of the Middle Skeena River. In *Skeena River Prehistory*, edited by G.F. MacDonald and R.I. Inglis, Archaeological Survey of Canada Mercury Series Paper 87, Canadian Museum of Civilization, Hull, pp. 169-180.

From Land to Sea: Late Quaternary Environments of the Northern Northwest Coast

Knut R. Fladmark

ABSTRACT

Paleoenvironmental factors potentially may limit human presence in any region or strongly affect cultural adaptations. I report the timing and extent of Late Pleistocene ice advances, major sea level changes, and the developmental histories of the Stikine, Nass, and Skeena River systems. The evolution of terrestrial biotic systems since about 15,000-20,000 B.P., revealed by palynological studies, is also considered. Because of significant variation, the Queen Charlotte Islands, southeastern Alaska, and the B.C. mainland coast, extending inland to about Telegraph Creek – Hazelton, are treated separately. An emergent land-bridge connected the Queen Charlotte Islands to the mainland in the early Holocene, ending in a very rapid rise in sea levels about 9000-10,000 B.P., possibly recorded in Haida flood legends. Other potentially catastrophic events described in native traditions include the Aiyansh lava flow ca. 220 B.P. in the Nass valley and the Rocher Déboulé landslide in the Skeena valley about 3500 B.P.

RÉSUMÉ

Certains facteurs paléoenvironnementaux sont en mesure de limiter la présence humaine ou d'affecter fortement les adaptations culturelles dans n'importe quelle région. Je mets en lumière, entre autres, la chronologie et l'étendue des avancées glaciaires du Pléistocène récent, les grandes variations du niveau de la mer, et les étapes du développement des systèmes fluviaux de la Stikine, de la Nasse et de la Skeena. On prend aussi en considération l'évolution des systèmes biotiques terrestres depuis environ 15000-20000 A.A., qu'ont révélée les études palynologiques. En raison de variations significatives, on

In *Perspectives on Northern Northwest Coast Prehistory*, edited by Jerome S. Cybulski. Hull: Canadian Museum of Civilization, Archaeological Survey of Canada, Mercury Series Paper 160, pp. 25-47, © 2001.

traite séparément les îles de la Reine Charlotte, le sud-est de l'Alaska et la côte principale de la C.-B. jusqu'à Telegraph Creek – Hazelton dans l'intérieur des terres. Au début de l'Holocène, un pont terrestre en émergence reliait les îles de la Reine Charlotte au continent, mais fut inondé par une élévation rapide du niveau de la mer vers 9000-10000 A.A., événement auquel font peut-être allusion les légendes haïdas des inondations. D'autres événement potentiellement catastrophiques rapportés dans les traditions autochtones comprennent les coulées de lave d'Aiyansh vers 220 A.A. dans la vallée de la Nass et les coulées de terre du Rocher Déboulé dans la vallée de la Skeena vers 3500 A.A.

INTRODUCTION

The shorelines and river valleys along which most archaeological sites occur on the northern Northwest Coast have experienced significant changes in form and location throughout the Late Pleistocene and Holocene in response to various environmental factors. The changes have included regional fluctuations in glaciers and sea levels, as well as localized landslides and volcanic eruptions. This paper will review paleoenvironmental variables for the Queen Charlotte Islands, southeastern Alaska, and the northern mainland coast of British Columbia since the late Pleistocene (Fig. 1), and provide brief summaries of palynological sequences.

LATE PLEISTOCENE GLACIATIONS

QUEEN CHARLOTTE ISLANDS

Haida Gwaii, as the Queen Charlotte Islands are known to their native inhabitants, is separated from the mainland coast of British Columbia by the 55-140 km width of Hecate Strait. Currently beset by strong currents and storms, it is too wide to allow crossings by land mammals or by people lacking sophisticated watercraft. Thus, insular biotic and, to some degree, cultural successions have followed distinct endemic trends throughout the late Quaternary. The islands' distance from mainland centers of glaciation also has suggested an incomplete ice cover during the Late Wisconsinan allowing the survival of some plants and animals through that period.

The idea of a glacial refugium on the Queen Charlotte Islands was first raised by Calvin J. Heusser (1955:435-37, 1960:97) after a bog revealed a pollen record going back almost 11,000 years. The earliest flora already were quite diverse, implying that plants had existed on the islands during the preceding glacial period. That idea also was supported by highly disjunct insular fauna, including a unique species of caribou (*Rangifer dawsoni*) and subspecies of black bear (*Ursus americanus carlottae*), implying lengthy isolation from mainland populations (Heusser 1960: 201-205). In that regard, it should be noted that while the zoologist Bristol Foster (1965:35-37) also recognized the distinctiveness of the "Dawson caribou," he thought that they first reached the islands only about 10,000 years ago. Nevertheless, he still felt that several other endemic species and subspecies of smaller mammals, including ermine (*Mustela erminae haidarum*), pine marten (*Martes american nesophila*), and shrew (*Sorex obscurus*), had survived in insular refugia (ibid., pp. 38-46). Over the last 30 years, other biologists have continued to support the concept of a Charlottes refugium, based on the unique characteristics of insular biota (e.g., Calder and Taylor 1968:112, Moodie and Reimchen 1976:472-474, O'Reilley et al. 1993:682).

In contrast, traditional geological opinion has seen a solid wall of Late Wisconsinan ice sealing the entire Pacific coast with no possibility of any significant refugia. Thus, the first Quaternary geological studies on the Queen Charlotte Islands concluded that they had been completely glaciated, with only some rocky nunataks remaining ice-free (Alley and Thompson 1978:16-17, Nasmith 1970:7, Sutherland-Brown 1968:28-34, Sutherland-Brown and Nasmith 1962:214-218). However, since the early 1980's other Quaternary scientists have reevaluated the evidence and concluded that the Late Wisconsinan ice cover on the islands was indeed less than total and of relatively short duration (e.g., Mathewes et al. 1985:791, Clague 1989c:72).

Critical to the question of a Charlottes refugium is the fact that northeastern Graham Island has yielded the oldest postglacial palynological site in British Columbia (Mathewes 1989:83, Warner, Mathewes and Clague 1982:675). There, at the southern end of the Cape Ball locality, which stretches along 5-6 km of eroding sea-cliff, radiocarbon dates between 16,000 ± 570 and 14,700 ± 700 B.P. on plant remains in postglacial silts provide a minimum age for local deglaciation (Clague, Mathewes and Warner 1982:1791-1792, Mathewes et al. 1985:791, Mathewes 1989:87). About 3 km further north, basal deposits consisted only of outwash sands and silts, indicating a position now beyond the maximum glacial front. Those sediments were topped by thin layers of peat dated at 13,700 ± 100 and 13,350 ± 200 B.P. At other locations, up to 2 km further north, buried peat beds dating back to 12,400 ± 100 B.P., were covered by almost 2-3 m of "marine, littoral and estuarine" sediments. That indicates terrestrial plant growth at a time of significantly lower sea levels, with the vegetated surface later inundated by rising water (Barrie et al. 1994:126, Mathewes and Clague 1982:1186-1188). In general, the Cape Ball locality confirms that the islands sustained significant plant life by at least 16,000 B.P. and could have served as an origin point for the later dispersal of spruce, western and mountain hemlock, pine, and alder out to other parts of the north coast (Heusser 1989:103).

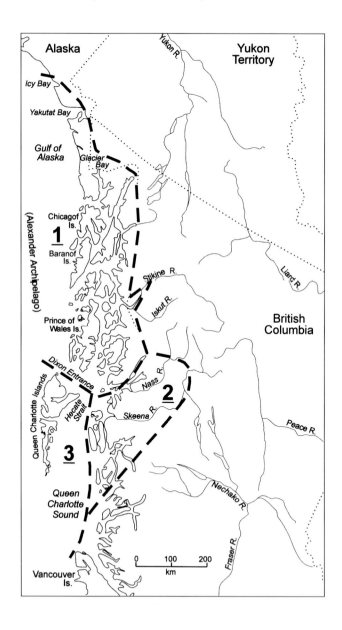

Fig. 1. Subareas of the northern Northwest Coast: (1) southeast Alaska; (2) northern mainland; (3) Queen Charlotte Islands.

SOUTHEASTERN ALASKA

North of the Queen Charlotte Islands, much of the mainland coast of south-eastern Alaska is a rugged fjord land with many modern glaciers reaching tidal water. In the late 1960's and early 1970's, one perspective saw a Late Pleistocene ice sheet covering the region, with an outer edge roughly paralleling the present mainland shoreline north of the Alexander Archipelago (e.g., Péwé 1975:16, Prest 1969). However, an alternative opinion saw much of the northeastern coast of the Gulf of Alaska as being no more intensely glaciated during the Late Wisconsinan than during the climax of the Neoglacial about A.D. 1800 (Péwé, Hopkins and Giddings 1965:359). More recent studies have suggested an intermediate position between those two extremes. Thus, examination of the ca. 100 km wide continental shelf north of Cross Sound has indicated eight U-shaped submarine valleys, presumably eroded by glaciers (Carlson et al. 1982:219, Molnia 1986:219-222). A lack of evidence for glacial erosion between those troughs implies that intervening subaerial shelf areas remained free of ice even at the maximum stage of glaciation (Molnia 1986:224-225).

South of Cross Sound, the numerous islands of the Alexander Archipelago add greatly to the complexity of the coastline. Here, there also have been divergent opinions about the extent of Late Wisconsinan glaciation. Thus, while some researchers have seen a thick ice cap stretching out to the edge of the continental shelf (e.g., Péwé 1975:16), others have argued for a less than total ice cover (e.g., Mann 1986:254-261). As for the Queen Charlotte Islands, biologists have suggested that biotic refugia existed in parts of the Alexander Archipelago during the last Pleistocene (e.g., Heusser 1960:204). Unique species of small mammals are most common in outer parts of the archipelago, while islands closer to the mainland tend to be dominated by continental species. That implies that animals survived in those outer coastal settings through at least part of the Late Wisconsinan glaciation, developing characteristics distinct from mainland populations.

It also has been thought that Alaskan brown bears originally expanded south along the coast in early postglacial times, while black bears spread northwards, since there is no evidence for them in the Beringian refugium. In addition, the current presence of black-tailed deer in the Alexander Archipelago suggests an original northwards movement along the coast (Klein 1965:13-16). Recently, important new information about the history of bears in the Alexander Archipelago has come from caves on northern Prince of Wales Island. They revealed remains of black bears (*Ursus americanus*) dated from 11,565 ± 115 to 6415 ± 130 B.P. and of brown bears (*Ursus arctos*) dated from 12,295 ± 120 to 9769 ± 75 B.P. That indicates that both species co-inhabited the island in the Late Pleistocene and Early Holocene, although brown bears no longer live there. Their mtDNA also shows a closer genetic relationship to modern polar bears than to the grizzlies of the adjacent mainland, again suggesting an original southward dispersal along the coast. The caves also had remains of two other animals no longer found on the Alexander Archipelago or the adjacent Alaskan mainland, red fox (*Vulpes vulpes*) and caribou (*Rangifer tarandus*) (Heaton, Talbot and Shields 1996:188-191). This indicates that a complex and unique terrestrial fauna survived on the island during the late Pleistocene (Baichtal 1993, Busch 1994, Heaton, Talbot and Shields 1996:188-191). Also, as pointed out by Heaton, Talbot and Shields (1996:190-191), bears and humans are both omnivores, with very similar resource requirements. If bears could live on Prince of Wales Island during the Late Wisconsinan, so could people.

NORTHERN BRITISH COLUMBIA MAINLAND

The northern mainland coast of British Columbia was totally glaciated during the Late Wisconsinan maximum, with inland ice thicknesses reaching 1500-2000 m. However, the ice would have progressively thinned westwards, terminating on the emergent land of Hecate Strait (Clague 1984a:44). About 14,500-15,000 B.P., the area around the mouth of the Skeena River seems to have been rapidly deglaciated, as ice masses were broken up by rising sea levels (Clague 1984b:260). Shells from glaciomarine sediments at Prince Rupert, dated at 12,700 ± 120 B.P., suggest ice withdrawal before that time. The remaining glacier in the lower Skeena River valley disappeared after a calving bay developed at least 10,600-10,700 years ago (Clague 1984a:47-49). The Bulkley River confluence about 130 km inland also became ice-free "a few hundred to a thousand years later" (Gottesfeld, Mathewes and Gottesfeld 1991:1584, Clague 1984a:45). It seems that glaciers in both the lower Skeena and the Kitsumkalum-Kitimat troughs retreated in contact with the sea. A prominent end-moraine formed across the southern end of that trough at Kitimat, representing a brief period of stability in the retreating ice front at about 11,000 B.P. That was followed by renewed rapid recession which stabilized again near Terrace between about 10,400 and 10,800 B.P., in relation to a marine shoreline still about 200 m above present (Clague 1984a:49).

SEA LEVEL CHANGES

Second only to glaciations, major sea level changes critically affected the extent and nature of inhabitable coastal terrain and food resources. Regional Late Quaternary sea levels responded to a complex interplay of eustatic, isostatic, and tectonic factors, with the momentary position of the land/sea interface at any one place representing the net effect of local manifestations of all those factors (e.g., Morrison 1968:41-48, Clague 1975:17). In particular, highly varied isostatic effects between a relatively heavily glaciated inner coast and lightly glaciated off-shore islands, produced very divergent sea level trends across even short east-west distances (e.g., Clague 1983:324-326, 338, 1989b:44-45, Fladmark 1975:170, 1983:73-74).

QUEEN CHARLOTTE ISLANDS

The importance of past sea level positions to native occupants of the Queen Charlotte Islands is shown by the many archaeological sites along its raised shorelines. The following section reviews those sea level changes over about the last 10,000 to 11,000 years, starting in Queen Charlotte Sound and then moving north through Hecate Strait to Dixon Entrance.

The bottom of Queen Charlotte Sound shows a series of U-shaped elongated depressions, suggesting erosion by Late Wisconsinan glaciers from the mainland, leaving three intervening raised ice-free banks (Luternauer and Murray 1983:22-3, 58). Because sea level was at least 100-110 m lower than present at ca. 13,700-10,000 years ago, most of those banks were then dry land (Josenhans et al. 1993:122-127). In fact, a piece of root in growing position and other samples of wood dredged from depths of ca. 100 m, dated between 10,650 ± 350 and 9940 ± 75 B.P., indicate forests once grew on those now submerged land-surfaces (Luternauer et al. 1989b:359). Freshwater lakes also filled inner fjord basins of southern Moresby Island, now 105 m below sea level, as late as 10,360 ± 80 B.P. However, about 200-300 years later they were flooded by ocean water, as shown by dated marine shells lying above lacustrine sediments in core samples (Josenhans et al. 1995:78-81).

In Hecate Strait, early sea levels as low as -100 to -110 m also are indicated by submerged river valleys and wave-cut terrace features seen in bathymetric charts (Barrie and Bornhold 1989:1253). In fact, a broad low-relief "Hecatian Land-Bridge" would have existed if a 100-110 m drop in sea level occurred at the same time across the entire strait, providing an access route to the islands for bears, caribou, and, possibly, people (Fig. 2). Currently, it would not be possible for caribou or bears to cross from the mainland, necessitating a significantly reduced water barrier or land bridge some time in the Late Quaternary (Klein 1965:15, Foster 1965:257). The fact that deer did not reach the islands until introduced by Europeans, indicates that their earthward move into the Alexander Archipelago occurred only after sea levels had risen and the present barrier of Hecate Strait was established in the early Holocene (Klein 1965:16).

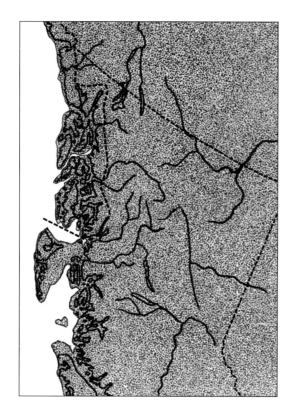

Fig. 2. The northern Northwest Coast at -100 m sea-level position.

In a series of core samples from about 30 m deep in western Hecate Strait, the highest sediments were Holocene sandy gravels with shell fragments, deposited in a marine environment. The next lowest were fluvial sands and silty sands. One core, from about 20 km east of Graham Island, contained abundant wood fragments and roots, dated by the accelerator mass spectrometry (AMS) method to 13,790 ± 150 and 13,190 ± 100 B.P. (Barrie et al. 1994:125). There also were high frequencies of sedge (*Cyperaceae*) and varying amounts of grass and other herbaceous pollen. That is similar to pollen assemblages from Cape Ball, indicating that a tundra-like vegetation, with scattered shrubs, covered northeastern Graham Island and the Hecatian Land Bridge about 13,700 to 10,500 B.P. (ibid., pp. 126-128). To the north, Dixon Entrance would not have seen much emergent land even with a 100-110 m sea level drop. However, it was entirely ice-free by about 12,900 B.P. and until about 10,500-10,200 B.P. maintained sea levels significantly lower than present (Barrie and Conway 1993:20).

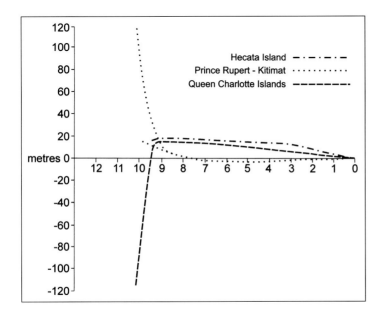

Fig. 3. Northern Northwest Coast sea levels.

Thus, late Pleistocene and early Holocene sea levels around the Queen Charlotte Islands were significantly lower than present and then went through rapid upward adjustments (Luternauer et al. 1989a:66-68). They seem to have climbed an average of 6.3 cm/yr. between 10,000 and 9000 years ago (Josenhans et al. 1995:88) (Fig 3). That rate of rise would have been visible to any observers, amounting to about 100 m in less than 1000-1500 years, possibly providing a source for the "flood legends" in some Haida traditional histories (Luternauer et al. 1989b:359). The Charlottes sea level first passed the present position about 9500 B.P. and had climbed 15 m higher than present by 500 years later (Josenhans et al. 1995:88) (Fig.3). It stayed near there until about 5500 B.P., producing a raised beach terrace all around the islands, and then fell to the present level (Luternauer and Murray 1983:4). The prominence of that +15 m raised beach level and lack of intermediate beaches between it and near the modern shoreline, hints of an ongoing steady uplift driven by tectonic factors (Clague 1989a:67-8, Luternauer and Murray 1983:19, Yorath and Chase 1981). Indeed, the sea level may still be falling slowly, as suggested by shell-fish remains found in living positions 0.5-2.0 m above the modern intertidal zone (Clague, Mathewes and Warner 1982:1792-1794).

SOUTHEASTERN ALASKA

Information about past sea levels in southeastern Alaska is still very preliminary (Mobley 1988:261). Because of varied glacial loading and isostatic effects, the region must have experienced significant east to west variations (Clague 1975:19) with tectonic factors increasing localized variability. The Gulf of Alaska is one of the most seismically active regions on earth, having been affected by eight earthquakes stronger than 7.3 on the Richter scale since 1896, resulting in instantaneous displacements between 15 m upward and two meters downwards. In addition, an orogenic uplift of about one centimeter per year is ongoing as the Pacific plate slowly subducts beneath the North American plate (Molnia 1986:220).

Some of the islands of the Alexander Archipelago, as well as the mainland coast, experienced significant glacioisostatic depression in the late Pleistocene. Thus, on Kupreanof Island near the center of the archipelago, marine shells found 62 m above present sea level dated at 12,400 ± 800 B.P., while others on Chicagof Island, further to the north and west at 70 m., dated at 12,130 ± 110 B.P. On Baranof Island, in the west, withdrawal of Late Wisconsinan ice more than 13,000 years ago, was followed by a sea level at least 61 m above present. However, about 10,300 B.P. the island began to emerge and a prominent beach terrace, now 9 m above sea level, formed by 9500 B.P. (Swanston 1989:47-51). In fact, a well-defined raised beach terrace seems to have developed on all islands after about 9500 B.P. but now lies at different elevations across the archipelago because of varied isostatic effects. Prince of Wales and Hecata Islands, at the southern end of the archipelago, seem to have experienced sea level changes similar to those of the adjacent Queen Charlotte Islands. Thus, their shorelines were lower than present until about 10,000 B.P., rose to 15 m above present by about 9500-8500 B.P., and then slowly fell to the present position (Swanston 1969:31, Mobley 1988:265) (Fig.3).

The mainland coast of southeastern Alaska was affected by much more pronounced glacioisostatic depression and rebound effects. Thus, near Juneau, beach gravels estimated at 10,000 to 12,000 years in age now lie 150-183 m above the present shoreline (Miller 1973:C17) while a ca. 17 m high beach terrace dates to 9700 ± 800 B.P. Near Wrangell, at the mouth of the Stikine River, a ca. 21 m high terrace also dates to 9700 ± 350 B.P. (Swanston 1989:51). At Ketchikan, at the southern mainland end of the Alaska panhandle, a 10 m high beach terrace yielded dates of 8420 ± 130 B.P. and 7230 ± 115 B.P. (Swanston 1989:51, Mobley 1988:261) with even higher terraces occurring over 60 m above sea level (Mann 1986:254-255).

NORTHERN BRITISH COLUMBIA MAINLAND

At the end of the last glaciation, the northern mainland coast of British Columbia also experienced pronounced isostatic depression. About 10,500 B.P., the sea level stood about 200 m above present in the Kitimat-Terrace area (Clague 1983:325, 337, 1984a:51, 1984b:263-264). The Skeena River valley west of Terrace was a marine fjord which joined an arm of the sea extending up the Kitsumkalum-Kitimat trough, creating an island of the intervening terrain (Clague 1984a:11). Beaches and marine deltas around Kitimat had fallen to about 120 m above present by 10,100 B.P. and to 35 m above present by 9300 ± 90 B.P. (Clague 1983:328, 337, 1984a:45, 51).

At the same time as inner coastal settings were isostatically depressed hundreds of meters, relative sea levels were significantly lower further west (Heusser 1960:193, Clague et al. 1982:604). Initially, low levels just beyond the periphery of the ice-sheet were partly due to crustal forebulge effects, when an uplifted "bulge" of land, peripheral to the area of isostatic depression, migrated eastwards on the heels of the retreating Cordilleran glacial complex. As the ice melted and the peak of that bulge moved inland, sea levels further west rose (Clague 1983:333).

The present sea level position seems to have been initially attained on the northern mainland coast about 8000-8500 B.P. However, it may have continued to fall, remaining a few meters below present until about 5000 B.P., and slowly risen since. That would explain a lack of archaeological sites in Prince Rupert Harbour which predate ca. 5000 B.P. despite intensive research (Clague 1984a:51-52, Clague et al. 1982:605). By the late 1970's, archaeology had revealed more than 40 shell-midden sites within a few meters of the present high tide line, continuously occupied for nearly 5000 years. However, the fact that many are now being eroded by wave action suggests that the sea level was somewhat lower when they were formed (Fig. 3).

LATE QUATERNARY VEGETATION SEQUENCES

The following offers a brief summary of Late Quaternary vegetation sequences for the northern Northwest Coast beginning with the very long record from Cape Ball on northeastern Queen Charlotte Islands. As previously noted, around 16,000 to 13,000 years ago that area had patches of tundra-like herbaceous grass-sedge meadow, set between exposed, wind-blown areas (Mathewes 1989:83). Notably, the oldest pollen assemblage included several plants no longer found on the islands. For instance, thrift (*Armeria*) occurs widely along the mainland coast today, but not on the Charlottes. There also were some seemingly odd associations of species, with plants currently restricted to alpine-subalpine settings found together with those of modern lowland swampy environments (Mathewes and Clague 1982:1190).

Vegetation became more complex around Cape Ball at 12,000-13,000 B.P. with relatively frequent willow macrofossils implying a dwarf-shrub tundra, while a single Sitka spruce needle (*Picea sitchensis*) hints of some stunted conifers (Mathewes 1989:85). About 12,000 years ago there was a significant increase in pollen abundance, particularly of grasses, sedges, and lodgepole pine, at the same time as thrift made its last appearance. Relatively frequent macrofossils of spruce and western hemlock (*Tsuga heterophylla*) appeared before 10,000 B.P. That may represent a period of maximum Holocene climatic cooling, seen in most Queen Charlotte Islands pollen sequences between about 10,700 and 10,200 B.P., corresponding to the Younger Dryas event (Mathewes, Heusser and Patterson 1993:104).

Red cedar was of major importance to the people of the Northwest Coast in ethnographic times. While small quantities of cedar-type pollen (*Cupressaceae*) are visible in Charlotte's sequences from about 10,000 B.P. and grew slightly in frequency 6500 to 1500 B.P., it was only after 1500 B.P. that they showed a sharp increase to post-European contact levels (Hebda and Mathewes 1984:712). That implies that islanders may have had significantly less access to cedar than mainland contemporaries until about 1500 B.P., with important implications concerning their houses, canoes, and totem poles.

Most reconstructions of late Pleistocene - Holocene vegetation sequences in southeastern Alaska still seem largely based on Calvin Heusser's 1960 pioneering studies. In what he defined as the Late-Glacial period of 10,000 to 11,000 B.P., the Alexander Archipelago was dominated by ferns, sedges, willows, and alder, with lodgepole pine the only conifer, suggesting an open parkland-like vegetation

(Heusser 1960:118-119). Sitka spruce showed up about 9500 B.P., paralleling a period of alder dominance which lasted until about 7500 B.P. From 8200 to 3500 B.P., the most common tree shifted from alder to Sitka spruce, and then to western and mountain hemlock. Western hemlock has been the dominant tree since 3500 B.P., associated with Sitka spruce. Areas of muskeg also expanded after that time, reflecting Neoglacial climatic conditions (Heusser 1985:154). The last 1000 years saw a vegetation dominated by hemlock, spruce, lodgepole pine, and sphagnum moss (Heusser 1960:118-123, 178, Ager 1983:131).

More recent research in Glacier Bay and Yakutat Bay also has suggested a significant reversal of a postglacial warming trend between 10,800 and 9800 B.P. marked by a shift from earlier pine forests to a tundra-like environment, with large numbers of grasses, sedges, and *Artemesia*. It lasted until about 10,000 B.P. when renewed warming caused herbaceous elements to decrease and alder to once again increase (Engstrom, Hansen and Wright 1990:1384, Peteet 1986:118). That provides further evidence for a regional Younger Dryas-like cooling interval (Mathewes 1993).

A 10,300-year-long pollen sequence also was obtained from the northern end of Lynn Canal at the head of the Alaska panhandle. It revealed six vegetational zones with the oldest at 10,870-10,330 B.P. being an open lodgepole pine woodland with lots of shrubs, including willow and alder. Zone 2, at 10,330-9480 B.P., still represented a pine woodland, although Sitka spruce grew greatly in numbers, paralleled by a decrease in ferns, grasses, sages, and sedges. Later, spruce and alder increased in dominance, while pine decreased, followed by a later surge in hemlock before 2900 B.P. (Cwynar 1990:1106-1107).

That study noted how rapidly lodgepole pine must have spread north along the coast at the end of the last glaciation, presuming an origin in western Washington and southern British Columbia, in order to reach Lynn Canal by 10,500 B.P. (ibid., p. 1109). Another analysis also indicated that lodgepole pine became a pioneer species even further north in the Yakutat Bay area, by spreading along the coast about 11,000 to 10,000 B.P. (Peteet 1991:790-794). However, as noted before, lodgepole pine pollen occurred at Cape Ball on the Queen Charlotte Islands as early as 12,000 to 13,000 B.P. and that would represent a more likely point of origin for such a northward expansion into Alaska.

There is still relatively little palynological information available for the northern mainland coast of British Columbia. In the 1950's, Calvin Heusser sampled three peat sections on the Skeena River estuary and another on the outer mainland coast.

Most were dominated by willow, alder, and lodgepole pine at ca. 11,000-10,000 B.P. Lodgepole pine, Sitka spruce, western hemlock, alder, and ferns characterized the period between 10000 and 8200 B.P., while between about 8200 and 3500 B.P. varying proportions of Sitka spruce, Mountain and Western hemlock, alder, and ferns appeared over time (Heusser 1960:104-105).

Only one later palynological study has been published for an equivalent bog woodland sampling site near Prince Rupert (Banner, Polar and Rouse 1983:938-940). There, a community of pine, alder, ferns, and, perhaps, small numbers of spruce, hemlock, and cedar, appeared sometime before 8500 B.P. That was followed by a richer array of spruce, alder, hemlock, skunk cabbage, and ferns, subsequently replaced by a less diverse assemblage of cedar, western hemlock, and pine. The forest continued to degrade over time, ultimately leading to the modern yellow cedar bog woodland, representing an overall cooling and wetting climatic trend (ibid., p. 946).

THE NEOGLACIAL IN SOUTHEASTERN ALASKA

In terms of later Holocene paleoclimates, the Neoglacial period represented a significant cooling trend over the last 2000 to 4000 years which resulted in major glacial re-advances in southeastern Alaska. Thus, in Icy Bay, at the northern end of the Alaska panhandle, glaciers overran preexisting forests about 1900 B.P. and culminated on the outer coast. About 300 years later, they withdrew far back into the fjord system until A.D. 1230. That was followed by a re-expansion to a position much more advanced than today, representing a "Little Ice Age" maximum of about A.D. 1250-1850 (Porter 1989:366-369). In fact, when visited by Captain Vancouver in 1794, Icy Bay did not exist, having been entirely filled with glaciers.

Yakutat Bay is another large coastal indentation 80 km south of Icy Bay, fronting Hubbard Glacier, the longest tidewater glacier in North America. There, an initial Neoglacial advance dated to about 2000 to 1200 B.P. A later "Little Ice-Age" re-advance peaked about A.D. 1700, followed by an ongoing retreat after A.D. 1888 (Mann 1986:259). Many Tlingit stories recount interactions with a dynamic ice-contact environment in that area (de Laguna et al. 1964:17-18). Further south, Holocene glaciers also twice occupied Glacier Bay, successively damming the tributary Muir Inlet, causing it to fill with a freshwater lake (Goodwin 1988:67). Around 800 B.P., the ice expanded to a maximum position near the mouth of the bay and stayed there until at least A. D. 1799 (Mann 1986:257-258, Lawrence 1958:99).

The Stikine is the largest river crossing the mainland portion of the Alaska panhandle and glacial damming events could have affected it in the Neoglacial. In fact, Tlingit oral histories recount a time when people traveling down the river found it blocked by glaciers with the water flowing through a tunnel beneath the ice (Kerr 1948:17). As the story goes, two old women volunteered to drift through the tunnel on a raft and after two days emerged on the other side to be jubilantly greeted by others who had walked across the glacier (Peck 1982:70-71).

HOLOCENE HISTORY OF THE NASS AND SKEENA RIVER VALLEYS

As focal points of resource access and communication corridors, the Nass and Skeena Rivers were critical to native settlement and subsistence patterns on the northern mainland coast. However, those river systems must have changed significantly since the first people appeared on their shores. Here as elsewhere in the Cordillera, important paleoenvironmental variables affecting rivers included glaciations and rising or falling drainage base levels (i.e., sea levels), as already described, as well as sporadic catastrophic events such as volcanic eruptions and landslides.

In fact, the Nass River valley is the scene of one the most recent volcanic eruptions in Canada when the Aiyansh Lava Flow issued from a vent in the headwaters of the Tseax River about 60 km north of Terrace. It flowed down a narrow tributary of that river, impounding 16 km long "Lava Lake," and continued another 18 km north to the Nass River. There, it spread out, forming a broad, blocky ca. 30 km² lava plain, pushing the river to the north side of the valley (Sutherland-Brown 1969:1460). A young age for that event, suggested by the freshness of the lava and its lack of plant cover, was confirmed when a buried tree was dated to 220 ± 130 B.P. (ibid., p. 1467). It also was well remembered by the Nisga'a people as late as the 1940's: "One day long ago a great lava eruption took place at Gitwinsilkqu on upper Nass River. The molten mass pushed the waters of the river back across the valley . . . overwhelmed villages and fishing hamlets in its path and the people fled to the surrounding hills" (Barbeau 1950:76).

Like other rivers draining the western Cordillera, the Skeena has been affected by sporadic large scale earth movements, impacting human settlement and subsistence patterns. Southwest of Hazleton, the cloud-laced peak of Mt. Rocher Déboulé rises 2330 m above the river valley. The unstable rocks and sediments of that steep mountain slope provide an ideal setting for mass wastage and, on the north side of the mountain, a particularly large late Holocene debris fan has been radiocarbon dated to 3580 ± 150 B.P. (Gottesfeld et al. 1991:1584-1587). Certain Gitksan traditions may refer to that event (ibid., p. 1591). The basic story recounts how the people of the legendary village of "Temlaham" (or "Tum-L-Hama") at the foot of Rocher Déboulé hunted mountain goats above their village. Eventually "they grew careless," making fun of the spirits of the animals (Barbeau 1924:224-226) and the chiefs of the Mountain Goat people exerted punishment:

> Into this peaceful scene, one day, came fear. Unseemly events were taking place far back in the forest. It soon attracted the attention of the people, and as they watched, they saw great trees thrown high above the forest top. The disturbance came nearer. Some gigantic force was coming down the valley of the creek. As it came the forest was torn apart, trees uprooted, trampled down. A wide gash in the greenery told of its passing. Closer and still closer to the river came the turmoil and at last a bear came out on the river's margin. A bear. But, unlike any bear the People had ever seen. A giant grizzly bear; one capable of uprooting trees, of snapping giant trunks as though they were they were grasses. The bear paused; and glared at Tum-L-Hama . . . The bear moved from house to house, killing all who opposed him. Only when he came to the westerly edge of the town did he turn and re-enter the river. Then he crossed the swirling waters and disappeared into the forest (Robinson and Wright 1962:18-20).

SUMMARY AND CONCLUSIONS

This paper has attempted to summarize late Pleistocene and Holocene glaciations, sea level changes, events affecting river systems, and general trends of plant succession in the northern Northwest Coast over about the last 13,000 to 15,000 years. The region formed a very dynamic natural context for human endeavours with significantly shifting ice fronts, rising and falling sea levels, and changing biota. Those natural variables influenced cultural adaptations, defined the basic availability and nature of places suitable for occupation, and controlled the long-term survival of such sites in the geoarchaeological record. Notably, some environmental changes, including sea level adjustments, happened far more rapidly than usually considered in "uniformitarian" perspectives. Coupled with occasional truly catastrophic events such as volcanic eruptions and land-slides, that suggests that archaeologists could afford to pay greater attention to the inherently chaotic nature of some environmental processes when attempting to understand cultural changes over time and human interactions with past natural worlds (cf. Harris 1990:1-4).

ACKNOWLEDGEMENTS

I am indebted to the many Quaternary scientists of varied specialties who obtained and initially reported the information summarized here. In particular, they include in alphabetical order, John J. Clague, Calvin J. Heusser, Heiner Josenhans, J. L. Luternauer, and Rolf W. Mathewes.

REFERENCES CITED

Ager, T.A. (1983). Holocene vegetational history of Alaska. In *Late Quaternary environments of the United States. Vol.2, The Holocene*, edited by H.E. Wright, Jr., University of Minnesota Press, Minneapolis, pp. 128-141.

Alley, N.F., and B. Thomson (1978). *Aspects of Environmental Geology, Parts of Graham Island, Queen Charlotte Islands*. Resource Analysis Branch Bulletin 2. British Columbia Ministry of the Environment, Victoria.

Baichtal, J.F. (1993). An Update on the Pleistocene and Holocene Fauna Recovered from Caves on Prince of Wales and Surrounding Islands. Abstract of paper read at 20th Annual Conference of the Alaska Anthropological Association, Anchorage.

Banner, A., J. Polar, and C.E. Rouse (1983). Postglacial paleoecology and successional relationships of a bog woodland near Prince Rupert, British Columbia. *Canadian Journal of Forest Research* 13:938-947.

Barbeau, M. (1924). *The Downfall of Temlaham*. The MacMillan Company of Canada, Ltd. Toronto.

Barbeau, M. (1950). *Totem poles; According to Crests and Topics*. National Museum of Canada Bulletin 119, Vol. 1, Anthropological Series 30.

Barrie, J.V., and B.D. Bornhold (1989). Surficial geology of Hecate Strait, British Columbia continental shelf. *Canadian Journal of Earth Sciences* 26:1241-1254.

Barrie, J.V., and K.W. Conway (1993). Postglacial geology of Dixon Entrance, northwestern British Columbia continental shelf. *Geological Survey of Canada Paper 93-E, Current Research, Part E, Cordillera and Pacific Margin*:15-21.

Barrie, J.V., K.W. Conway, R.W. Mathewes, H.W. Josenhans, and M.J. Johns (1994). Submerged Late Quaternary terrestrial deposits and paleoenvironment of northern Hecate Strait, British Columbia continental shelf, Canada. *Quaternary International* 20:123-129.

Busch, L. (1994). A glimmer of hope for coastal migration. *Science* 263:1088-1089.

Calder, J.A., and R.L. Taylor (1968). *Flora of the Queen Charlotte Islands. Part 1, Systematics of the Vascular Plants.* Canada Department of Agriculture Research Branch Monograph 4, Part 1. Ottawa.

Carlson, P.R., T.R. Bruns, B.F. Molnia, and W.C. Schwab (1982). Submarine valleys in the northeastern Gulf of Alaska: Characteristics and probable origin. *Marine Geology* 47:217-242.

Clague, J.J. (1975). Late Quaternary sea-level fluctuations, Pacific coast of Canada and adjacent areas. *Geological Survey of Canada Paper* 75-1C:17-21.

Clague, J.J. (1983). Glacio-isostatic effects of the Cordilleran Ice Sheet, British Columbia, Canada. In *Shorelines and Isostacy*, edited by D.E. Smith and A.G. Dawson, Institute of British Geographers, Special Publication No. 16, Academic Press, New York, pp. 321-343.

Clague, J.J. (1984a). *Quaternary Geology and Geomorphology, Smithers – Terrace – Prince Rupert Area, British Columbia.* Geological Survey of Canada Memoir 413. Ottawa.

Clague, J.J. (1984b). Deglaciation of the Prince Rupert – Kitimat area, British Columbia. *Canadian Journal of Earth Sciences* 22:256-265.

Clague, J.J. (1989a). Cordilleran ice sheet (Quaternary geology – Canadian Cordillera). In *Quaternary Geology of Canada and Greenland*, edited by R.J. Fulton, Geology of Canada 1, Geological Survey of Canada, Ottawa, pp. 40 41.

Clague, J.J. (1989b). Quaternary sea-levels (Quaternary geology – Canadian Cordillera). In *Quaternary Geology of Canada and Greenland*, edited by R.J. Fulton, Geology of Canada 1, Geological Survey of Canada, Ottawa, pp. 43-47.

Clague, J.J. (1989c). Quaternary geology of the Queen Charlotte Islands. In *The Outer Shores. Based on the Proceedings of the Queen Charlotte Islands First International Symposium, University of British Columbia, August 1984*, edited by G.S. Scudder and N. Gessler, Queen Charlotte Islands Museum Press, Queen Charlotte City, pp. 65-74.

Clague, J.J., J.R. Harper, R.J. Hebda, and D.E. Howes (1982). Late Quaternary sea levels and crustal movements, coastal British Columbia. *Canadian Journal of Earth Sciences* 19:597-618.

Clague, J.J., R.W. Mathewes, and B.G. Warner (1982). Late Quaternary geology of eastern Graham Island, Queen Charlotte Islands, British Columbia. *Canadian Journal of Earth Sciences* 19:1786-1795.

Cwynar, L.C. (1990). A late Quaternary vegetation history from Lily Lake, Chilkat Peninsula, southeast Alaska. *Canadian Journal of Botany* 68:1106-1112.

Davis, S.D. (1989). Introduction. In *The Hidden Falls Site, Baranof Island, Alaska*, edited by S.D. Davis, Alaska Anthropological Association Monograph Series, Fairbanks, pp. 1-22.

De Laguna, F., F.A. Riddell, D.F. McGeein, K.S. Lane, and J.A. Freed (1964). *Archaeology of the Yakutat Bay Area, Alaska*. Bureau of American Ethnology Bulletin 192.

Engstrom, D.R., B.C.S. Hansen, and H.E. Wright, Jr. (1990). A possible Younger Dryas record in Southeastern Alaska. *Science* 250:1383-1385.

Fladmark, K.R. (1975). *A Paleoecological Model for Northwest Coast Prehistory*. Archaeological Survey of Canada Mercury Series Paper 43. Canadian Museum of Civilization, Hull.

Fladmark, K.R. (1983a). A comparison of sea-levels and prehistoric cultural developments on the east and west coasts of Canada. In *The Evolution of Maritime Cultures on the Northeast and Northwest Coasts of America*, edited by R.J. Nash, Simon Fraser University Department of Archaeology Publication 11, Burnaby, pp. 65-77.

Foster, B. (1965). *The Evolution of the Mammals of the Queen Charlotte Islands*. British Columbia Provincial Museum Occasional Papers 14. Royal British Columbia Museum, Victoria.

Goodwin, R.G. (1988). Holocene glaciolacustrine sedimentation in Muir Inlet and ice advance in Glacier Bay, Alaska, U.S.A. *Arctic and Alpine Research* 29 (1): 55-69.

Gottesfeld, A.S., R.W. Mathewes, and L.M. Johnson Gottesfeld (1991). Holocene debris flows and environmental history, Hazleton area, British Columbia. *Canadian Journal of Earth Sciences* 28:1583-1593.

Harris, S.L. (1990). *Agents of Chaos: Earthquakes, Volcanoes and Other Natural Disasters*. Mountain Press Publishing Company, Missoula.

Heaton, T.H., S.L. Talbot, and G.F. Shields (1996). An Ice Age refugium for large mammals in the Alexander Archipelago, southeastern Alaska. *Quaternary Research* 46 (2):186-192.

Hebda, R.J., and R.W. Mathewes (1984). Holocene history of cedar and Native Indian cultures of the North American Pacific coast. *Science* 225:711-713.

Hebda, R.J., and R.W. Mathewes (1986). Radiocarbon dates from Anthony Island, Queen Charlotte Islands, and their geological and archaeological significance. *Canadian Journal of Earth Sciences* 23:2071-2076.

Heusser, C.J. (1955). Pollen profiles from the Queen Charlotte Islands, British Columbia. *Canadian Journal of Botany* 33:429-449.

Heusser, C.J. (1960). *Late Pleistocene environments of North Pacific North America*. American Geographical Society, Special Publication No. 3S.

Heusser, C.J. (1985). Quaternary pollen records from the Pacific Northwest Coast: Aleutians to the Oregon-California border. In *Pollen Records of Late Quaternary North American Sediments*, edited by V.M. Bryant and R.G. Holloway, American Association of Stratigraphic Palynologists Foundation, Dallas, pp. 141-185.

Heusser, C.J. (1989). North Pacific coastal refugia–the Queen Charlotte Islands in perspective. In *The Outer Shores. Based on the Proceedings of the Queen Charlotte Islands First International Symposium, University of British Columbia, August 1984*, edited by G.S. Scudder and N. Gessler, Queen Charlotte Islands Museum Press, Queen Charlotte City, pp. 91-106.

Josenhans, H.W., J.V. Barrie, K.W. Conway, R.T. Patterson, R.W. Mathewes, and G.J. Woodsworth (1993). Surficial geology of the Queen Charlotte Basin: evidence of submerged preglacial lakes at 170 m. on the continental shelf of western Canada. *Geological Survey of Canada Paper 93-1A, Current Research, Part A: Codillera and Pacific Margin*:119-127.

Josenhans, H.W., D.W. Fedje, K.W. Conway, and J.V. Barrie (1995). Post glacial sea-levels on the Western Canadian continental shelf: evidence for rapid change, extensive subaerial exposure and early human habitation. *Marine Geology* 125:73-94.

Kerr, F.A. (1948). Lower Stikine and Iskut River Areas, British Columbia. *Geological Survey of Canada Memoir 246*.

Klein, D.R. (1965). Postglacial distribution patterns of mammals in the southern coastal regions of Alaska. *Arctic* 18:7-20.

Lawrence, D.B. (1958). Glaciers and vegetation in south-eastern Alaska. *American Scientist* 46:89-122.

Luternauer, J.L., J.J. Clague, K.W. Conway, J.V. Barrie, B. Blaise, and R.W. Mathewes (1989a). Late Pleistocene terrestrial deposits on the continental shelf of western Canada: Evidence for rapid sea-level change at the end of the last glaciation. *Geology* 17:357-360.

Luternauer, J.L., K.W. Conway, J.J. Clague, and B. Blaise (1989b). Late Quaternary geology and geochronology of the central continental shelf of western Canada. *Marine Geology* 89:57-68.

Luternauer, J.L., and J.W. Murray (1983). *Late Quaternary Morphologic Development and Sedimentation, Central British Columbia Continental Shelf*. Geological Survey of Canada Paper 83-21. Ottawa.

Mann, D.H. (1986). Wisconsin and Holocene glaciation of Southeast Alaska. In *Glaciation in Alaska: The Geologic Record*, edited by T.D. Hamilton, K.M. Reed, and R.M. Thorson, Alaska Geological Society, Anchorage, pp. 237-265.

Mathewes, R.W. (1989). Paleobotany of the Queen Charlotte Islands. In *The Outer Shores. Based on the Proceedings of the Queen Charlotte Islands First International Symposium, University of British Columbia, August 1984*, edited by G.S. Scudder and N. Gessler, Queen Charlotte Islands Museum Press, Queen Charlotte City, pp. 75-90.

Mathewes, R.W. (1993). Evidence for Younger Dryas-age cooling on the North Pacific coast of America. *Quaternary Science Reviews* 12:321-331.

Mathewes, R.W., and J.J. Clague (1982). Stratigraphic relationships and paleoecology of a late-glacial peat bed from the Queen Charlotte Islands, British Columbia. *Canadian Journal of Earth Sciences* 19:1185-1195.

Mathewes, R.W., L.E. Heusser, and R.T. Patterson (1993). Evidence for a Younger Dryas-like cooling event on the British Columbia coast. *Geology* 21:101-104.

Mathewes, R.W., J.S. Vogel, J.R. Southon, and D.E. Nelson (1985). Accelerator radiocarbon date confirms early deglaciation of the Queen Charlotte Islands. *Canadian Journal of Earth Sciences* 22:790-791.

Miller, R.D. (1973). *Gastineau Channel Formation, A Composite Glaciomarine Deposit near Juneau, Alaska*. United States Geological Survey Bulletin 1394-C. Washington.

Mobley, C.M. (1988). Holocene sea-levels in Southeast Alaska: Preliminary results. *Arctic* 41 (4):261-266.

Molnia, B.F. (1986). Glacial history of the northeastern Gulf of Alaska – a synthesis. In *Glaciation in Alaska: The Geologic Record*, edited by T.D. Hamilton, K.M. Reed, and R.M. Thorson, Alaska Geological Society, Anchorage, pp. 219-235.

Moodie, G.E., and V. Reimchen (1976). Glacial refugia, endemism, and stickleback populations of the Queen Charlotte Islands, British Columbia. *The Canadian Field Naturalist* 90:471-474.

Morrison, R.B. (1968). Means of time-stratigraphic division and long-distance correlation of Quaternary successions. In *Means of Correlation of Quaternary Successions*, edited by R.B. Morrison and H.E. Wright, Proceedings of the 7th INQUA Congress (1965) 8, University of Utah Press, Salt Lake City, pp. 1-113.

Nasmith, H. (1970). Pleistocene geology of the Queen Charlotte Islands and southern British Columbia. In *Early Man and Environments in Northwest North America*, edited by R.A. Smith and J.W. Smith, The University of Calgary Archaeological Association, Calgary, pp. 53-64.

O'Reilley, P., T.E. Reimchen, R. Beech, and C. Strombeck (1993). Mitochondrial DNA in *Gasterosteus* and Pleistocene glacial refugium on the Queen Charlotte Islands, British Columbia. *Evolution* 47 (2):678-684.

Peck, C., Sr. (1982). Two women and the glacier. In *Alaska's Glaciers*, edited by R.A. Henning, B. Olds, and P. Renick, Alaska Geographic 9(1) pp. 70-71.

Peteet, D.M. (1986). Modern pollen rain and vegetational history of the Malaspina Glacier District, Alaska. *Quaternary Research* 25:100-120.

Peteet, D.M. (1991). Postglacial migration history of lodgepole pine near Yakutat, Alaska. *Canadian Journal of Botany* 69:786-796.

Péwé, T.L. (1975). *Quaternary Geology of Alaska*. United States Geological Survey Professional Paper 835. Washington.

Péwé, T.L., D.M. Hopkins, and J.L. Giddings (1965). The Quaternary geology and archaeology of Alaska. In *The Quaternary of the United States*, edited by H.E. Wright and D.G. Frey, Princeton University Press, Princeton, pp. 355-373.

Porter, S.C. (1989). Late Holocene fluctuations of the fjord glacier system in Icy Bay, Alaska, U.S.A. *Arctic and Alpine Research* 21 (4):364-379.

Post, A. (1976). The tilted forest: Glaciological-geologic implications of vegetated Neoglacial ice at Lituya Bay, Alaska. *Quaternary Research* 6:111-117.

Prest, V.K. (1969). *Retreat of Wisconsin and Recent Ice in North America*. Geological Survey of Canada, Ottawa.

Prest, V.K. (1984). The late Wisconsin glacier complex. *Geological Survey of Canada Paper* 84-10:21-36.

Robinson, W., and W. Wright (1962). *Men of Medeek*. Northern Sentinel Press Ltd., Kitimat.

Sutherland-Brown, A. (1968). *Geology of the Queen Charlotte Islands, British Columbia*. British Columbia Department of Mines and Petroleum Resources Bulletin 54. Victoria.

Sutherland-Brown, A. (1969). Aiyansh lava flow, British Columbia. *Canadian Journal of Earth Sciences* 6:1460-1468.

Sutherland-Brown, A., and H. Nasmith (1962). The glaciation of the Queen Charlotte Islands. *Canadian Field-Naturalist* 76:209-219.

Swanston, D.N. (1969). A Late Pleistocene glacial sequence from Prince of Wales Island, Alaska. *Arctic* 22 (1):25-33.

Swanston, D.N. (1989). Glacial stratigraphic correlations and Late Quaternary chronology. In *The Hidden Falls Site, Baranof Island, Alaska*, edited by S.D. Davis, Alaska Anthropological Association Monograph Series, Fairbanks, pp. 47-60.

Warner, B.G., R.W. Mathewes, and J.J. Clague (1982). Ice-free conditions on the Queen Charlotte islands, British Columbia, at the height of the Late Wisconsin Glaciation. *Science* 218:675-677.

Yorath, C.J., and R.L. Chase (1981). Tectonic history of the Queen Charlotte Islands and adjacent areas - a model. *Canadian Journal of Earth Sciences* 18: 1717-1739.

Revisiting an Old Concept: The North Coast Interaction Sphere

Patricia D. Sutherland

ABSTRACT

The concept of a "north coast interaction sphere" is re-examined in light of recent interpretations of social and economic change on the northern Northwest Coast, particularly those relating to the evolution of cultural complexity and ranked society. The archaeological evidence which has been used to support such arguments is summarized and compared to that of the western Arctic Inuvialuit, a maritime hunting society in which status was attained through accomplishment rather than heredity. It is argued that archaeological evidence does not support interpretations of the early evolution of social complexity as known from the historic period on the northern Northwest Coast. The existence of a prehistoric interaction sphere should not be considered as marking the beginning of the ethnographic pattern of social complexity and ranked societies.

RÉSUMÉ

On ré-examine le concept de «la sphère d'interaction dans le nord de la côte» à la lumière des interprétations récentes reliées au changement social et économique qui ont eu lieu dans le nord de la Côte Ouest, particulièrement en ce qui a trait à l'évolution de la complexité culturelle et de la hiérarchie sociale. On passe en revue l'enregistrement archéologique qui a été utilisé pour appuyer de tels arguments et on le compare à celui des Inuvialuit de l'arctique occidental, société de chasse maritime où le rendement plutôt que l'hérédité

In *Perspectives on Northern Northwest Coast Prehistory*, edited by Jerome S. Cybulski. Hull: Canadian Museum of Civilization, Archaeological Survey of Canada, Mercury Series Paper 160, pp. 49-59, © 2001.

donnait accès au statut. On affirme que l'enregistrement archéologique n'appuie pas les interprétations reliées à l'évolution ancienne de la complexité sociale telle qu'elle se manifestait à la période historique dans le nord de la Côte Ouest. Il n'est pas de mise de considérer que l'existence de l'interaction préhistorique marque le début du mode ethnographique de la complexité sociale et des sociétés hiérarchisées.

INTRODUCTION

In 1969, following several seasons of field work in northern British Columbia, including excavations in Prince Rupert Harbour and on the Queen Charlotte Islands, George F. MacDonald (1969) proposed the concept of an "area co-tradition" for the northern Northwest Coast. Basic to this concept was the notion that the same cultural pattern which characterized the northern coast historically, or what Drucker (1955) called the "Northern Province," was also shared by the prehistoric peoples who occupied the area.

As archaeological research progressed, this concept was replaced by that of a "north coast interaction sphere" (Fladmark 1975; Fladmark et al. 1990). It was thought that until approximately 3000-2500 B.P. cultural developments in the areas occupied historically by the Tsimshian and Haida were separate and distinct. The interaction sphere which was postulated to have been established at this time consisted of an exchange of ideas, goods and people maintained through trade, warfare, and intermarriage. It was considered that this development marked the beginning of the so-called "ethnographic pattern" on the northern Northwest Coast (MacDonald and Inglis 1981).

This paper revisits the concept of the "north coast interaction sphere" in light of recent archaeological research and interpretation that has taken place during the past two decades.

RECENT RESEARCH ON THE NORTHERN NORTHWEST COAST

The most notable development in archaeological work on the coast of British Columbia in recent years has been the elaboration of arguments dealing with the development of social complexity. Efforts to trace the origins of the "ethnographic pattern" have been a central interest since the earliest days of archaeological work on the northern coast and, indeed, the concepts of "area co-tradition" and "north coast interaction sphere" were attempts to place elements of the ethnographic pattern into an archaeological context. More recently, however, interpretation has focused on the development of the central core of this pattern: the system of social ranking which was fundamental to all aspects of life on the Northwest coast during the ethnographic period.

Social ranking is a factor which is difficult to detect archaeologically. Interpretations have generally been based on material factors which are directly or indirectly associated with social complexity. They includesize of residential and community units, material markers of social status as revealed in dwellings and burials, evidence of warfare, and evidence of trade for exotic and highly valued goods which are assumed to have had an unequal distribution within a society. The use of such indirect markers has usually led to interpretations postulating the development of social ranking beginning at some time between 3500 and 2500 years ago.

While scholars working on the northern coast have been developing these interpretations, the focus of my research has shifted from northern British Columbia to Arctic Canada. This work has familiarized me with cultural sequences which share certain characteristics with those of the Pacific coast but which have been interpreted in a much different manner. Most relevant to the present discussion is the history and traditional culture of the Inuvialuit, the occupants of the outer portion of the Mackenzie River Delta and adjacent regions of the western Arctic coast.

The Inuvialuit are the most easterly of the relatively dense Eskimo population groups which inhabit the Western Arctic. They traditionally lived in large multifamily winter houses and summer communities which ranged up to 1000 or more people, engaged in long-distance trade involving the movement of goods between the Central Arctic and Siberia, carried out warfare with neighboring Indian and Inuit groups, and were buried in a complex fashion involving the inclusion of personal items such as labrets, sleds, kayaks and even whaling boats ten metres or more in length (Stefansson 1914; McGhee 1974). Most of these elements are those which are used by archaeologists working on the northern Northwest Coast as markers for the development of a ranked society. Yet, the traditional social organization of the Inuvialuit was not based on hereditary rank. Only one village was said to have had a hereditary chief (Stefansson 1914:165-72) and this interpretation seems to have been based on a rather vague knowledge of succession practices. Accomplishment in hunting and the ability to provide for family and associates were the bases for social status marked by the term umealik, literally, a man who owned or controlled an umiak or whaling-boat (Stefansson 1914:164).

The material correlates of Inuvialuit social organization show distinct similarities to those which have been used to suggest the existence of prehistoric ranked societies on the northern Northwest Coast. This leads one to suggest that if the "ethnographic pattern" in this region had been similar to that of the Inuvialuit rather than that of the Haida and Tsimshian, the archaeological evidence would not have encouraged an interpretation of evolving ranked societies over the past few millennia.

RECONSIDERING THE "NORTH COAST INTERACTION SPHERE"

The link between the concept of the "north coast interaction sphere" and the interpretation of hereditary social ranking appears to centre on evidence of trade and warfare. There seems to be general agreement that these activities are key elements in the development of social complexity throughout the region. Most of the research has focused on developments in traditional Tsimshian territory. It might be usefully complemented by a summary of what we know of the prehistoric development of trade and warfare in traditional Haida territory on the Queen Charlotte Islands.

The isolated location of Haida Gwaii, separated from the mainland for several thousand years in the past by a dangerous body of water, allows the presence of materials emanating from the mainland to be interpreted as obvious evidence of long-distance communication. The cultural sequence on the Queen Charlotte Islands goes back at least 9000 years (Fedje et al. 1996) and throughout that span of time retains its distinctive character in comparison to adjacent mainland sequences. The prehistory of Haida Gwaii can be described in terms of three subsequent traditions: a newly recognized but poorly understand complex of materials which begins to appear about 9200 years ago (Fedje et al. 1996); the Moresby Tradition from approximately 8000 to 5000 years ago, defined primarily on the basis of a microblade industry; and the Graham Tradition beginning about 5000 years ago and characterized by shell midden accumulation and a wide range of bone and antler artifacts, as well as both ground and chipped stone tools (Fladmark et al. 1990).

Evidence of contact with the mainland appears relatively early with the occurrence of a microblade fragment of obsidian from the Late Moresby Tradition site of Cohoe Creek (Ham 1990). To date, this is the only such find, and would suggest occasional and sporadic contact rather than systematic trade across Hecate Strait during this period. In the Graham Tradition as represented at Blue Jackets Creek and beginning around 4000 years ago, contact with the mainland is evidenced by the presence of obsidian artifacts, ribbed stones which appear in Prince Rupert Harbour assemblages, and artifacts manufactured from the tissue of animals which are not indigenous to the islands, such as porcupine incisor tools (Sutherland 1980). The larger amounts and greater variety of materials suggest more contact with adjacent mainland regions at this time. Given the evidence for widespread and well developed occupation of traditional Tsimshian territory during this period, it seems very likely that most of this material was obtained by trade with mainland populations.

Long-distance trade in both utilitarian and exotic materials, therefore, has a long history on the northern coast and began much earlier than the dates proposed by various models for the development of complex ranked society. The archaeological evidence in both the Moresby and Graham traditions, however, suggests a much smaller scale of trade than that known from the historic period. If evidence of trade is to be used as a measure of social complexity, we must suspect that the scale of the trade indicated by archaeological materials would not be consistent with the development of hereditary ranked social units.

In mainland sequences, located in areas with access to a broader range of materials, archaeological evidence of trade is more difficult to recognize. However, the scale of trade in all archaeological periods dating earlier than a few centuries ago would appear to be on a similar level to that evidenced on the Queen Charlotte Islands. In terms of trade, a "north coast interaction sphere" appears to have been developing as early as, perhaps, 4000 years ago, but it is unlikely that these trading contacts were carried out in the context of developing social complexity leading directly to that of the ethnographic period. The scale of trade evidenced archaeologically is more on the level which characterized the ethnographic Inuvialuit than the level of historic Northwest Coast peoples.

Archaeological evidence of warfare is another measure which has been used to postulate the type of community interactions which characterized the ethnographic period. According to Cybulski's (1999) analysis of skeletal trauma in burials from the Prince Rupert Harbour area, warfare was endemic in the period between 3100 and 1500 years ago. Archer (1992) reports the abandonment of communities in the later portion of this period, possibly related to resettlement to more defensible locations. Evidence of conflict appears significantly earlier at Namu on the central coast (Cybulski 1996). The burials from Blue Jackets Creek on the Queen Charlotte Islands show no indication of the trauma noted for adjacent mainland groups and evidence suggesting involvement in warfare is limited to a few stone club fragments (Severs 1974). The archaeological evidence, therefore, suggests that warfare may have occurred at different periods and different scales of intensity in various regions of the Northwest Coast. Interpreting this evidence as signaling the development of complex societies is rather problematic. Recent excavations in the Mackenzie Delta region of the western Canadian Arctic have produced evidence of inter-community violence on a similar scale among ancestral Inuvialuit (Morrison and Arnold 1994). As in the case of trade, warfare may have been a component of a developing interaction sphere without being related to the development of ranked societies.

Burials have provided scope for further interpretation of status differentiation as a sign of increasing social complexity. On the Nass River, for example, Cybulski (1992:71) notes the appearance of labret use in female burials from midden deposits at the Greenville site, dating from approximately 1500 years ago, as a signal of continuity with the practices of the ethnographic period and as a measure of the development of ranked society. Midden interments also occur at Blue Jackets Creek on the Queen Charlotte Islands, and labret wear is also apparent on the teeth of some individuals buried there (Severs 1974). In contrast to Greenville, relatively complex burial practices are evidenced as early as 4000 to 5000 years ago at Blue Jackets Creek with burials accompanied by grave goods such as shell disc beads, beads of sea otter teeth, obsidian, and, in one case, by artifacts made from caribou metapodials incised with geometric designs.

The development of complex burial practices also appears as early as 4000 to 5000 years ago at the Pender Canal site on the southern coast (Carlson and Hobler 1993). In other areas, the development appears to occur at a somewhat later date and in each region the practice takes a distinctive form. Interaction between regions may be suspected as a means of transmitting the general ideas of burial practice, and such elements as labret use and complex burial can be seen as evidence of a "north coast interaction sphere." Yet, as in the case of trade and warfare, there is not a necessary or even probable link between these practices and the development of ranked societies. To return to the Mackenzie Delta model, it should be remembered that labrets were worn by all men in Inuvialuit society. Burials were differentiated by the nature of equipment provided for the grave, ranging from sleds and kayaks for most hunters to umiaks for men who had achieved the status of umealik.

Leaving aside for the moment the arguments relating to an interaction sphere, perhaps the most direct material evidence for the existence of complex corporate groups is that relating to the size and nature of residential units. The most revealing evidence comes from Coupland's (1988) analysis of the prehistory of Kitselas Canyon on the lower Skeena River. Here, the Paul Mason phase (3200-2700 years ago) is seen as transitional from temporary camps to permanent villages of small and egalitarian residential units. Some evidence of differentiation is seen in the Kleanza phase (2500-1500 years ago), but then there is a hiatus of some 1200 years until the historic period. Historic villages in the area were five times the size of those of the Kleanza phase, suggesting a major increase in social complexity.

In the past I have undertaken analysis of three shell midden sites located in three regions of the northern Northwest Coast: Blue Jackets Creek on the Queen Charlotte Islands, Dodge Island in Prince Rupert Harbour, and Greenville on the Nass River. All three sites provided evidence of prolonged residential use, and between them they cover the period from approximately 4000 to 1500 years ago. In none of these sites is there evidence for the type of large structures, or differentiated residential units, which characterized the ranked societies of the ethnographic period in the region (Severs 1974, Sutherland 1978, Cybulski 1992).

SUMMARY

In recent years, the principle interest of most scholars working on the prehistory of the northern Northwest Coast has focused on the evolution of cultural complexity, and in particular of ranked society. Many of the arguments relating to this question deal with the interactions of social groups both within and between the areas inhabited historically by nations such as the Tsimshian and Haida. Evidence for the development of an "area co-tradition" or a "north coast interaction sphere" has been used to support the idea of an evolving social complexity taking place over the past 2500 or 3500 years and leading directly to the hereditary ranked social units of the historic period.

This paper suggests that we might more closely examine the link between regional interaction, as evidenced by trade, warfare, and similar levels of burial ceremonialism, and the evolution of social complexity. As noted above, the levels of trade, warfare, burial differentiation, and even labret use, which are evident on the northern Northwest Coast throughout much of the prehistoric period, are on a scale similar to those of non-ranked peoples such as the Mackenzie Delta Inuvialuit. By concentrating on the long-term evolution of social ranking, we may be missing evidence for more complicated and more interesting processes. Working on the assumption of continuous development, and searching for a distinct point in that development which marks the appearance of ranked society, is likely not the most useful approach to understanding north coast prehistory.

Present evidence suggests that interaction between the peoples of various regions of the Northwest Coast has an ancient history, evidenced by sporadic trade extending more than 5000 years into the past. This interaction reached new levels, in terms of trade and the spread of ideas, in the period between approximately 3500 and 2500 years ago, and in some regions this development was accompanied by warfare. I would argue that the development of a "north coast interaction sphere" should be viewed as a period of dynamic change, but should not be confused with evidence for the development of ranked societies. Certainly, at the end of this period, there are no convincing archaeological indications to support such interpretations. The complex social organization which characterized the ethnographic pattern appears to be a relatively late development and one which has not been traced archaeologically beyond the past few centuries.

Recent research reported elsewhere in this volume suggests that the prehistory of the northern coast does not appear to fit a model of smooth and continuous development over the past several thousand years, leading gradually to the cultures of the historic Tsimshian and Haida. Instead, as Maschner (1991:924) stated nearly a decade ago "the development of the ethnographically known Northwest Coast pattern is the product of a long and turbulent history." I would add that the elements which comprise "the north coast cultural pattern" did not develop at the same time as part of an evolving complex, but at different times and in different situations as part of an ongoing process of historical and evolutionary change. Archaeologists might usefully reassess the importance of unique events and situations in the development of specific historical traditions, rather than neglecting such events in the search for evidence of cultural patterns.

ACKNOWLEDGEMENTS

I wish to thank Jerome Cybulski and George MacDonald for giving me the opportunity to work on research collections in their care and for discussions we have had on the prehistory of the North Coast.

REFERENCES CITED

Archer, D.J.W. (1992). Results of the Prince Rupert Harbour Radiocarbon Dating Project. Unpublished manuscript, Resource Information Centre, Heritage Conservation Branch, Government of British Columbia, Victoria.

Carlson, R.L., and P.M. Hobler (1993). The Pender Canal excavations and the development of Coast Salish culture. *BC Studies* 99:25-52.

Coupland, G. (1988). *Prehistoric Cultural Change at Kitselas Canyon*. Archaeological Survey of Canada Mercury Series Paper 138. Canadian Museum of Civilization, Hull.

Cybulski, J.S. (1992). *A Greenville Burial Ground: Human Remains and Mortuary Elements in British Columbia Coast Prehistory*. Archaeological Survey of Canada Mercury Series Paper 146. Canadian Museum of Civilization, Hull.

Cybulski, J.S. (1996). Conflict and Complexity on the Northwest Coast: Skeletal and Mortuary Evidence. Paper Read at the 61st Annual Meeting of the Society for American Archaeology, New Orleans.

Cybulski, J.S. (1999). Trauma and warfare at Prince Rupert Harbour. *The Midden* 31 (2):5-7.

Drucker, P. (1955). *Indians of the Northwest Coast*. American Museum Science Books. The Natural History Press, New York.

Eldridge, M. (1991). The Glenrose Cannery Wet Component: A Significance Assessment. Unpublished manuscript (Permit 1990-24), Resource Information Centre, Heritage Conservation Branch, Government of British Columbia, Victoria.

Fedje, D., J.B. McSporran, and A.R. Mason (1996). Early Holocene Archaeology and Palaeoecology at the Arrow Creek Sites in Gwaii Haanas. *Arctic Anthropology* 33 (1):116-142.

Fladmark, K.R. (1975). *A Paleoecological Model for Northwest Coast Prehistory*. Archaeological Survey of Canada Mercury Series Paper 43. Canadian Museum of Civilization, Hull.

Fladmark, K.R., K.M. Ames, and P.D. Sutherland (1990). Prehistory of the northern coast of British Columbia. In *Handbook of North American Indians, Vol. 7, Northwest Coast*, edited by W. Suttles, Smithsonian Institution, Washington, pp. 229-239.

Ham, L.C. (1990). The Cohoe Creek site: A Late Moresby Tradition shell midden. *Canadian Journal of Archaeology* 14:199-221.

MacDonald, G.F. (1969). Preliminary culture sequence from the Coast Tsimshian area, British Columbia. *Northwest Anthropological Research Notes* 3 (2):240-254.

MacDonald, G.F., and R.I. Inglis (1981). An overview of the North Coast Prehistory Project (1966-1980). *BC Studies* 48:37-63.

Maschner, H.D.G. (1991). The emergence of cultural complexity on the northern Northwest Coast. *Antiquity* 65:924-934.

McGhee, R. (1974). *Beluga Hunters: An Archaeological Reconstruction of the History and Culture of the Mackenzie Delta Kittegaryumiut*. Institute of Social and Economic Research, Memorial University of Newfoundland, St. John's.

Morrison, D., and C. Arnold (1994). The Inuktuiut of the Eskimo Lakes. In *Bridges Across Time: The NOGAP Archaeology Project*, edited by J.-L. Pilon, Canadian Archaeological Association, Occasional Paper 2, Victoria, pp. 117-126.

Severs, P.D.S. (1974). Archaeological investigations at Blue Jackets Creek, FlUa-4, Queen Charlotte Islands, British Columbia, 1973. *Canadian Archaeological Association Bulletin* 6:165-205.

Stefansson, V. (1914). The Stefansson-Anderson Arctic Expedition, Preliminary Ethnological Report. *Anthropological Papers of the American Museum of Natural History* 14 (1).

Sutherland, P.D. (1978). Dodge Island: A Prehistoric Coast Tsimshian Settlement Site in Prince Rupert Harbour, British Columbia. Unpublished manuscript (Ms. 1345), Information Management Services (Archaeological Records), Canadian Museum of Civilization, Hull.

Sutherland, P.D. (1980). Understanding Cultural Relationships Across Hecate Strait, Northern British Columbia. Paper presented at the 13th Annual Meeting of the Canadian Archaeological Association, Saskatoon.

Defending the Mouth of the Skeena: Perspectives on Tsimshian Tlingit Relations

Susan Marsden

ABSTRACT

This paper explores the possible coincidence of the oral record of the Gitksan, Nisga'a, and Tsimshian (*adawx*) and the Tlingit (*at.oow*) with the findings of Northwest Coast archaeology. In particular, key events in the common history of the Tsimshian and the Tlingit are examined in the light of archaeological work on the Skeena River and at Prince Rupert Harbour. Consideration is also given to recent geological studies in the region. Discussion includes the potential role of oral history in archaeological projects and the need for a rigorous methodology in the review and interpretation of the oral record.

RÉSUMÉ

Cet article explore la possibilité que la tradition orale des Gitksans, des Nisga'as, des Tsimshans (*adawx*) et des Tlingits (*at.oow*) coïncide avec les découvertes archéologiques sur la Côte Ouest. On examine particulièrement les événements clefs de l'histoire commune des Tsimshans et des Tlingits à la lumière des fouilles archéologiques effectués sur la rivière Skeena et à Prince Rupert Harbour. On accorde aussi une considération aux récentes études géologiques effectuées dans la région. La discussion tient compte du rôle potentiel qu'a joué l'histoire eu égard à la mise en œuvre des projets archéologiques et le besoin d'une méthodologie rigoureuse face à la réévaluation et à l'interprétation de la tradition orale.

In *Perspectives on Northern Northwest Coast Prehistory*, edited by Jerome S. Cybulski. Hull: Canadian Museum of Civilization, Archaeological Survey of Canada, Mercury Series Paper 160, pp. 61-106, © 2001.

INTRODUCTION

The oral historical and cultural record of aboriginal peoples has informed anthropology and archaeology since the founding of these disciplines, yet scholars, for the most part, have failed to understand the aboriginal institutions that have ensured the preservation and transmission of that knowledge. As well, most scholars have assumed a qualitative difference between written and oral history, the latter being considered relatively recent, informal, fragmentary, and, therefore, comparatively unreliable.

Rather than continue to filter the oral record through this academic lens, this paper revisits the oral histories of northern Northwest Coast First Nations, the *adawx* of the Gitksan, Nisga'a, and Tsimshian and the *at.oow* of the Tlingit, approaching them as the product of a formal intellectual institution that defines their content, form, and integrity.[1] For these nations (see Fig. 1), it is the responsibility of the extended kinship group, or *wilnat'aał*, within each clan to perpetuate the memory of their history.[2] The record of the extraordinary, often epic, events that shaped the unique identity of each group is composed as *adawx* and validated in a feast, or potlatch, where other *wilnat'aał* witness the telling of the *adawx* and acknowledge its legitimacy. These formal historical documents are then passed on through the chiefs, who in each ensuing generation validate them again in their feasts.

Through the feast, therefore, the chiefs know their own groups' histories in the context of the histories of all the other groups within their clans, tribes (villages) and nations. For northern Northwest Coast First Nations, this historical context defines current social, political, and economic relationships and shapes the decisions that will define those relationships in the future. The legitimacy of

---

[1] The northern Northwest Coast is defined in this paper to include the territories of the Haida, Tlingit, Tsimshian, Tahltan, Tsetsaut, Nisga'a, Gitksan, Haisla, and Heiltsuk. Events described in the *adawx* and *at.oow* took place in the territories of these nations.

[2] The Tsimshian *wilnat'aał* and the Tlingit clan (sib) refer to a group of Houses which share the same ancestry and history. Although the Tlingit change their sib name as they move to new locations and the Tsimshian do not formally name their *wilnat'aał* but represent it through their crests, in both nations it is the ancestry and history of this group that are perpetuated in *adawx* and *at.oow*. Phratries are also the same institution among the Tsimshian and Tlingit. The Tlingit, however, have a strong moiety system and only two phratries, the Raven and the Wolf (predominately in the south) and the Raven and the Eagle (predominately in the north), the Wolf and Eagle sometimes being considered the same phratry. Four phratries are found among the Tsimshian, Gitksan, and Nisga'a: the Eagle, Wolf, Killerwhale/Fireweed and Raven/Frog. However, a strong moiety system also underlies the social institutions of these nations.

territorial holdings, the nature and scope of marriage and clan alliances, and access to territory, trade, status, and wealth all flow from the historical identity of the group. The *adawx* and *at.oow*, therefore, are not merely remembered events, related periodically on ceremonial occasions. They record, define, and perpetuate the very fabric of society.

This paper attempts to acknowledge the full significance and rich intellectual content of the *adawx* and *at.oow*, to provide an academic form in which the original aboriginal voice is not subsumed by that of the non-aboriginal scholar, and to examine a greater role for archaeology and other disciplines in research that parallels and dates the oral record. As a case in point, this paper examines the extensive oral record that chronicles a period of migration of Athapascan peoples into the territories of the Tlingit and a further movement of Athapascan and Tlingit groups into the territories of the Gitksan, Nisga'a, and Tsimshian.

The paper first presents the *adawx* and *at.oow* that describe a period of warfare among the Wolf, Eagle, and Raven clan groups then established at the headwaters of the Stikine River. These groups were probably Tsetsaut and Tahltan but may have assimilated other Athapascans from outside the region. Those facing defeat abandoned the area and travelled downriver to the coast, where, as the *adawx* describe, some of them joined peoples long established on the coast and others more recently arrived there from the north. The *adawx* also describe further hostilities, culminating in a major battle within Tlingit territory at Tutxank in what is now southeast Alaska, and the subsequent move of the defeated peoples south to the border of Tsimshian and Tlingit territory.

The paper then presents *adawx* that describe the migration into Tsimshian territory of Raven, Wolf, and Eagle clan groups and the resulting wars between them and the Tsimshian at the mouths of the Skeena and Nass rivers and in coastal areas to the south. The accounts reveal a complex process by which the Tsimshian absorbed many of the invading peoples. The *adawx* also describe another wave of migration, by the same Athapascan peoples from the headwaters of the Stikine, down the Skeena River into Gitksan, Tsimshian, and Nisga'a territory, and the effects of that final migration among the Tsimshian.

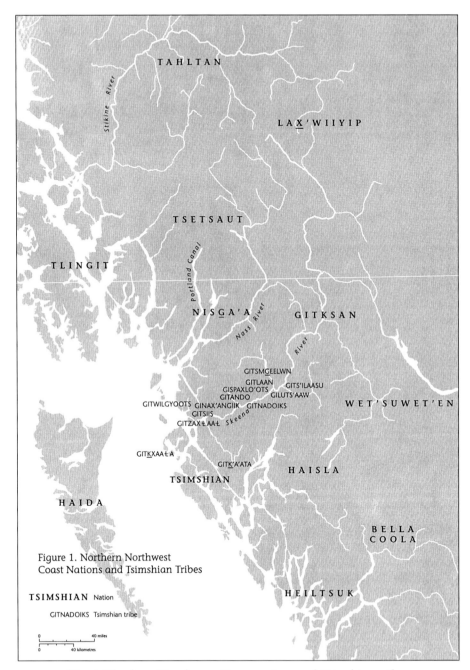

TAHLTAN

LAX̲'WIIYIP

Stikine River

TSETSAUT

TLINGIT

Portland Canal

NISG̲A'A

Nass River

GITKSAN

River

GITSMG̲EELWN
GITLAAN   GITS'ILAASU
GISPAXLO'OTS   GILUTS'AAW
GITANDO
GITWILGYOOTS GINAX'ANGIIK   GITNADOIKS   WET'SUWET'EN
GITSIIS
GITZAX̱ƚAAƚ Skeena

GITK̲XAAƚA

GITK̲'A'ATA

TSIMSHIAN   HAISLA

HAIDA

BELLA
COOLA

Figure 1. Northern Northwest
Coast Nations and Tsimshian Tribes

TSIMSHIAN Nation

GITNADOIKS Tsimshian tribe

HEILTSUK

| 0   40 miles |
| 0   40 kilometres |

Fig. 1. Northern Northwest Coast nations and Tsimshian tribes.

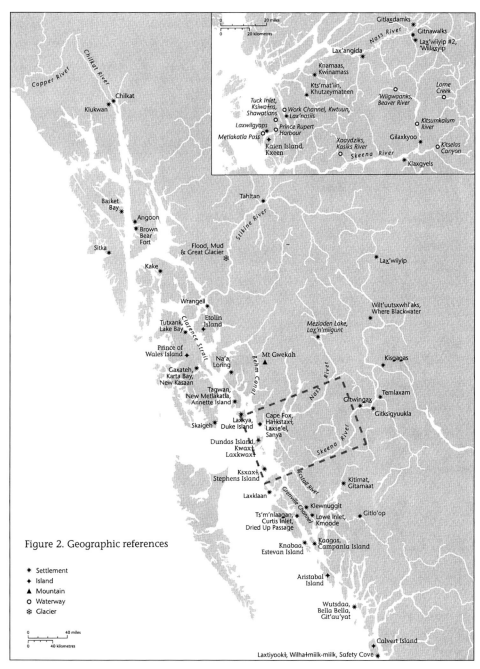

Figure 2. Geographic references

* Settlement
+ Island
▲ Mountain
○ Waterway
❋ Glacier

Fig. 2. Geographic references.

THE ADAWX RECORD

MIGRATION

The *adawx* that describe this period of migration consistently begin at the headwaters of the Stikine River, at the boundary of the Northwest Coast geographic region, beyond which, as a rule, events are not recorded by *adawx* and *at.oow*. Lax'wiiyip, meaning "open landscape" or "plateau" is the name of the general area at the headwaters of the Stikine where groups of the Wolf, Eagle, and Raven clans made their villages. Two specific areas or villages, Daxk'leo and Takun, are also mentioned but not specifically located by the *adawx* (for all places located by the *adawx* see Fig. 2). Disputes over salmon rivers and hunting grounds eventually caused a rift between the peoples at Lax'wiiyip and ended in many of them being forced to leave their homeland.

The *adawx* told by the descendants of those peoples speak of their movements and settlements and together tell the history of the period. George McCauley and Mary Ałaxsgaax (Wolf clan, Gitkxaała (Kitkatla)) described the events at the headwaters of the Stikine that precipitated the migration, in their history of the Tsimshian Wolf clan House of Nisgałoot of Gitkxaała:[3]

> In olden days, these people used to live together with the Ganhada people at the head of the Stikine River and their chief was Nisgałoot. The Laxgibuu (Wolf) clan was then at the head of all the people because it was numerous and they were great hunters. The Ganhada (Raven) people were very jealous of them because of their wealth, always having plenty of furs and also owning a salmon river from which they gathered great quantities of fish, and this fish they allowed no one else to catch. They traded this fish to the Ganhada and the Laxskiik (Eagles) who lived farther up the river. The Laxgibuu also had the best hunting grounds, and they always got a large quantity of furs. The other clans only got a few, and this made them very jealous of the Laxgibuu chief. So they, the Ganhada and the Laxskiik, planned to wage war upon the Laxgibuu (Beynon and Barbeau n.d. d, no. 2).

The Wolf clan groups at Lax'wiiyip were outnumbered and faced defeat. As a result, many of them abandoned their territory, and, accompanied by the families of their Raven clan spouses, some travelled overland to the headwaters of the Nass

---

[3] In the citations that follow, the spelling of the words in the various Northwest Coast languages have been standardized in the current orthography to assist the reader.

and Skeena Rivers and then later down the Skeena to the coast. Others, either accompanied or followed by groups of the Raven and Eagle clans, travelled down the Stikine but found their way blocked by a glacier. As described by George McCauley and Mary Ałaxsgaax, some of those people decided to go overland toward the north, while others passed through a narrow tunnel in the ice:

> As soon as the Laxgibuu heard this [that their village had been attacked], they all got into their canoes and fled down the river, and they were chased by the Laxskiik and the Ganhada who had now beaten them. Then the Laxgibuu came to a large glacier under which the water flowed. Many of the Laxgibuu fugitives did not want to go through this passage. They went up into the hills. Some went away to the head of the Nass River, and others went north. Only Nisgałoot and some of his nephews went with him and also some of the women. They went through the ice passage (under the glacier). When they had done this, they lived for a short time on this side of the glacier, and they sang a dirge song, and they then went down to the salt water, and still farther south (Beynon and Barbeau n.d. d, no. 2).

In the *at.oow*, "Basket Bay History," Robert Zuboff (Shaadaax', Raven clan, Kak'weidi) told of the origins of the Tlingit Dakl'aweidi of the Wolf clan who travelled over the glacier toward the north and came down the Chilkat River, and of the Raven clan Deisheetaan, the ancestors of the Kak'weidi at Basket Bay, who went under the glacier and down the Stikine River (for migration routes see Fig. 3):[4]

That land of ours,	It was long ago,
that land of ours	it's been long,
is called Kak'w;	since the histories have been told of us;
but in English	we are named for it,
Basket Bay . . .	Kak'weidi.
This is how the history is told,	For the things that happened
about	to the Tlingit
Basket Bay, from the time it's been ours,	in the beginning,
from the time it's been ours,	many say
ages.	we migrated here

---

[4] Those who migrated into Tlingit territory are already identified here as Tlingit, even though they could still be considered Tahltan or Tsetsaut, or, if they were new to Tahltan or Tsetsaut territory at the headwaters of the Stikine River, Athapascan from a nation north or west of the Stikine. Rather than complicate this paper with designations such as Athapascan/Tlingit, the reader is asked to keep in mind the relatively recent Athapascan origin of many people designated as Tlingit.

through the south,
the south.
And, you know, there are many
          who migrated down the Stikine
River,
down the Stikine River.
The story of my fathers is always told,
of when they migrated down the Stikine.
At one place, there,
in the river,
the river flowed under a glacier.
This is where they tied a raft together.
They put the elderly women on it.
One's name was Awasti and the other
Koowasikx,
these elderly women.
They are the first ones who were pushed
under
          the glacier.
Having drifted under it and through to the
other side,
they started singing.
Floating under the glacier
gave them their song.
Based on this
a raft was made.
Some went on it.
Under it, under the glacier, they floated,
down the river.
But many of them
were afraid
to float under the glacier.
That is why they started over it,
some started over the glacier.
These are the ones who came down the
Chilkat,
          the relatives of my fathers,
the Dakl'aweidi.
They became the Chilkats.
The name that came from those
          who went over the glacier
is Sitka [glacier] indeed,

those who came down through Chilkat,
are named Sitka.
Those of us
who are Deisheetaan,
still
tell it like this,
as coming from the South,
from the south.
I wonder where we came out, those of us.
I wonder where we came out.
From there we finally went northward,
northward,
we began searching.
They tried many places.
Villages were founded in many places.
At that time
across from Brown Bear Fort,
when it froze,
they walked over the ice
at that time,
at the point when they moved across.
Well! There are many who are our relatives,
these Deisheetaan,
some are living in the Interior.
Since long ago,
they have been living there.
There are many,
Nahoowu lives there
and this namesake of mine.
Shaadaax' is also there,
in the Interior.
You know, thinking about them,
if they've been living there a long time,
maybe we separated and migrated from
them.
That is why I'm thinking about them.
That is why we
gathered here on the coast.
This is where I will end
this story (Dauenhauer and Dauenhauer
1987:63-70).

Moses Klukshan (Wolf clan, Daḵl'aweidi) added that of the Daḵl'aweidi who went north, some first went under the glacier and then later dispersed north to Kake and Klukwan, while others became the Nanyaayi at Wrangell:

> The ancestors of this clan came from the interior, up the Stikine River. They were few in number. They were moving down the river but came to where the river ran under a glacier that reached across the valley. They sent a young man to see if the glacier could be crossed. He found where the river ran from under the glacier . . . There were two old women (one was named Awaste) among them and it was decided to send them into the tunnel-channel to test it . . . they got into the skin-covered canoe and told two young men to get them two canoe poles. These they decorated with feathers. They put spruce twigs and feathers in their hair; this was to test the head room of the ice roof of the channel . . .

So they passed under the glacier and gave thanks for the new land they had found . . .

> They lived for quite a time at a place on the river called Cagwatsan . . . Then the feuds started and the people scattered to different parts of southeast Alaska. Many of the Daḵl'aweidi moved to Kake. One of the Daḵl'aweidi was named Natlsitlaneh. He was the first to carve the killer whale totem . . . The people traveled and moved toward the north several times. But they could find only poor salmon (i.e., no red salmon). When some of them came to Klukwan they found that both sockeye and king salmon ran in the river. Here they settled. But the Nanyaayi remained at Wrangell (Olson 1967:28-29).

Among the feuds referred to are those between the Wolf clan group, Daḵl'aweidi, and an Eagle clan group, Nexadi, which travelled with them down the Stikine River. Relations between them continued to be characterized by feuds and battles, with competition for salmon streams and access to seal trapping areas leading readily to a breakdown in marriage alliances, and war and dispersion. The location of the feuds was said variously to have been Tutxank, Na'a, and Laxse'el. The most consistent location of the definitive battle was Tutxank at Lake Bay. As a Tlingit elder only identified as GB (Raven clan, Tihittaan) related:

> The Daḵl'aweidi clan was the predominant (owning) one of Etolin Island and part of Prince of Wales Island. Many pictographs of the killer whale, their principal crest, may be seen in that area. Their chief village was Tutxank below Lake Bay.

> The legendary home of the clan was far up the Stikine, about a hundred and fifty miles. Their village, still occupied by a few of the clan, was called Takun. In their migration they came down the river on a raft and reached a point where a glacier blocked the valley . . . The passage was negotiated safely and the rest of the people followed.

With the Dakl'aweidi clan were the Nesadi of Kake and the Nexadi of the
Sanyakwan. The Nexadi settled first at a place on the Stikine near Boundary. Later
they moved to Sanya (Cape Fox) area.

The Dakl'aweidi settled at Tutxank. At that place an incident occurred that caused
the clan to split . . . The two groups (the two clans) lived on opposite sides of the
stream . . . The two groups had a blood feud. After the fighting was over both
sides went out into the channel. They wept because they were going to separate.
One group pointed with their paddles to the south. They went that way and gave
rise to the Tantakwan. The other group pointed to the north and went that way.
They became the Dakl'aweidi of Angoon and Klukwan (Olson 1967:32-33).

The feud is described in some detail in an *adawx* told by an unidentified
Tsimshian elder. The battle was said to have taken place at Na'a, a bay and village
just south and across Clarence Strait from Tutxank:

At the village of Na'a (now known as Loring, Alaska), the Laxgibuu (Wolf) had a
village. They had weirs in the river, where they caught seals. There was a rapid at
the mouth of the lagoon, and, as each tide receded, seals were caught in the traps,
sometimes many seals. The Laxskiik (Eagles) then approached the Laxgibuu
(Wolf), for their prince to marry one of their princesses, so that they may share in
the common catch of seals. This was agreed to, and it was understood that they
would share half and half. If they caught only one seal they would divide it in
halves, and must always get an equal division of the seals caught. This arrangement
worked well for some time. Then friction erupted between the Wolf chief and his
Eagle wife, and he beat her. Taking his spear, he stabbed her many times, and
wounded her in many places. A bridge crossed the river, and the wounded woman
returned over it to the house of her uncle. Soon after, she died . . . [Then Waka, her
brother, took revenge and killed the Wolf chief husband].

The Laxgibuu (Wolf) chief's nephew now led his people to retaliate upon the
Laxskiik (Eagles). For this he put on a cloak of Grizzly Bear with a grizzly-bear
head, while Waka wore his war garments of white ermine under which was a
tough sea-lion hide. The two leaders had agreed that if either one was defeated, the
other would take possession of the war headgear of the other who was defeated.
The Grizzly-Bear headdress had abalone pearls in the ears and the eyes. Then the
two fighters stood on this bridge between the two villages, and met in single
combat in the middle of the bridge. After struggling for a long time the Eagle
warrior Waka overcame the Wolf and he cut the head off of his opponent, and he
returned to his own village amid shrieks imitating those of the eagle after
capturing its prey. It is for this reason that we (Laxskiik) are privileged to wear the
Eagle crest to this day.

Both parties now fought for many days. Then the Eagles prepared for flight, as they were being defeated (Beynon and Barbeau n.d. a, no. 126; see also, n.d. a, no. 63).

The Eagle clan escaped on a raft with their crest objects, including two stone eagles. They used one of the stone eagles and some coppers as an anchor and these were lost when they were forced to escape again. A number of personal names and crests commemorate this journey.

Charley Jones (Wolf clan, Nanyaayi) also referred to the battle, placing it at Lake Bay:

> There was a settlement at Lake Bay on Prince of Wales Island. Living there were people of the Nexadi, Nesadi, Dakl'aweidi and Katkaayi clans. Part of the settlement . . . was below Lake Bay where there is a narrow channel. There were houses on both sides and a bridge across.

> [Here the people] . . . from the opposite sides of the creek got ready and the battle began as the tide was low. Many were killed and many bodies floated on the incoming tide. The fight went on for several days.

> After the fighting the clans dispersed. Some of the Katkaayi went to Sitka, another group to the south where they became one of the clans of the Tsimshian . . . Some of the Nexadi came to Wrangell; others went to the Sanya tribe (Olson 1967:36).

The Nexadi Eagle clan group that came down the Stikine River may have established itself at Tutxank and Na'a by joining a Nexadi Eagle group there. Members of the same clan were bound to help each other, and throughout the period, those migrating into new areas were absorbed by those of the same clan already settled there. In the case of the Nexadi, there was a group of the Eagle clan in the area since the time of the flood. According to Billy Johnson (Caguk, Nexadi), the Nexadi survived the flood "on the mountain called Gwekah at the head of Rudyerd Bay" off Behm Canal (Olson 1967:36). As well, the clan origin legend of the Nexadi "begins at Gaxateh in Karta Bay near New Kasaan" (Olson 1967:34), directly across Clarence Strait from Na'a.

There are indications that another group of the Eagle clan migrated into the region from the far north around the same time as those from the Stikine River. John Tate (Salaaban, Eagle clan, Gispaxlo'ots) and Sam Bennett (Nisp'iins, Killerwhale clan, Giluts'aaw) described their arrival:

> Originally these people had come from the far north, and they first met in combat with the Raven clans at Xai'x (Kake) Alaska. They travelled down the coast, and

for a time stayed with the Stagyin (Stikine) tribe of the mouth of the Stikine River. Again there was more trouble between the people, as they had no fishing sites and could not get any salmon. So they moved on farther south and came to Na'a (Loring). Here again they got into difficulties, this time with the Laxgibuu (Wolf) people who were too numerous. Once more they took to flight. They went farther in the direction of the South Wind, Haaywaas or Rain-Wind. They settled at what is now called, Cape Fox, Hałkstaxł (Beynon and Barbeau n.d. a, no. 53).

Like the Nexadi Eagle clan group from the Stikine River, those from Kake may also have joined the original Nexadi among the Sanya.

The pressures resulting from the influx of the new peoples intensified as they continued to search for new territory and alliances. Eventually, other Tlingit clans already established in the region were drawn into the conflict. The Ganaxadi chief, Kaga, was driven from his village at Skaigeh, on the south end of Prince of Wales Island, by Kadanaha, a chief of one of the Wolf clan groups that had migrated down the Stikine River. In his new village on nearby Duke Island, Kaga was challenged to a game of *xsan* by Anda', one of the chiefs of Kadanaha's group, now established at Skaigeh. *Xsan* is an ancient gambling game among Northwest Coast peoples and was often the arena for intense interclan rivalry and the transfer of considerable wealth. Herbert Wallace (Nisyaganaat, Raven clan, Gitsiis), who "heard this narrative from many Gidaganits (Tlingit) and also from some of the Tsimshian," described the events which followed the game of *xsan* between Kaga and Anda' and Kaga's second forced move, this time to Dundas Island:

> At the village of Laxkya (Lagyiil), On-Eyebrows (Duke Island), the people were gambling xsan. Among them was a young Laxgibuu (Wolf) chief of the Gidaganits (Tlingit) named Anda'. They were gambling with Kaga, a Ganhada chief of the Gidaganits. They became angered at one another during the game, and Kaga killed the Laxgibuu chief. They then entered into civil war (lipnawaada) with one another. Kaga becoming weaker, gave up the conflict and compensated the Laxgibuu by giving them his territory on Laxkya. He left here and went to the island of Kwaxł [Dundas Island] and there formed a village of his own. After he had lived there sometime and built a da'ax [terraced house], he then sent word to the Laxgibuu (Wolf) to come and visit him. He wanted to have a permanent peace between them, to have no more wars. When the Laxgibuu arrived, he entertained him and took his sister and placed her alongside the Laxgibuu chief, to become his wife . . .

> [The Wolf chief, not wanting peace, killed Kaga's sister. Kaga retaliated by killing the Wolf clan chief.] . . . The Laxgibuu people were going to retaliate. They wanted to take the village of Kaga but they lacked the courage to do it, because they were

the first at fault, having burned the woman given to them by Ḵaga. That is the reason why the Gidaganits people came to be established in the village at Laxkwaxł (Beynon and Barbeau n.d. d, no. 21).

David Swanson (Killerwhale clan, Giluts'aaw) also related the *adawx* of these events:

> Close to their new village [on Duke Island] was an island with a flat top. This they converted into a fort, which they were to use later in battle as well as a shelter. Now the daughter of Ḵaga, a Ganhada of the Gidaganits married Ḵadanaha, a Laxgibuu Gidaganits. Ḵaga [Ḵadanaha is probably meant here], some time later, beat his wife out of jealousy. This was the cause of civil war between the Laxgibuu and the Ganhada. Ḵaga, being outnumbered, was defeated by the Laxgibuu. Then he went to Laxkwaxł (North Dundas Island). Here he built a fort, and he used as fishing station Warks Canal, Kts'mat'iin (farther north) and Ksiwałn (Tucks Inlet) further up (from Prince Rupert, on the same Arm) (Duff n.d., Gitwilkseba).

INVASION AND DEFENCE OF TSIMSHIAN TERRITORY

Ḵaga was the first of the Gidaganits (Tlingit) to invade the Tsimshian. According to Matthew Johnson (Lagaxnits, Eagle clan, Gispaxlo'ots) and Henry Pierce (Laans, Killerwhale clan, Gispaxlo'ots), Ḵaga made "many raids upon the Tsimshian and the Tlingit . . . [he] erected for himself a fortified house, which was known as Da'axs Ḵaga: Terraced House of Ḵaga, Kwaxł (Dundas Island)" (Beynon and Barbeau n.d. b, no. 27). It cannot have been long after, however, that the Wolf and Eagle clan groups also began to press south. James Lewis (Ḡaymtkwa, Killerwhale clan, Gitḵxaała) and an elder, J. Nelson, described the circumstances:

> And the Wolf clan of the Tlingits came down away to Kaien Island and Gwisḵ'aayn was the real head chief. And their opposite phratry [clan], with whom they intermarried was the Eagle phratry . . .
>
> And it was from these that some of the groups [*wilnat'ał*] of the Wolf clan came from and went to strange countries and there they made new villages and lived there and whoever was the leader or headman of the group became the chief of the newly made village (Beynon n.d., no. 227).

Benjamin Tate (Nee'gmdaw, Killerwhale clan, Giluts'aaw) described the nature of the Tlingit incursions into Tsimshian territory from their foothold on Dundas Island:

> While the Tlingits were living on Dundas Island, they lived very close to the Tsimshian, and also the Gitḵxaała and the Tlingit were always raiding the

Tsimshian and the Gitḵxaała. And the Tlingit were a great many and they had not yet joined into the Tsimshian tribes. They never raided a large village, only watching when one group went to their camp, either Tsimshian or Gitḵxaała, and it was these that the Tlingit attacked and killed, and the Tsimshian and all the other tribes were afraid of the Tlingit (Beynon n.d., no. 66).

At different times during the invasion, Tlingit Raven clan groups made villages or seasonal camps on Dundas Island, Kts'mat'iin (Khutzeymateen Inlet), Work Channel, Ksiwałn (Shawatlans, adjacent to Tuck Inlet) and the Knamaas (Kwinamass) River,[5] while groups of the Wolf and Eagle clan made them on Kts'mat'iin, Work Channel, Tuck Inlet, probably Klewnuggit, Lowe Inlet and Curtis Inlet, and on Dundas Island, Stephens Island, and, possibly, at Metlakatla Pass.

It is difficult to determine exactly which Tsimshian tribes were established in these coastal areas at the time, but it seems that the area at the mouth of the Skeena River was largely Gitwilgyoots territory and that the Killerwhale clan group led by Yahan, Ligiutkwaatk, and Saxsa'axt was the leading group among the Gitwilgyoots tribe. Their territory included a large part of the coastal region at the mouth of the Skeena and eulachon grounds at the mouth of the Nass. Other groups, the Killerwhale clan of the Gispaxlo'ots and Ginax'angiik tribes for example, held territory there as well, but it was not until the Tlingit were driven from the region that all the Skeena River tribes built winter villages at Metlakatla Pass.[6]

On the islands to the south of the mouth of the Skeena River, the Killerwhale were the leading clan among the Gitḵxaała tribe, the leading chief at that time being Wisaa'i. Ts'ibasaa, the famous chief of Temlaxam origin, had joined the Gitḵxaała by that time, but it was probably not until after his successful leadership in defending them from the Tlingit that he replaced Wisaa'i as the leading chief. The Wolf clan, whose chief was Hagilaxha, were the leading group among the Gitḵ'a'ata tribe, and their territory extended up the mainland along Grenville Channel. The same Wolf clan group was also represented at Gitḵxaała and their territory, on Pitt Island along the other side of Grenville Channel, gave the Wolf clan effective control over the area.

---

[5] According to Matthew Johnson and Henry Pierce, "Knamaas was the property of Niswaksenaałk. He had acquired this territory from the Gidaganits (Tlingit), who were the original owners. The last Gidaganits chief here was Ḵaga, a Ganhada (Raven). With him here lived other chiefs: Kogdits, Tsawits, and 'Wiiksenaałk. They had here a sort of permanent village, as the fishing and hunting was very plentiful" (Beynon and Barbeau n.d. b, no. 27).

[6] An analysis of the possible sociopolitical organization at the time cannot be considered here but the relationship between clan and tribe (village) may have been quite different before this period.

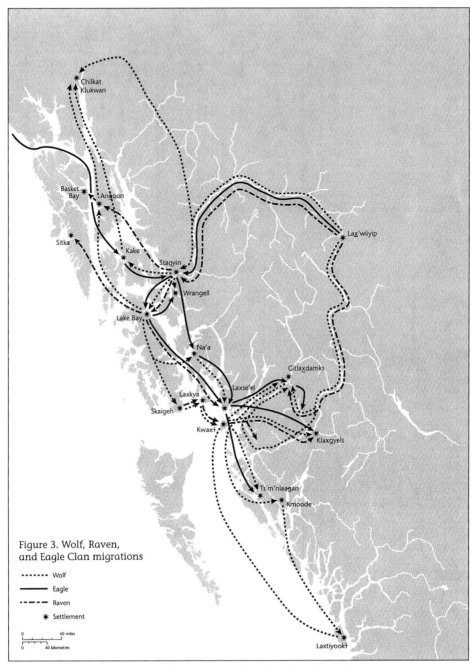

Figure 3. Wolf, Raven,
and Eagle Clan migrations

- - - - - - Wolf

———— Eagle

— - — Raven

✳ Settlement

Chilkat
Klukwan

Basket
Bay

Angoon

Sitka

Kake

Stagyin

Wrangell

Lake Bay

Na'a

Gitlaxdamks

Laxse'el

Laxkya

Skaigeh

Kwaxɫ

Klaxgyels

Lax'wiiyip

Ts'm'nlaagan

Kmoode

Laxtiyookɫ

0   40 miles

0   40 kilometres

Fig. 3. Wolf, Raven, and Eagle clan migrations.

As the raids on their villages intensified, the Tsimshian at the mouths of the Skeena and Nass Rivers were forced to retreat to defensive positions up the Skeena, while those on the southern coast responded by moving to fortified sites on nearby islands. After establishing themselves in defensive positions throughout their territory, the Tsimshian began to regroup, forming alliances with neighbouring tribes and peoples and developing innovative strategies to defeat the Tlingit and drive them out of their lands.

In the south, Ts'ibasaa established his village on a fortified site at Knabaa (Estevan Island at the south end of Banks Island). Nearby on Aristabal Island was the village of 'Wakaas, a Raven clan chief of the Wutsdaa (Heiltsuk). Henry Collison ('Wakaas, Raven clan, Gitkxaała) described how, after an initial defeat at the hands of the Tlingit Wolf clan chief Gwisk'aayn and his Eagle clan allies, Ts'ibasaa invited 'Wakaas to join Gitkxaała, thereby forming an alliance with 'Wakaas' powerful relative Hamdziit at Wutsdaa:

> Well after this then Ts'ibasaa invited 'Wakaas to come and live with him at Knabaa . . . he moved to here and then they were now numerous and the nephews and nieces of 'Wakaas married to the nephews and nieces of Ts'ibasaa and they now increased to a great many and now the Gitkxaała were strong now that they were joined by the group of 'Wakaas.
>
> There was now an increase in the Raven clan among the Gitkxaała and then 'Wakaas assumed his name among the Gitkxaała and Tsi'basaa affirmed him as being the chief of the Gitkxaała.[7] And now all of the people knew that it was part of the House of Hamdziit of the Wutsdaa and there was now many Wutsdaa names among the Gitkxaała. Well, it was 'Wakaas who showed the people how to make all the people brave. 'Wakaas fed the children with the hearts of wolves and this made them brave and it also gave to them that they would have a keen sense of smell . . . (Beynon n.d., no. 226)

Ts'ibasaa was now ready to retaliate against the Tlingit. Henry Collison described the definitive battle for the Gitkxaała and the rout of the Wolf clan group of Gwisk'aayn from their territory:

> And there was among the Gitkxaała a warrior by the name of Gamayaam [a relative of Ts'ibasaa] and when the raiding Stikine [Tlingit] came, he killed many Stikines and this the Stikines knew and they really wanted to capture Gamayaam

---

[7] The meaning here is probably that he became chief among the Gitkxaaôa. There is no indication that 'Wakaas was ever the leading chief of this tribe.

alive and take him. So that was why Gwisk̲'aayn came again to make war upon the Git̲k̲xaała people to come and massacre them.

When they came to Kxeen [Kaien Island] and they camped here a while at the mouth of a creek here and all the Stikine gathered here and it was then that the chief Gwisk̲'aayn said to his warriors, "Who of you will take G̲amayaam alive . . ?"

Well next day and then the Stikines set out to go to where the Git̲k̲xaała lived at K̲aagas [Campania Island, another fortified site adjacent to Knabaa on Estevan Island]. The Stikines did not know of the village of Knabaa and this was where 'Wakaas the G̲anhada chief lived now and also Ts'ibasaa lived there at Knabaa [a fort site]. Well, when the Stikines got to the fort at K̲aagas, they tried to take this by quietly attacking it and almost all of the [Stikine] Wolf clan and Eagle clan were here and they were in great numbers.

. . . the raiders quickly surrounded the fort with their canoes and shot up at it with their arrows. They tried to climb up but they were unable to do so as there was only one trail and the rest of the sides of the fort was steep rock. The Git̲k̲xaała people had gathered a great many stones and now this was what they threw down on top of the canoes of the Stikine.

When the Stikine knew that they were not able to take the fort, they then at once planned to await until their water was finished and then they would perish as soon as the water was finished. Well, the Git̲k̲xaała knew at once the thought of the Stikine and then they started to save all their urine and when they had done so, they just without any reason would throw this from the fort and this made it appear that water was plentiful with them and they had no regard to save the water.

Well, this the raiding Stikine saw and then they thought that there was a well inside of the fort and they knew they would not be able to overcome this and they gave it up . . . (Beynon n.d., no. 226)

Meanwhile, Ts'ibasaa and 'Wakaas on Knabaa had been preparing for battle and they now intentionally allowed their whereabouts to be discovered by the raiders. Henry Collison continued:

Then all of the warriors of the House of 'Wakaas arose and also of the House of Ts'ibasaa and amongst them was G̲amayaam, the Git̲k̲xaała warrior. And G̲amayaam was the one that led the Git̲k̲xaała. And after all of the women and children were hidden then all the warriors gathered together to get ready to meet those that were approaching, that was the raiding strangers . . . Now that the raiders were right below the village, the Git̲k̲xaała seemed all to be excited and they all ran about and seemed to want to escape and were all excited and really

seemed to be startled and excited how they acted and the raiding Stikine paddled
strenuously . . .

Well just as soon as all the Stikine raiders' canoes landed and then all the Gitꓘxaała
warriors ran down and then they fought against the Stikine warriors and it was
unexpected how they acted. And instead the Stikines started to escape and again
went into their canoes and the Gitꓘxaała jumped into the water after them and
caught all the canoes of the raiders and broke them into small pieces and there
were many Stikines killed and it was then that the great brave Stikine that was to
take Ǥamayaam alive, he was hiding in the bow of Gwisk̲'aayn's canoe . . . And
then [the Stikine escaped] and there were many that died and were taken by the
Gitꓘxaała (Beynon n.d., no. 226).

Gwisk̲'aayn and his people may have been part of Ḵadanaha's group or a
distinct Wolf clan group from the same region at the headwaters of the Stikine.
Gwisk̲'aayn was eventually forced to return to the mouth of the Stikine River
where he established his permanent village, but many of his people over time
settled among the Tsimshian and the Nisga'a.

During this same period, some of the Wolf clan invaders tried to establish
themselves along Grenville Channel just north of Ḵaagas and Knabaa. It seems
that it was through the indigenous Wolf clan groups that the invading Tlingit were
able to gain a foothold in Gitꓘxaała and Gitk̲'a'ata territory. Although they may
have joined those of their clan long established there, they continued to make raids
on other villages in the region. James Lewis and Heber Clifton ('Waxmoon,
Killerwhale clan, Gitk̲'a'ata) described the response of the Gitk̲'a'ata to the attacks
and the alliances they formed to drive away the invaders:

. . . And all the tribes that would go to Gitamaat were always watched by all the
Wolf clan and now there were many Wutsdaa, Gitlo'op and Gitamaat and
Gitk̲'a'ata who were killed by the Wolf clan.

Well all these tribes were worn out at what the Wolf clan had done to them and
they were really afraid to go anywhere close to the Wolf clan village so that then
Nta'wiiwalp, chief of the Gitk̲'a'ata, called for help; he invited all of the chiefs of
the Wutsdaa, Gitlo'op and Gitamaat and they discussed the thing that they will do
to the Wolf clan, who were now about to destroy them. And when all the chiefs
came together then all the chiefs agreed as one that they would clean off all the
Wolf clan and that they would altogether as one make war upon the Wolf clan
village.

This was what Hamdziit, chief of the Wutsdaa said, "The Wolf clan have now
done too much and it will be well to clean them off from here and we will kill
them all." . . . When it was spring . . . [they] gathered together and the Wolf clan

never knew of them gathering together to make an attack on the Wolf clan. And the Wolf clan were about to set out to visit where others of the Wolf clan lived at Lowe Inlet and it was then those that were to raid together, attacked, these four tribes, and because it was so unexpected, the Wolf clan now seemed very weak, when they were attacked, so they escaped in flight and left their village.

So it was then that the Gitk̲'a'ata moved down and lived where the Wolf clan had lived and here they live to this day. Well it was then that the power of the Wolf clan went down and all the Wolf clan escaped to Lowe Inlet and they possessed this river. And it was then that all the different tribes tried to chase away all of the Wolf clan, because they were very much warlike people and besides they were a strange tongue; they were Tlingits and this was really why all the other tribes were after them . . . (Beynon n.d., no. 228).

As the Git̲kxaała and Gitk̲'a'ata were meeting with success in the south, the Tsimshian tribes at the mouth of the Skeena began to retaliate as well, eventually driving the Tlingit from their territory and reestablishing themselves on Kaien Island and at Metlakatla Pass, where they were joined by their Skeena River allies. The defeat of the Tlingit by the Tsimshian at the mouth of the Skeena River was led by Aksk, a warrior of the Gitwilgyoots tribe. Aksk was from the House of Spiingan (also called Xmu or Gilax'aks). This House was part of an ancient *laxmoon* (saltwater) Killerwhale group, among whom were also the Houses of Ligiutkwaatk, Yahan, and Saxsa'axt of the Gitwilgyoots and the House of Wisaa'i at Git̲kxaała. The ancient home of this people is said to have been on Stephens Island, which remained their territory after they moved to the mouth of the Skeena River.

The narrative below, compiled from two accounts, one told by Herbert Wallace, the other by Heber Clifton, begins after the Tsimshian retreated up the Skeena River. Aksk and his family took refuge among the Gitzax̲łaał tribe on the Ecstall River:

They went to the headwaters of Niskiwa's [territory], later known as Tsisyak [Ts'msyaak, at the headwaters of the Ecstall River] . . . They arrived there at a large cavern, of which they made their refuge . . . [Aksk] took this young girl as his wife. . . [There they raised five sons.] He taught his sons how to become warriors and how to hunt. . . He brought them up with one ambition, that is to retaliate on the Gidaganits.

After they were grown up, he was prepared to move back to the Ksyeen [Skeena River]. . . The Gitzax̲łaał outfitted these young people with a canoe and food and sent them on. They knew that the Gitwilgyoots had a village on the Ksyeen, just below X̲aaydziks [Kasiks River] . . . On this location was the fortress (t'oots'ip) of the Gitwilgyoots, a huge mountain-like island. It was very difficult of approach. This band had now grown in numbers, as the young people had married and increased. They built a house on this fortress.

All the young people had to learn the art of warfare and prepare their weapons and handle them. . . The house was built at the edge of the rocky island and the canoes were tied to the doorway, and the paddles were always at the doorway. All the young people were constantly practicing canoeing in these treacherous waters . . . They had already built cache houses along the Xaaydziks River and the house was full of spears and war implements. They had gathered into this house many stones which to throw upon anyone attacking the fort.

One day many canoes approached which they recognized as Gidaganits canoes. The Gidaganits attacked the island fort. They were many in numbers. The young people in the fort kept throwing stones and spears at these besiegers. But the Gidaganits, in spite of this, were able to approach the island. Aksk, finding out that they were unable to overcome the foe, closed his trap door and went to the other entrance, where the canoes were tied up. They all escaped into their canoes . . . They were able to escape from the Gidaganits, but the raiders burned their village. The fugitives came up from their fortress and went up the river to where the Gitsiis had their village . . .

The following year, Aksk said, "We shall move now, down to the salt water, to the coast … They took two canoes and lashed them together, making a raft on which they piled timber for the building of a house. They then came to a place on Kaien Island (Prince Rupert) and were going to build a village there (where the white beacon stands, and where the cemetery of Prince Rupert is).

Here he erected a fortified place. He built his house on a mound (right opposite where the Cooperative Cold Storage Plant now stands, in Prince Rupert) . . . Then he made a huge trap door which was many timbers thick, and he suspended it from the rafters of the house right over the doorway of the house so that it would drop upon the clear space below and would crush everything it would fall upon. Each corner was lashed so that it could be quickly released . . . Aksk now gathered dry rotted wood and fashioned these to the size of human beings, and then placed them in the sleeping places and covered each of these figures with cedar bark mats. They resembled sleeping figures. He gathered many pieces of kelp and strung each piece from a platform he had built in the rafters and each end of the kelp was tied to the head of the pieces of wood resembling sleeping human forms. Through these pieces of hanging kelp came sounds of snoring. In every way these appeared as sleeping forms. Aksk was now ready to meet his enemies the Tlingit.

In order to attract their attention, he made a huge smoke screen of green boughs and the smoke went high into the sky. It was seen by some Tlingit who lived at Dundas, and they became curious as to who was causing the smoke. They came in and soon saw where the smoke was rising from, and they located the large house . . . That night, the scouts returned to where the Tlingit were hiding. Aksk realized that they were now going to attack, and he told his people, "Tonight, we will beat our drums and pretend we are having our halaayt dances and sing very loudly. This will give the Tlingit the idea that we are not aware of their approach, and also they will think that we are a large number . . . When we have finished and apparently retired to our sleeping places, you will go up into the rafters on the long platforms and you, my oldest nephews will each hold a corner of the lashes for the great trap door. When I say, "Let go," you will each unfasten your lashes, and let the door drop on top of the raiders. Then those who are making the snoring noises through the kelp down upon the wooden forms, will shoot their arrows upon the attackers . . .

The first invaders crept to the sleeping forms and speared them. But they could not withdraw their spears from the rotted wooden forms. They now gathered at the doorway. When they all got under the heavy trap door over the entrance, Aksk called out "Wah! (Now)" and the lashes were cut at each corner, and the trap fell upon the Tlingit wounding and killing many . . . Those that escaped were easy victims for Aksk's followers who shot them from the rafters. Few escaped . . . . So the Tlingit that fled were very few and they left some of their canoes behind. Aksk now set off in pursuit and was able to capture several canoes. He took them to his house. Among the captives was the nephew of the Tlingit chief Na'nadzu. Aksk took two of the captives and sent them to their country, to tell the chiefs that compensation must be made to Aksk for those that had been killed in the first attack of his Skeena village. Should they fail, then the captives now held here would be killed.

In the meantime other Tsimshian heard of the invasion. They now moved down to where Aksk had built his house. So that there was now a number of houses and many more people added to the group of the warrior Aksk . . .

When the Tlingit messengers arrived at their village, they told the chief Na'nadzu [what had happened and what Aksk had said] . . . The Tlingit chief called in the head men and said, "We will gather all our wealth and also prepare the captives we took from the Tsimshian village on the Skeena. These we will return. For those whom we killed and scalped we will give compensation. We will take many canoes and leave our captives with canoes." So the Tlingit now made everything ready . . .

Then one day, there came to this village a great many canoes. The canoe folk were singing their peace songs and throwing eagle down upon the waters, signifying peace. They sang their songs for a long while. Then Aksk together with his followers stepped down to the beach and met the Tlingit, and, after a short exchange of halaayt songs, the Tlingit were led to Aksk's house, in which was beating the halaayt drum, announcing their approach. The Tlingit gave their

Gawagaani [peace] songs and dance and began, first, to return all the living captives, and give compensation for the ones who had been killed on the Skeena village of Aksk.

While there were other battles between the Tsimshian and the Gidaganits, from this time when defeated by Aksk, the Gidaganits withdrew farther north. Where formerly they had their villages at Ksxaxł (Stevens Island) and Kwaxł (Dundas Island) they now deserted these settlements. The Tsimshian established their main group of tribal villages at Metlakatla Passage and on what is known now as Tuck's Inlet. Instead of associating himself with Saxsa'axt, the Gispwudwada [Killerwhale] chief of the Gitwilgyoots, Aksk became associated with Nisloos, the Laxskiik chief of the same tribe, there now being two separate villages. One of Saxsa'axt [who] lived where the present site of Metlakatla stands and the other at Kxeen (the present site of the Prince Rupert Cooperative Cold Storage plant at Prince Rupert) (Beynon and Barbeau n.d. d, no. 23; n.d. c, no. 91).

Herbert Wallace and Heber Clifton both named some of the Tlingit chiefs driven off by Aksk. Na'nadzu is probably the same name as 'Anadzu, said to be one of the Wolf clan chiefs related to 'Anda and Kadanaha who came under the glacier and down the Stikine River (Duff n.d., Gitlaan Origins). This group is also called the Git-skaigeh after their village at the south end of Prince of Wales Island to which they presumably returned after their defeat by the Tsimshian. Yiłkenigi, Tsigi or Hałtsigi were said to be members of the Eagle clan and "Tagwan was their central village (now New Metlakatla on Annette Island, Alaska)" (Beynon and Barbeau n.d. d, no. 23). They were probably Eagle clan groups who migrated together with others of the Wolf clan and were found together with them in each of the areas where they settled.

As Heber Clifton related, after the rout of the invading Tlingit, the Skeena River tribes had begun to establish themselves at Metlakatla Pass. Henry Pearce (Gawala, Eagle clan, Gispaxlo'ots) described the process:

When their neighbouring tribes who had lived along the banks of Skeena River heard that the Gitwilgyoots had occupied this place. This fame induced them to go and look over the land suitable for location. Some of these tribes set out at once to seek a new place. . . and choose a good land for their village site. Many other tribes followed, and made other settlements along both sides of Metlakatla passage. Each tribe took possession of that land out side their village site where to hunting and fishing. For these people lived mainly by hunting and fishing, and roamed in their own selected territory from place to place in search of game. By this time. All these tribes [who] were formerly living in Skeena River now had permanent homes and living in large villages. Houses have been build in every village, each sheltering many families. By this time. Each tribe has two villages, one at Metlakatla and another one up in Skeena River (Duff n.d., William Kelly manuscript).

As Henry Pearce related, some of the tribes that now established themselves at Metlakatla Pass had previously located their summer and winter villages on their Skeena River territories. The new location of the winter villages of all the Skeena River tribes now consolidated the Tsimshian defensive position at the mouth of the Skeena. It remained for the Tsimshian to reassert themselves at the mouth of the Nass River. Some time after Aksk's victory at the mouth of the Skeena, the Gitsiis tribe discovered groups of Tlingit at Work Channel and Kts'mat'iin. The Raven clan of the Gitsiis formed a war party and attacked the Tlingit villages, killing many and routing the rest. According to the account told by John Tate, the Gidaganits at Kts'mat'iin were the Eagle clan group which originated in the far north and fought at Kake, and who eventually settled at "Cape Fox, Hałkstaxł":

> Kts'mat'iin, a long inlet almost cutting through the peninsula to the Skeena River, was first the property of the Laxskiik (Eagle) Gidaganits (Tlingit). Originally these people had come from the far north, and they first met in combat with the Raven clans at Xai'x (Kake) Alaska . . . [From here they moved south to Hałkstaxł where they decided to move again]. At once they gathered all their belongings together and set out to look for another site, where there was safety from foreign raids, and also where there was a plentiful supply of salmon and mountain game such as mountain goats and deer and bear. In the distance there was a very high mountain. They headed for it, and when they had paddled and sailed, they came to the mouth of a huge inlet. They travelled up and finally reached the head and found a large river where there was much salmon.
>
> Nobody seemed to live here. They had passed one river, but there were several villages on it, Knamaas. They passed by and then came to place in a valley (ñgut'iin) and called it Kts'mat'iin. They found a plentiful supply of game and food, and also a great supply of seal. This was the best discovery they had made as yet in their travels. So they established a big village here. It was secure from an attack and could only be reached by the entrance. They did not know how close to the Skeena they were, nor that, on the other side of the divide, were the Tsimshian villages. They had now settled here.
>
> At the Gitsiis village on the Skeena . . . there was a Gitsiis man [Gwishayaax of the Raven clan] who was constantly gambling and loosing steadily. He had no possessions left, as he had gambled away everything, even his wife and family. Very downhearted he went up into the hills, wandering at random. He did not care where he was going. He journeyed up and over the hills and down into the other side. Behold, he saw a large body of water. He did not know where it was or what the name of it was, but he kept on travelling down the other side of the

mountain. Smoke seemed to be rising a long way off. He was still some distance from this body of water, when he heard a strange sound as of chopping, but with a different sound. If it were a stone axe, it would sound as thuds, but this was different, like a bell sound. He grew interested in this and began travelling in the direction of the sound. Approaching very cautiously, he saw a man making a canoe, not in the usual way that canoes were made, and it was a large canoe. The Gitsiis now watched from a distance the strange canoe maker, but kept hidden, as he thought he may be a spirit. Just before dark the canoe-maker walked about the canoe he was making, gathered his tools and hid them. When the Gitsiis saw the strange man going away, he followed him and saw him get into a canoe and paddle away. He watched the direction he went towards a large village in the distance. The Gitsiis then went back on his trail to the spot where the tools were hidden, and he found a copper axe and many copper wedges, also a copper hammer. He marveled at these, as he did not know how these were made. He chose a place where he could hide, another day, and watch the canoe-maker, so that he could learn how to use these tools.

He did this every day until the canoe was ready to be shaped by boiling. All the while the Gitsiis went down to the shore near where the village stood. He would sit there in the morning and count the canoes, as they headed down the inlet. At night, he would count them returning. Thus he knew how many canoes there were . . . He now knew all that he wanted, and he returned to his own village on the Skeena. When he got there he went to the chief Nisyaganaat and said, "I have wonderful things to tell you, having discovered a new country. Many strange people there speak in a strange tongue, also using strange tools in making canoes and having unknown weapons . . . In two days walking from here, we can arrive there, and then make our plans as to how to attack . . . [The Gitsiis attacked the Tlingit and none escaped.] It was thus that the Gitsiis came into possession of this new territory from the Gidaganits which has since remained the property of the Gitsiis tribe.[8] This was the first time that copper tools were introduced among the Tsimshian (Beynon and Barbeau n.d. a, no. 53).

THE TLINGIT AMONG THE TSIMSHIAN

At some point during hostilities between the Wolf and Eagle clan groups and the Tsimshian, the Tlingit Raven clan chief, Kaga had been driven again from his village, this time on Dundas Island, by the Tlingit Wolf clan group led by Kadanaha. He must also have been displaced from his fishing stations at the mouth

---

[8] This reference to the 'property of the Tlingit' refers to the time of their invasion. A comprehensive review of the *adawx* concerning this region and the statements of territorial ownership recorded over the last century identify ownership from ancient times of these areas by the direct ancestors of Tsimshian and Nisga'a groups (see, also, Duff n.d., Gitsiis Territories).

of the Nass River by the Eagle clan groups that were afterwards driven out by the Gitsiis. David Swanson described how Ḵaga and his people were forced to hide in the hills on the mainland where they were discovered and taken in by a number of Tsimshian tribes:

> The Laxgibuu people came to Dundas to be revenged for the death of their chief. They drove Ḵaga and his tribe to the mountains here, and they became associated with the Tsimshian, being scattered all over the hills in the neighbourhood. They also feared the Tsimshian, until they were found by the Ganhada Tsimshian, who took them in, and they were distributed among the Ganhada of various tribes. Down to the present time, it was a custom for the wilaaysk (kinsmen) to give assistance to one another. In battle the people of the same crest will not slay one another . . .
>
> This is how the crest of Mool'xan (Gitwilkseba) and 'Ayaaex (which are Tsimshian names assumed by Ḵaga) originated. The reason for taking this name of Mool'xan was that, when hiding in the woods on the mainland, his fire would appear at various places. (Mool'xan is the term applied to firing the whole interior of a tree.) Here he became a Gitwilkseba and his village on the Skeena was near Klaxgyels. He and his people formed a village by themselves. Their head chiefs were Nis'wiibaas and Ḵapligidaał.
>
> Ts'maaymban, of the Gitwilgyoots found a number of Ḵaga's party in the woods along the coast where they were hiding. This is mentioned in his own myth [*adawx*]. But he is not himself of Gitwilkseba origin, but the same as the Gitlaan House (Duff n.d., Gitwilkseba).

Charles Abbott (Txaldaw, Killerwhale clan, Gispaxlo'ots) also commented on the origins of Ḵaga and his people and on their amalgamation with their clan relatives among the Tsimshian:

> . . . On the saltwater the whole of Kwtuun (Works Channel) and Kts'mat'iin and Knamaas and all the territories between these valleys was the property of the Gidaganits, who were in course of time overcome by different Tsimshian raids, mostly under Gitsiis leaders. All of these new territories between these valleys became the property of the Ganhada Gitsiis, and many of these Ganhadas were of Gidaganits origin and became amalgamated into the Gitsiis tribe and retained their old rights on the saltwater territories (Duff n.d., Gitsiis Territories).

The successful defence of the mouth of the Skeena and the Nass rivers by the Tsimshian began a period of readjustment in which the nature of Tsimshian society underwent dramatic change. Although often summarized in a sentence or two, the process almost certainly took place over decades, if not centuries. Figure 4 identifies the Tlingit Raven, Wolf, and Eagle clan groups which over a period of time, and in various ways, became Houses among the Tsimshian. In some cases, other Houses later split off from them and moved to other tribes; the figure, therefore, does not identify the full number of Houses which trace their descent to this influx of Tlingit groups.

A number of *adawx* describe the ways in which the groups became members of Tsimshian tribes. They reflect the legal system of the Tsimshian in which clan or marriage alliances are necessary before foreign groups can become Tsimshian. As well, new Houses can only be established in a Tsimshian tribe through a feast, or potlatch, in which the distribution of wealth, the telling of *adawx*, and the display of crests, songs and *naxnox* (spirit powers) demonstrate the power and status they will bring to the tribe.

The oral record contains few references to the process by which Ḵaga and his people joined a number of Tsimshian villages. Generally speaking, it can be described as one in which various leaders under Ḵaga joined preexisting Raven clan Houses in each tribe. Ḵaga himself formed the House of Ligigasgyoo among the Gitwilgyoots (Barbeau and Beynon n.d. B.F. 41.10; Duff n.d., Gitlaan Origins). Of the other tribes Ḵaga's people joined among the Tsimshian, the Gitsiis, the Gitlaan, the Gits'ilaasu (Kitselas), and the Gitzaxłaał, their presence among the Gitzaxłaał was the most remarkable, as there they became the leading House of Nishoot which played a prominent role among the Tsimshian in later periods. Those that joined the Gitlaan and the Gitsiis also rose to positions of leadership in the Houses of Nis'waksenaałk and Nisyaganaat respectively. The efforts of some of Ḵaga's people to form their own tribe, the Gitwilkseba, ended in failure and the various Houses were eventually absorbed into neighbouring tribes. The House of Ḵoom was formed among the Gits'ilaasu and became the leading Raven clan House in later days. They also eventually reached into Gitksan territory where they became part of the Raven clan at Gitwingaẋ (Kitwanga) and Gitksigyuukla (Kitsegukla).

The Wolf clan groups were not as successful in penetrating Tsimshian society. William Moore (Oyai, Wolf clan, Gitwinksihlxw) described how many of those who were not driven north settled among the Nisga'a and only Nislaganoos rose to prominence among the Tsimshian:

> For a time, they stayed at Na'a (Loring). They knew they had other [clan] relatives farther south with whom they hoped to unite and thus again grow strong in numbers ... This Laxgibuu (Wolf) band arrived at the mouth of the Nass River ... and they stopped at the mouth of this river, Liisms. Here some members of the

clan separated and went on further south, these under the leadership of Nislaganoos. These afterwards became the Gitlaan tribe and established themselves first at Knamaas, and then at Skeena River points. The households that went up the Nass River passed under the leadership of Niskinwaatk and joined with others of their group who had already come to the Nass River. They were a large group. These became separated into smaller bands. Among these was a group who established itself at Lax'angida. This was the Gwaxsu family, who were also a large group. The reason why they separated was that they were too numerous (Beynon and Barbeau n.d. d, no. 7).

Nislaganoos established a foothold among the Gitlaan by marrying into the Raven clan group of Ḵaga, their old enemies, who, in becoming Gitlaan, had maintained their position at Knamaas. Enoch Maxwell (Killerwhale clan, Gitlaan) explained the process:

> There they joined the Gitlaan branch and settled down. Not very long afterwards Niswaksenaałlk married two sisters of Nislaganoos, who were Lax'nlał and 'Wutixskaks. He divided his power and gave it eventually to his sons, who adopted the name of Nislaganoos and took the senior chieftainship of the Gitlaan tribe and of all the Tsimshian at that time. Nislaganoos' house was called ñiptaksk, a Gidaganits or Tlingit term (Beynon and Barbeau n.d. d, no. 4).

Those who joined the Gispaxlo'ots, Gitnadoiks, and Ginax'angiik established only a minor presence in each tribe.[9] Among the Gitsiis and the Gitḵxaała they joined long established Wolf clan groups, as described by George McCauley and Mary Ałaxsgaax:

> They lived at Laxse'el (Cape Fox), and from there they went hunting the sea otter. They travelled still farther south and stayed with the Gitsiis tribe, at the Wark's Canal, at a place known as Lax'nasiis and some stayed here and became members of this tribe (the Gitsiis). Others went farther south and they joined in with the Gitḵxaała after they had given a huge feast. Ts'ibasaa who was the head chief of the Gitḵxaała took them in and they became Gitḵxaała. They were not very many and had no wealth. So they never became chiefs among the Gitḵxaała (Beynon and Barbeau n.d. d, no. 2).

Some of the Wolf clan who remained formed peaceful alliances with Gitḵxaała Houses and eventually joined them at Laxklaan. Nisgałoot, a nephew of

[9] According to Charles Abbott, "The Laxgibuu (Wolves) with whom the Thunderbirds had been in civil war fought among themselves at Laxse'el, after the Thunderbirds had gone. They also took to flight, and went up the Nass . . . From among these Wolf people that migrated to the Nass [then across to the mid-Skeena] came the house of Xnes and of Ts'ikshawtks. They were the only two Wolf houses among the Gispaxlo'ots." (Beynon and Barbeau n.d. a, no. 52)

Gwis<u>k</u>'aayn, formed an alliance with Ts'ibasaa, his former enemy, and remained among the Tsimshian. James Lewis described his assimilation by the Git<u>k</u>xaała:

> Well, this was what one of the eldest nephews of Gwis<u>k</u>'aayn did, he went to a new country looking for a place in which fur-bearing animals were plentiful, that is marten and mink. Well, after many days of canoeing they came to a place which was a long inlet and they headed here and then they found where a large river ran down into the head of it and there they went. It was now the middle of winter and there was no more fresh salmon for all the people and only a few had any dried salmon.
>
> Nisgałoot was the name of the leader of the Wolf clan group and when he landed he saw there was a waterfall at the mouth of this river. And then first he laid there. And then he walked over to the other side of the waterfall searching for trails of animals and then he found that this river was full of coho salmon and the man was very happy, as he now found a country of plenty. And then he made what the ancient people used to catch salmon, to trap it [lagant] . . . Well this plentiful country had been found by the Wolf clan and Nigałoot at once named this territory here as Ts'm'nlaagan (In Place of Salmon Trap – Curtis Inlet), as it was here that he trapped salmon.
>
> And then they lived here and although Gwis<u>k</u>'aayn had returned back to the Stikine River as he now was really defeated in battle with the Tsimshians and many of his people stayed behind and lived in the direction of the Git<u>k</u>xaała now. Well they had not yet all met, the Git<u>k</u>xaała and the Wolf Clan of Stikine River, and there lived very close by one of the chiefs of the Git<u>k</u>xaała who was Ts'ibasaa at one of his villages. And one day while canoeing about the Wolf clan suddenly met with the Git<u>k</u>xaała. Now the Git<u>k</u>xaała themselves had not lived here in the past, they had just come fleeing from war parties and they made their village at Dried Up Passage and this was the first time Ts'ibasaa and Nisgałoot met, and now between them there was peace, between the two tribes and they invited each other to each others feasts . . . [These two groups began to intermarry.] . . .
>
> When this [halaayt] season came, then all of the Git<u>k</u>xaała gathered together here [at Laxklaan] and sometimes the Wolf clan chief joined in the halaayts, as he now was really part of the tribe now but he really kept as his own village Kts'm'nlaagan and whenever he went to the village of Laxklaan, he seemed only to visit and he lived permanently at Kts'm'nlaagan and he always joined in everything that the Git<u>k</u>xaała done (Beynon n.d., no. 227).

The Eagle clan, which had always been outnumbered by the Wolf clan in earlier villages, rose to prominence among the Tsimshian, especially among the Gispaxlo'ots. According to Charles Abbott:

The Gispaxlo'ots tribe at one time had as their royal House that of Waxaayt, now extinct. On the Skeena River, the original Gispaxlo'ots people were: Suhalaayt (Gispwudwada), 'Wiiget (Gispwudwada), Nistoo (Ganhada), Nismasgaws (Ganhada), Sagipaayk (Ganhada) and Gamayaam (Gispwudwada) . . . There were no Laxskiik (Thunderbird or Eagle) nor Laxgibuu (Wolf) clansmen in the Gispaxlo'ots tribe in those days. The Thunderbird Houses of Nis'wa'mak and Xpi'lk (royal), together with. . . [Xyuup, Nisa'walp, Xpaws, Gawala, 'Li'n'saanxs and Nismootk] . . . came from Laxse'el in flight to the Nisga'a on the Nass River and the Tsimshian on the Skeena . . . The groups that had migrated south from Laxse'el were known as Gwinhuut (Beynon and Barbeau n.d. a, no. 52).

Enoch Maxwell explained how the Eagle clan group of Nis'wa'mak joined the Gispaxlo'ots:

Sgagweet did not originally belong to the Gitando tribe, but lived with Nis'wa'mak who became a Gispaxlo'ots a short time after these arrived. Waxaayt, a Gispwudwada, was then the chief of the Gispaxlo'ots. He married a niece of Nis'wa'mak. She and Waxaayt had a son and Waxaayt himself gave him a name, Hats'iksnee'x. When the boy grew up to be a young man, his father called all the people together and said, "You see my son. When I die, he shall become my successor." On the death of Waxaayt, his son took his place, as the leading House of the tribe, and assumed the name Xpi'lk. In this way the Laxskiik (Eagles) became the royal family in the Gispaxlo'ots, and later Xpi'lk took the name of his uncle Nis'wa'mak (Beynon and Barbeau n.d. a, no. 47).

As Herbert Wallace explained, it was Nis'wa'mak who came from the north and who was later joined by Ligeex from the Wutsdaa. These Houses together eventually raised the Gispaxlo'ots tribe to the leading position among the Tsimshian.

In the olden times, the Gispaxlo'ots tribe of the Tsimshian had a chief of their own, near Metlakatla. He was called Waxaayt of the Gispwudwada, a Gitksets'oo Gispwudwada. As for Ligeex, he came from Wutsdaa (Bella Bella, to the south) at a place named Git'au'yat. (At the beginning, the Gispaxlo'ots had no hunting territories nor fishing stations whatsoever on the Skeena River, whereas all the other Tsimshian tribes had. . .

I repeat: Nispilas, a Laxskiik, was already a chief there among the Gispaxlo'ots before the arrival of Ligeex. Another Eagle or Thunderbird (Laxskiik) chief there was Nis'wa'mak, who had come from Alaska. He was a Gwinhuut Thunderbird. It is not remembered whether Nispilas or Nis'wa'mak had come first to the Gispaxlo'ots. Yes! Nispilas was from Wutsdaa (Bella Bella, south), and Nis'wa'mak, a Gwinhuut from Alaska. Nispilas has a song saying that he has originated at Git'au'yat (Bella Bella). Here it is: My adawx tells me that I came

from Git'au'yat, and there is a sign on a cliff to show that I am from that place."
This spot is very close to Bella Bella. Really Nispilas was of the same family as
Ligeex. They came to Gispaxlo'ots at different times. Nispilas arrived before the
flood, Little Ligeex after the flood . . . Before Nispilas arrived, Waxaayt was the
head chief. He had said to Nispilas, "You will be the chief, and I will resign for
you." So Nispilas became the head chief.

Nis'wa'mak has another story. He was a Gwinhuut, and it is not known surely at
what time he arrived here. But it was later than Nispilas. After he had settled here,
there were two chiefs at the head of the tribes, Nispilas and Waxaayt. At the time
when Ligeex came to Metlakatla, the two head chiefs were Nispilas and
Nis'wa'mak. Ligeex stayed with Nispilas, his uncle. But he eventually took the
power from Nispilas and succeeded him. It is then that he assumed the name of
Big Ligeex and he became head chief. From that time on, the Gispaxlo'ots had
two Houses of head chiefs, standing next to each other, that of Big Ligeex and that
of Nis'wa'mak . . .

Herbert Wallace concluded by describing how two other Gwinhuut leaders
established Eagle clan Houses, one among the Nisga'a and one in the Gitsmgeelwn
(Kitsumkalum) tribe among the Tsimshian:

The head chief of Gitnawalks, a village on the Nass river, named Mineeskxw,
rightly traces back his ancestry to the Gwinhuut, in Alaska. From that village and
Mineeskxw's household a man went to Gitsmgeelwn. His name was
Ksgoogmdziiws. Before his coming there, the Gitsmgeelwn had a Thunderbird
(Laxskiik) chief of their own, named Nisk'iil, who received him, his [clan] cousins,
in his House. Later Ksgoogmdziiws had an affair with one of Nisk'iil's daughters
and there was nearly a fight over it. Ksgoogmdziiws was about to leave the village,
when his cousin, Nisk'iil took a large copper and gave it to him. And the trouble
came to an end (Beynon and Barbeau n.d. a, no. 63).

Kastu'ini from the Gwinhuut Eagle clan group also joined Gitsmgeelwn. The
adawx told by Samuel Kennedy (Ksgoogmdziiws, Eagle clan) shows how they were
driven from one place to another before they were taken in by the Gitsmgeelwn:

Kastu'ini was then the chief of this band. Frightened of the carcass or remains of
this huge monster, these wanted to migrate to another place. So they returned
towards the Nass River. Then they built a village – its name I forget – at the mouth
of this river. These Gidaganits were warriors, and they invited the Tsimshian tribes
to join them on the Nass where to fish. So together with these other people, they
lived on the Nass, for a time, among themselves. They gathered the eulachon.
Having extracted the oil, they threw the remnants in the river. These remnants
were picked up by the Tsimshian, who were then on the verge of starvation . . .

[Ḵastu'ini and a Nisga'a of the Killerwhale clan had a competition with coppers. The Tsimshian helped the Nisga'a and Ḵastu'ini was defeated. The Tsimshian] were hoping to drive away Ḵastu'ini and his warriors, because they wanted to prevent him from remaining on the Nass. Then Ḵastu'ini determined to take flight, gathering all of his shields and packing them for the voyage. The Shark crest on his house he took down and burnt, while his chief woman took her roasting stick, and she threw it into the water singing, "Ha'i'ert, this will become the property of the slave people who are jealous of us," referring to the Tsimshian tribes. This flight became known as Huudm hayetsk, the Flight of Copper Shields. There was in it no one killed, but only the competition of wealth and coppers. They came to the waters of K'ikyeen. This river they followed to its source. They were pursued and chased by the Tsimshian. Tlaagai had on, at this time, his war raiment of ermine, which had been acquired in their encounter with the Laxgibuu (Wolf) clan [at the battle at Tutxank]. When the Tsimshian were in close pursuit, he would tear off one of the ermines and throw it behind him. As the Tsimshian came upon this, they would stop in their pursuit and fight among themselves, as to who would take possession of the remains . . . They had now come to a river named Nigwanks ['Wiigwaanks], known now as Beaver River . . .

They went on down . . . until they arrived at the lake of Gitsmgeelwn. As they fled down the course of the Kitsumkalum River . . . they came on then the village of the Gilaxkyoo, Robin Village, in which the people were then living . . . they recognized these people to be Laxskiik, Eagles . . .When these Gwinhuut approached he [Nisk'iil, the Eagle chief] called out, "Is this you my relatives?" He was afraid of them. One of the newcomers answered, "We are of the Gidaganits people, and we are Laxskiik (Eagles). The old chief let it be known that he was also a Laxskiik, and they were all overjoyed in meeting one another. The chief then led them to his house in the canyon, and at the invitation of this chief, they all lived there a long time.

. . . From that time on to the present, this group remained among the Gitsmgeelwn tribe (Beynon and Barbeau n.d. a, no. 55).

THE FINAL WAVE OF MIGRATION

In the early period after Aksk had established an effective defensive position on Kaien Island and the Gitsiis had driven the Tlingit from the mouth of the Nass, groups of the Tsimshian Wolf clan established a large single clan village at Laxwilgyaps at Metlakatla Pass. There the Tsimshian encountered yet another wave of migrating peoples, this time from the upper Skeena River where "those who had gone overland," while others had gone under the glacier, had established themselves.

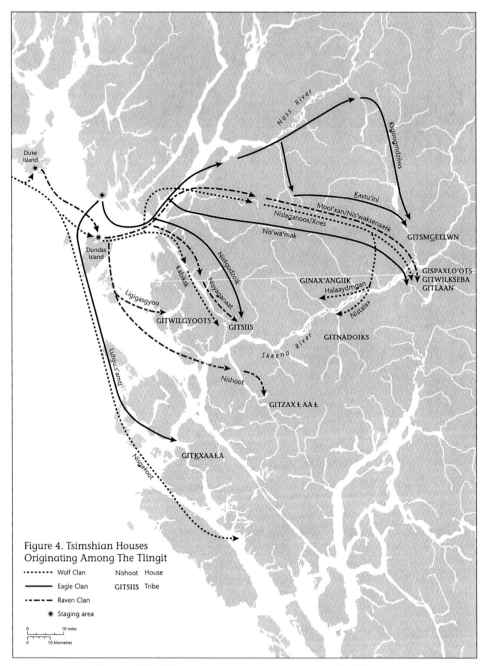

Figure 4. Tsimshian Houses
Originating Among The Tlingit

········· Wolf Clan   Nishoot House
──── Eagle Clan   GITSIIS Tribe
─ ─ ─ Raven Clan
     ✳ Staging area

0 ┝━━━━━┥ 10 miles
0 ┝━━━━━┥ 10 kilometres

Fig. 4. Tsimshian houses originating among the Tlingit.

Matthew Gurney (Kyeexw, Wolf clan, Gitlax̲damks) and Emma Wright (Hleex, Eagle clan, Gitlax̲damks) described the migration of the group down the Skeena River through the territory of their clan relatives among the northern Gitksan:

> The Lax Gibuu (Wolf) group that originally came from the headwaters of the Stikine River, instead of travelling down the river to the coast as did the other Wolf groups, went into the hills and overland and reached the headwaters of the Skeena River around the vicinity of what is now Kisgagas [a Gitksan tribe]. They stayed here for a time, and having no exclusive territory for their own large band, they followed the Skeena downstream. Along with them was the large group of Kyeexw. Together with them were the G̲anhada spouses of the Laxgibuu men, and some of these, when at Kisgagas, went farther inland to what is called 'Wilt'uutsxwhl'aks': Where Black Water, or Blackwater River (Beynon and Barbeau n.d. d, no.8).

Some remained among the Gitksan, where their descendants still reside, while others continued down river. Led by their chief, Tok̲, they travelled as far as Lorne Creek, upriver from Kitselas Canyon, where they "established their village which they called Lax'anmił, On-where-dry-plateau." They explored the surrounding area and discovered the Gitsmgeelwn territory, which was already inhabited, and the Nass River territory which was inhabited by "those that had lived with them on the Tahltan and had also taken to flight when they had fought with the Raven group at Tahltan." As Matthew Gurney and Emma Wright explained:

> These were under the leadership of Niskinwaatk . . . and Nisyok̲. They were very well established and had much territory of their own. As they recognized one another, they related their various adventures, and Tok̲ told of his village towards the Skeena, a few days travel from where the Nass village stood (Beynon and Barbeau n.d. a, no. 55).

According to James Adams (Ax̲tiwiluugoodi, Raven clan, Gitlax̲damks) and Kyeexw, those of the Raven clan, with whom the Wolf clan group led by Kyeexw were intermarried, Ksemxsan, Ax̲tiwiluugoodi, and Txa'analax̲hatk, also moved down the Skeena and joined the Wolf clan at the Gitsmgeelwn territory (Beynon and Barbeau n.d. b, no. 11b). According to Matthew Gurney and Emma Wright, they later moved from there:

> Ksemxsan then gathered his people together . . . They travelled for some time over the mountain and finally landed at what is now Gitlax̲damks. There they joined in with another group of G̲anhada, who had also come from the headwaters of the Stikine. They had stayed at Meziaden Lake, at a place they called Lax'n'miigunt (Place-of-wild-strawberries). The Ksemxsan clan is now the largest G̲anhada

group among the Nisga'a and has branches in all the present Nisga'a villages, also in the <u>G</u>anhada House of Niskimas of the Gitnadoiks tribe of the Tsimshian (Beynon and Barbeau n.d. b, no. 61).

The Wolf clan also abandoned the area on the middle Skeena River. Matthew Gurney and Emma Wright described how they divided into two groups; one joined their relatives in the Gitla<u>x</u>damks area, while the other travelled downriver to Metlakatla Pass:

> Some went down the Skeena, going to meet some of those whom they were certain had gone down to the coast. A greater number went overland to the Nass River, where they knew that there were people of their own clan already living. So thus they divided. Those that went to the coast by the way of the Skeena were led by <u>G</u>amlugides, while To<u>k</u>, who was the actual head of the group, went overland to the Nass River (Beynon and Barbeau n.d. d, no. 8).

James Adams described how <u>G</u>amlugides joined the Tsimshian at Laxwilgyaps:

> Those that went to the coast, came to where there were other Laxgibuu groups and there they made their home for a long while. These were of <u>G</u>amlugides . . . this group had established itself at Laxwilgyaps in the Metlakatla Passage. Their village was then under Asagalyaan, a Laxgibuu of the Gitsiis tribe. It was while here that they, under their chief <u>G</u>amlugides, became a foremost leader among all the Laxgibuu clans, having acquired power from the wolves (Beynon and Barbeau n.d. d, no. 11b).

Matthew Gurney and Emma Wright continued their account, relating how <u>G</u>amlugides eventually was forced to leave Laxwilgyaps:

> Then came ructions among themselves, as they had no hunting property of their own and were only taken in sufferance by the other Laxgibuu people when hunting and fishing. This trouble soon grew almost into open strife among the people . . .

> Then <u>G</u>amlugides gathered together his own group, telling them, "We shall go away from here and meet with To<u>k</u> on the Nass, where we will be free of any further evil influence which our enemies have brought upon us. They resent our being here, just as the Gitsmgeelwn tribe resented us on the Skeena and used their supernatural powers to bring about our destruction. In order to survive we had to escape." They had been here many years and there had a sprung up a very strong feeling against them, among other Laxgibuu (Wolf) groups. The Gitsiis tribe in whose village they were in, by sufferance, now plainly wanted them to move on . . . and then they set off. They finally got to the mouth of the Nass and there met with others whom they knew as being refugees like themselves from the Tahltan country, and they kept on travelling up the river until finally they came upon

where To<u>k</u> had built his village and called it La<u>x</u>'wiiyip (On the prairie), as was named the valley they had left behind, between the Skeena and the Nass River.

Now another group of Laxgibuu were also located on the Upper Nass, that is, the band that had come down the Stikine from Tahltan under the leadership of Niskinwaatk and Nisyo<u>k</u>. This group was large and numerous . . . These were the first Laxgibuu to build their village on the Upper Nass. The other group of Laxgibuu led by To<u>k</u> made their village on the opposite side of the river and there were now two villages of Laxgibuu. Though they were of the same common origin, having come from Tahltan at the headwaters of the Stikine river, and having taken to flight from the Raven (<u>G</u>anhada) clan, they had taken different routes in their flights, one group going down the Stikine River, and the other, over the hills to the headwaters of the Skeena River. Thus these two groups of Laxgibuu, while of the same origin, became on the Nass, two distinct groups (Beynon and Barbeau n.d. d, no. 8).

After <u>G</u>amlugides departure from Metlakatla there still remained numerous members of the Wolf clan under the leadership of Asagalyaan of the Gitsiis. At the same time the House of Nis'wa'mak of the Gwinhuut Eagle clan now established at Metlakatla was growing in prominence. The competition for territory, resources and power between the Wolf and Eagle clans again sparked hostilities. Herbert Wallace gave an account of the events that took place:

In ancient times, there was a village in which the Laxgibuu people all lived together. Across stood a Laxskiik village, whose head was Nis'wa'mak. Between these Wolf and Eagle villages was a trap to catch seals. It belonged to the Laxgibuu. But the Laxskiik coveted it. Yet the Laxgibuu would not let them have it. So Nis'wa'mak killed the Laxgibuu people and took full possession of the seal trap.

Nis'wa'mak was married to a sister of the chief of the Laxgibuu. (Bidał, in the House of Asagalyaan) . . . a child was born to her, and Nis'wa'mak asked his slaves what the child was. They replied, "A boy." The father grew angry and said, "Go and kill him," because he knew that if a son grew up, he would take the place as chief of the Laxgibuu and revenge his family upon him, and he would lose his seal trap . . . (Beynon and Barbeau n.d. d, no. 18).

Nis'wa'mak's wife hid one of her sons and he grew up to become a great warrior and a wealthy chief, taking his uncle's name, Asagalyaan. After hostilities broke out between them, Asagalyaan killed his father and made war on his father's people. Eventually the other tribes at Metlakatla Pass decided that Asagalyaan had become a threat to them as well. He was killed by an old warrior of the Gitlaan tribe and he and the other groups associated with him were dispersed among several

other tribes where they formed the Houses of Nisk'yaa among the Gitzax̱ł̣aał̣,
Asagalyaan and 'Nł̣ade among the Gitsiis, and La'is among the Giluts'aaw. While
Asagalyaan was originally Gitsiis, the others had to join Wolf clan Houses already
established in these other villages. As Herbert Wallace pointed out:

> It was a custom, whenever a person wished to leave one band or tribe, to join in
> with another, providing there were relatives there to receive them, that is, relatives
> of the same crest, such as Gispwudwada, etc. To do so, that person had to spend a
> large amount among the new tribe he wished to join (Beynon and Barbeau n.d. d,
> no. 18).

While this was taking place at Metlakatla, the arrival of G̱amlugides on the
Nass had created friction with his close clan relative, Toḵ. Nagwa'on, who was of
the same Wolf group as G̱amlugides made a bid for the leadership at Toḵ's
expense. Toḵ decided to leave the Nass and move further south, as Robert Stewart
(Txalaxatk, Eagle clan, Lax̱galts'ap) described:

> Nagwa'on was the head chief of a group of Laxgibuu (Wolf) and he wanted to be
> recognized as being the head chief of Nass River tribes . . . There was another
> group of Laxgibuu (Wolf) . . . under the leadership of Toḵ. While it was not as
> large in numbers as those of Nagwa'on, . . . for a long while it resisted the rights of
> Nagwa'on . . . [Toḵ and his group of Laxgibuu were eventually forced to leave]
> together with 'Wiihon, who was leader of the Gisgahaast [Fireweed/Killerwhale
> clan] group and ally of the Toḵ group of the Laxgibuu. These escaped to the
> mouth of the river. Th+ey then began to look for a more secure place. So they
> travelled on down the coast until they found Knamaas, but this they found
> already occupied. They went on south until they came to Kts'mat'iin. The Gitsiis
> tribe of the Tsimshian were already here, but the G̱anhada chief Galksik took one
> of the Laxgibuu women as his wife and through this alliance they lived here for a
> long while. Soon quarrels broke out over fishing and hunting territories. Before an
> actual battle occurred, Toḵ moved on down the coast. Some of the Laxgibuu who
> had married into the Gitsiis stayed at that tribe, becoming afterwards the Kaltk
> group of Laxgibuu which afterwards was subdivided into many Houses . . . The
> group travelled on down the coast and settled for a time at what is now called
> Lowe Inlet. Here they tried to control the area against invaders by stringing cedar
> bark rope across the narrow part of Grenville Channel, so that no strange canoes
> could get by. Soon these Laxgibuu and the Gisgahaast were outnumbered by the
> Tsimshian groups who were the Gitḵxaał̣a and the Gitḵ'a'ata. They were now
> trying to get these Laxgibuu people out of this location at Kmoode (Lowe Inlet)
> (Beynon and Barbeau n.d. d, no. 41).

The Gitḵ'a'ata, who thought that their original attacks on the Tlingit in their
territory had significantly reduced their enemy's numbers, were surprised to find

that there were still many of them at Lowe Inlet, not realizing it was yet another group, led by Tok. Heber Clifton described the Gitḵ'a'ata's response:

> With the Gitamaat and Gitlo'op they [the Gitḵ'a'ata] prepared to attack again. They were warned about a rope stretched across the entrance to Lowe Inlet. You will follow along the water's edge when coming from your village and when you come to where it is very narrow, you will take good care of where a rope is stretched across on the water and this is put across by the Wolf clan and upon the ropes ends are fastened deer hoofs and puffin bills and this makes a noise when the canoes come in contact with the rope and giving the alarm to the Wolf clan . .

> And they knew where the rope was stretched across by the Wolf clan, where it was a very narrow passage at Lowe Inlet . . . They all attacked together and took the Wolf clan without a struggle. Many of the Wolf clan escaped up into the hills and the raiders captured many women and children and killed many. Then the raiders broke up into pieces all of the canoes of the Wolf clan and razed all of the houses by fire and then they left . . . (Beynon n.d., no. 228).

As with the Raven, Wolf and Eagle groups among the other tribes, the Gitḵ'a'ata assimilated many of the defeated invaders. Heber Clifton related how some of the Tlingit Wolf clan remained and joined the Gitḵ'a'ata:

> Now some of the captives went to Gitamaat and some of others had gone to Gitḵ'a'ata and lived there and they really increased in number here. Well the Gitḵ'a'ata now were those who took the Wolf clan river of Lowe Inlet. And the Gitḵ'a'ata chief kept this plentiful territory for a long while . . . (Beynon n.d., no. 228).

Those remaining of the Wolf clan group led by Tok moved further south and eventually returned to the Nass River.

> These Laxgibuu . . . moved farther south, and for some time lived with the Wutsdaa tribe. It was not long after this that the Wutsdaa and this Laxgibuu band began to have trouble. They were once more forced to move, and they did until they came to what is known as Queen Charlotte Sound. At Calvert Island, they built a village at what is now Safety Cove. They called this Laxtiyookł. The waters of the source were Wilhałmiilk-miilk (Where Along Dance).

> These Laxgibuu now were tired of constantly moving round. They could no longer catch the eulachon or have eulachon oil, which was their staple food. They also were lonesome for their own people. They could not get the salmon as easily as they used to get it in their own rivers. So they now planned on returning to the Nass River. Together with the Gisgahaast group of 'Wiihon, their allies, they set out to return to the Nass. They stopped at many places. Some of them even settled

with the Gitk̲xaała Tsimshian. The others finally reached the mouth of the Nass, where for a time they lived at what is now Kincolith, and they were known as Gitiyooxł. Then the G̲anhada group, which already was at Kincolith, began quarrelling with them over fishing in the stream back of the village, where they got their salmon. As these quarrels became more frequent, the Laxgibuu, being outnumbered, they went up the Nass and, during the night, they passed the village of Nagwa'on and went on up the river. There they formed what has since been the Laxgibuu group Gitwil'nagyi'l (People Where as One). The Laxgibuu on the Nass became so numerous that they divided into two groups . . . (Beynon and Barbeau n.d. d, no. 41).

Matthew Gurney and Emma Wright explained this unusual situation:

Whereas they did not intermarry, they did not contribute to each others potlatches . . . When the funeral feast was on, the other Laxgibuu were guests along with the other clans (Laxskiik and G̲anhada) and received gifts as guests. . . The reason why this happened was necessity, as there were so many Laxgibuu people that, when a feast was given there were no guests (of our opposite clan) to entertain (Beynon and Barbeau n.d. d, no. 8 and no. 13).

After a complex process of warfare and accommodation unfolding over several decades, the invading peoples from the headwaters of the Stikine River and the northern coast were now dispersed throughout the territories of the Tlingit, Tsimshian, Gitksan and Nisga'a. With the battles finally at an end, the Tsimshian found themselves a more unified and complex nation with the proven capacity and resolve to defend their borders. The network of related groups now spread throughout the region, and the greater integration of the tribes within the Tsimshian nation, initiated a new period, characterized by closer economic ties, the development of a complex system of trade alliances, and an increasingly competitive system of social organization.

DATING THE *ADAWX*

It is evident that the contribution of *adawx* and *at.oow* to the understanding of Northwest Coast history is significant in itself. Combined with the findings of archaeology and other systems of dating, such as geology, paleobotany, and written history, the potential for new understandings is considerable. Here we examine geological and archaeological studies that may pertain to the period under discussion.

In the 1980's, preliminary geological work to date a neoglacial advance such as the *adawx* describe on the Stikine River was undertaken by the Gitksan Office of the Hereditary Chiefs. In a project prepared for Delgamuukw v. A.G., June Ryder identified three periods of neoglacial advance on the west coast of North America. The most recent, commonly referred to as the Little Ice Age, began approximately 900 years ago and ended around the eighteenth century. Earlier Holocene advances took place between 3000 (or 3500) and 2000 B.P. and between 7000 and 11,000 B.P.

In her examination of the glacial history of the Stikine River itself, Ryder used air photos and topographic maps to determine the possibility of a glacial advance that extended over the river. Ryder (1985) made the following comments in her final report:

> No clear evidence was found in the Stikine area for the greater extent of any glacier during earlier [than the late-Neoglacial advance] Holocene time. Clearly defined channels cut into bedrock by flowing water, and bedrock scarps on the eastern side of Stikine valley opposite Flood Glacier suggest that this glacier has probably extended across Stikine River since the maxima of the last Pleistocene glaciation, but this may have occurred either during late-Pleistocene glacier recession or during a Holocene readvance. Poorly defined linear depressions on the eastern side of Stikine valley opposite Mud Glacier may have carried meltwater at some former time, but they provide no significant evidence for a former greater extent of Mud Glacier.

> The possibility exists that moraines or other evidence of earlier Holocene advances of Great, Mud and Flood Glaciers have been eroded by Stikine River or buried by deposition of floodplain sediments.

As the results of the study were inconclusive, Ryder indicated that on site investigation might yield more pertinent information concerning a neoglacial advance of the Great, Flood or Mud glacier such as the *adawx* describe.

While archaeological evidence that might date the period described by the *adawx* is preliminary, there is an emerging consensus that between 2000 and 1500 B.P. there was a remarkable escalation in warfare along the Northwest Coast. These dates may provide a general time frame for the period in which the Tsimshian came under attack by groups invading from the north, while at the same time coinciding with the findings of geologists concerning neoglacial advances between 3000 and 2000 B.P.

Madonna Moss established 2000 to 1500 B.P. as an initial period for the appearance of fort sites along the northern northwest coast: "Our review suggests that discrete fort sites, which appear to represent a substantial investment of labor and logistical planning, appear on the North Pacific coast of North America during the last 1500 to 2000 years" (Moss and Erlandson 1992:86). Similar work at sites identified by the *adawx* as places of refuge during the Tlingit invasion might yield comparable results.

Jerome Cybulski identified a "high frequency of warfare" around the same time at Prince Rupert Harbour, based on his study of human skeletons excavated by George MacDonald in the 1960's and 1970's:

> . . . of those skeletons with injuries in the Prince Rupert Harbour sites, almost 60 percent manifested trauma plausibly attributable to episodes of interpersonal violence. Such trauma included depressed skull fractures from club blows, facial and anterior tooth fractures, defensive forearm "parry" fractures, defensive fractures of the outer hand, disarming fractures of the forearm and hand, and instances of decapitation (Cybulski 1990:58).

Cybulski also pointed out that "bone and stone clubs, bipointed ground stone objects, and ground slate daggers [located in the same sites as the skeletons] are clearly weapons" (Fladmark, Ames, and Sutherland 1990:234). Also found were copper covered cedar rods considered to be the remains of armour buried with:

> . . . a group of artifacts in a cemetery on the Boardwalk site (GbTo 31) about 1,800 years ago. It is one of the more intricate pieces of cultural history recorded in the shell-middens of Prince Rupert Harbour. The items might have belonged to a warrior. The cedar cylinders wrapped with copper may be the remnants of rod armour similar to that worn by Tsimshian warriors some 1,500 years later, while other elements likely represent weaponry for hand to hand combat. A human female skull and jaw, partly stained blue-green by copper salts, were in the same pit as the artifacts, possibly a trophy of war. The skull was not directly associated with other human bones or graves in the immediate area, some dating to about the same time as the artifacts and others to about 2,600 years ago (Cybulski 1993:6).

David Archer's work at Prince Rupert Harbour offers a possible date for the retreat of the Tsimshian up the Skeena prior to Aksk's defeat of the Tlingit. He established dates of between A.D. 1 and 400 for the permanent abandonment of 13 villages in the area, and a change in the settlement pattern thereafter:

> Of the village sites that have consistent, reliable dates, there are 13 that were all abandoned within the first few centuries A.D. To place this in context, only one site was clearly abandoned before this period. There appear to be two or three that

were abandoned in the centuries after A.D 500 and before the advent of Europeans, but certainly no more than this. The evidence points to a dramatic change in the local settlement pattern (Archer 1992:15).

In addition, there are specific findings at the location of the fort which was built by Aksk to defeat the Tlingit. It is a significant loss to the history of the Tsimshian that potentially extensive archaeological work in the area of Aksk's fort was curtailed by industrial development. Two sites were summarily excavated in the 1970's under urgent salvage requirements pending their imminent destruction by harbour development. One was the Lachane site, GbTo-33, which offered a rare opportunity for a match to a specific event in oral history. What was discovered shows the potential for correlation between the archaeological findings and the *adawx*.

According to the account of Aksk's fort recorded by Henry Tate, "they built a large square house . . . A little stream of water ran through one corner of the house" (Boas 1916:370). In a report on the salvage excavation at GbTo-33, Richard Inglis (1976:158) commented on the "tendency of northern tribes to build houses with wooden floors directly over flowing streams" and reported that "this waterlogged site, situated immediately between two house platforms, appears to be a refuse area where broken and unfinished artifacts were discarded."

Further, the fort that Aksk built was described as a log house, a "walkiik," and the huge trap door was made of whole logs lashed together, while in some accounts whole trees were used as a palisade. Inglis (1976:163) reported that "towards the bottom of level four was an extensive mass of large logs, tree stumps and branches. Some of the stumps clearly showed adzing on their ends." Thirty-three radio-carbon dates were obtained for GbTo-33, ranging in age from 4630 ± 105 to 560 ± 70 years B.P. (J. Cybulski, pers. comm., 1998). Dates of 2470 ± 90 to 1630 ± 100 years B.P. were associated with an adzed stump, wood bowls, basketry, and a zoomorphic carving found in the waterlogged portion of the site, Area C.

In the *adawx* recorded by Henry Tate (Boas 1916:370ff), the decapitation of the Tlingit slain by Aksk was described as follows:

> [When the young men returned from pursuing the Tlingit, they] cut off the heads of those they had slain in the canoes, and their father cut off the heads of those slain in the house; and when the ten young men came back from their pursuit they had four poles put up in their canoe, and many heads were hanging from these poles. They sang a song of victory . . . and the young men took the bodies of those they had slain and threw them on the beach, which was full of bodies. They took their scalps; and after they had done so, they took all the skulls and threw them in

the creek that ran by the side of the fort. They took all the canoes, crest helmets, decorated daggers, decorated armour, coppers, and elk skins of their enemies.

Jerome Cybulski (1996:5) reported specifically on human skeletal remains found at the Lachane site in an unpublished manuscript on file at the Canadian Museum of Civilization:

> Antemortem and perimortem skeletal trauma likely resulting from interpersonal violence was an important finding in the Prince Rupert Harbour skeletal collection as summarized and, in some respects, detailed elsewhere (Cybulski, 1990, 1992, 1994). The assemblage from the Lachane site provides the only direct archaeological evidence for the taking of heads, an often cited correlate of Northwest Coast warfare as known ethnographically (e.g., Codere, 1950:105; Drucker, 1951; de Laguna, 1990:215; Suttles, 1990:465).

Cybulski (1996:64-65) concluded his analysis of the remains of five individuals considered to have suffered decapitation as follows:

> The three known decapitations (i.e., those with cut neck vertebrae) included two males and a female, all in the young adult category. Burial 466 (without cut marks) and Burial 483 were identified as females, the first estimated at middle age, the second as a young adult. Their proximity to one another (in Area B of the site) suggested a single event. From the unusual body attitudes of the three in situ examples, one might further speculate that the victims were decapitated where they lay or that their corpses were unceremoniously dumped into a common pit in the general area of the cemetery.

> As reported and discussed elsewhere in this manuscript (p.19), a collagen-based radiocarbon age estimate of 1750 ± 40 years B.P. was obtained from Burial 481. This provides an acceptable "date" for the decapitation event at Lachane. This approximates a calendar age of A.D. 200, uncorrected for possible fluctuations in atmospheric C14 or marine reservoir influences.

Some of the objects taken from the defeated invaders, "crest helmets, decorated daggers, decorated armour, [and] coppers", may well have been new to the Tsimshian and therefore significant enough for them to have been buried with their warriors. Items in the cache at the Boardwalk site (GbTo-31) were a whale bone club, a slate spear or dagger, and two copper bracelets. As well, as noted above, the discovery of the Tlingit at Kt'smat'iin marked the first time that Gwishayaax of the Gitsiis had seen copper tools. There are only two known sources of "native copper" one at the headwaters of the Skeena River, the other on the Copper River in Eyak-Tlingit territory.

Dates between 2000 and 1500 B.P. for the events of this period are supported by the *adawx* record itself, which describes several periods and many events following the defeat and assimilation of the Tlingit by the Tsimshian. The changing nature of the social organization of the Tsimshian tribes, the development of extensive feasting, and economic and political alliances with neighbouring nations, and the increasing cohesion of the Tsimshian nation are described as taking place over many generations, and were complex processes, which indicate considerable time depth for their development. Dates more recent than 1000 B.P. would imply a compression of those processes, and many events described in the later *adawx*, thereby rendering incoherent the history of the later periods.

CONCLUSION

There is mounting evidence that, for 2000 years, extended kinship groups among the Tlingit, Tsimshian, Gitksan, and Nisga'a have passed on the history of a period of warfare and migration which was recorded by their ancestors in oral documents called *adawx* and *at.oow*. Through a remarkable cultural institution, which has ensured their preservation over centuries, the *adawx* and *at.oow* convey the history of the period to this day. By approaching *adawx* and *at.oow* without the cultural bias inherent in anthropology, but, instead, from within their indigenous context, the full extent and complexity of these historical documents becomes apparent. The detailed history they convey also provides a basis for discussion of such issues as the nature of Athapascan migration into the territories of coastal peoples, the important role of clan membership and marriage in the assimilation of new peoples into coastal societies, and the complexity of the sociopolitical and legal system of coastal nations such as the Tsimshian.

It is hoped that this paper has made a case for a role for archaeological research in dating the periods of history defined by the oral record. Many archaeologists have used the oral record to identify and locate sites, to formulate hypotheses, and to attempt to understand their findings. Archaeological literature has yet to analyse in detail the sources and intellectual processes involved in the use of oral history. What is suggested here is a more rigorous approach in which the study of *adawx* and *at.oow* is acknowledged as a distinct discipline that informs archaeological research both in its hypotheses and its conclusions.

Archaeological projects, and projects in related disciplines, planned with a view to dating a series of interrelated events in the *adawx*, could yield significant results, and, in so doing, add weight to the argument that *adawx* and *at.oow* constitute a unique and remarkable record of northern Northwest Coast history. Serious attention to this history might also slow the irrevocable loss of important archaeological sites such as Aksk's village on Kaien Island and ancient village and fort sites currently threatened by logging and other development throughout Tsimshian territory.

ACKNOWLEDGEMENTS

The cartography for this paper was done by Eric Leinberger.

REFERENCES CITED

Archer, D.J.W. (1992). Results of the Prince Rupert Harbour Radiocarbon Dating Project. Unpublished manuscript, Resource Information Centre, Heritage Conservation Branch, Government of British Columbia, Victoria.

Barbeau, M.C., and W. Beynon (n.d.). The Marius Barbeau and William Beynon Fieldnotes (1915-1956). Unpublished manuscript, Canadian Centre for Folk Culture Studies, Canadian Museum of Civilization, Hull.

Beynon, W. (n.d.). The Beynon Manuscript. Manuscripts from the Columbia University Library. University Microfilms International, Ann Arbor.

Beynon, W., and M.S. Barbeau (n.d.a). The Gwenhoot of Alaska in Search of a Bounteous Land. Unpublished manuscript, Canadian Centre for Folk Culture Studies, Canadian Museum of Civilization, Hull.

Beynon, W., and M.S. Barbeau (n.d.b). Raven Clan Outlaws of the North Pacific Coast. Unpublished manuscript, Canadian Centre for Folk Culture Studies, Canadian Museum of Civilization, Hull.

Beynon, W., and M.S. Barbeau (n.d.c). Temlarham: The Land of Plenty on the North Pacific Coast. Unpublished manuscript, Canadian Centre for Folk Culture Studies, Canadian Museum of Civilization, Hull.

Beynon, W., and M.S. Barbeau (n.d.d). Wolf-Clan Invaders from the Northern Plateaux among the Tsimsyans. Unpublished manuscript, Canadian Centre for Folk Culture Studies, Canadian Museum of Civilization, Hull.

Boas, F. (1916). Tsimshian mythology. In *Thirty-first Annual Report of the Bureau of American Ethnology, 1909-1910*, U.S. Government Printing Office, Washington, pp. 29-1037.

Codere, H. (1950). *Fighting with Property; A Study of Kwakiutl Potlatching and Warfare 1792-1930*. University of Washington Press, Seattle and London.

Cybulski, J.S. (1990). Human biology. In *Handbook of North American Indians, Vol. 7, Northwest Coast*, edited by W. Suttles, Smithsonian Institution, Washington, pp. 52-59.

Cybulski, J.S. (1992). *A Greenville Burial Ground: Human Remains and Mortuary Elements in British Columbia Coast Prehistory*. Archaeological Survey of Canada Mercury Series Paper 146. Canadian Museum of Civilization, Hull.

Cybulski, J.S. (1993). Notes on the Cache in Area A of the Boardwalk Site (GbTo 31). Unpublished manuscript, Information Management Services (Archaeological Records), Canadian Museum of Civilization, Hull.

Cybulski, J.S. (1994). Culture change, demographic history, and health and disease on the Northwest Coast. In *In the Wake of Contact: Biological Responses to Conquest*, edited by C.S. Larsen and G.R. Milner, Wiley-Liss, New York, pp. 75-85.

Cybulski, J.S. (1996). Context of Human Remains from the Lachane Site, GbTo 33 (Including Evidence for Decapitation). Unpublished manuscript (Ms. 3973), Information Management Services (Archaeological Records), Canadian Museum of Civilization, Hull, Québec.

Dauenhauer, N.M., and R. Dauenhauer, eds. (1987). *Haa Shuká, Our Ancestors: Tlingit Oral Narratives*. Vol. 1. Classics of Tlingit Oral Literature. University of Washington Press, Seattle and London.

De Laguna, F. (1990). Tlingit. In *Handbook of North American Indians, Vol. 7, Northwest Coast*, edited by W. Suttles, Smithsonian Institution, Washington, pp. 203-228.

Drucker, P. (1951). *The Northern and Central Nootkan Tribes*. Bureau of American Ethnology Bulletin 144. Washington.

Duff, W. (n.d.). Tsimshian File. Unpublished manuscript, University of British Columbia Museum of Anthropology, Vancouver.

Fladmark, K.R., K.M. Ames, and P.D. Sutherland (1990). Prehistory of the northern coast of British Columbia. In *Handbook of North American Indians, Vol. 7, Northwest Coast*, edited by W. Suttles, Smithsonian Institution, Washington, pp. 229-239.

Inglis, R.I. (1976). 'Wet' site distribution – the northern case, GbTo-33 – the Lachane site. In *The Excavation of Water-Saturated Archaeological Sites (Wet Sites) on the Northwest Coast of North America*, edited by D.R. Croes, Archaeological Survey of Canada Mercury Series Paper 50, Canadian Museum of Civilization, Hull, pp. 158-185.

Moss, M.L., and J.M. Erlandson (1992). Forts, Refuge Rocks, and Defensive Sites: The Antiquity of Warfare Along the North Pacific Coast of North America. *Arctic Anthropology* 29 (2):73-90.

Olson, R.L. (1967). *Social Structure and Social Life of the Tlingit in Alaska.* University of California Anthropological Records, Vol. 26. Berkeley.

Ryder, J. (1985). Recent History of Glaciers Adjacent to Stikine River in the British Columbia Coast Mountains with Particular Reference to Mud Glacier and Flood Glacier. Unpublished manuscript, Gitksan-Wet'suwet'en Tribal Council, Gitanmaax.

Suttles, W. (1990). Central Coast Salish. In *Handbook of North American Indians, Vol. 7, Northwest Coast*, edited by W. Suttles, Smithsonian Institution, Washington, pp. 453-475.

Swanton, J.R. (1908). Social conditions, beliefs and linguistic relationship of the Tlingit Indians. In *Twenty-Sixth Annual Report of the Bureau of American Ethnology, 1904-1905*, U.S. Government Printing Office, Washington, pp. 391-512.

Human Biological Relationships for the Northern Northwest Coast[1]

Jerome S. Cybulski

ABSTRACT

Three multivariate sets of morphological data were used to assess biological distances among four ancient and four recent aboriginal cranial samples by cluster analysis and multidimensional scaling. A subset of 17 nonmetric variants previously used to study the Nass River Greenville burial ground suggested functional or mechanical influences on potential genetic patterns. A variably different subset of 21 traits revealed a notably close association of Prince Rupert Harbour, Greenville, and Tsimshian, possibly reflecting ancestral-descendant connections from the Middle Pacific period through the period of historic contact. A notably looser, separate, though inconstant association was revealed for Haida, Tlingit, and ancient Namu. All data identified Blue Jackets Creek as an outlier quite distantly removed from the others. The position of a Bella Bella sample was ambiguous.

RÉSUMÉ

On fait appel aux ensembles multivariés des données morphologiques pour évaluer la distance biologique susceptible d'exister entre quatre échantillons anciens et quatre récents de crânes aborigènes en recourant à l'analyse par grappes et à l'échelle multidimensionnelle. Un sous-groupe de 17 variables non métriques utilisées auparavant pour l'étude des cimetières de Greenville sur la rivière Nass laissent entrevoir des influences fonctionnelles

[1] My 1996 symposium paper in Halifax was titled "Human Biological Relationships for the North Coast." The new title reflects extensive revision to the original, more comprehensive representation of the Prince Rupert Harbour and Haida samples, and the addition to the analyses of Tlingit and Bella Bella skulls.

In *Perspectives on Northern Northwest Coast Prehistory*, edited by Jerome S. Cybulski. Hull: Canadian Museum of Civilization, Archaeological Survey of Canada, Mercury Series Paper 160, pp. 107-144, © 2001.

et mécaniques sur les modèles génétiques potentiels. Un autre sous-groupe de variables de 21 caractères a révélé une association remarquablement étroite entre Prince Rupert Harbour, Greenville et Tsimshan correspondant peut-être à des liens ancestraux depuis le période *Middle Pacific* jusqu'à la période de contact. Une association remarquablement plus lâche, séparée, quoique versatile, a été révélée pour les Haïdas, les Tlingits et les anciens Namus. Toutes les données ont identifié Blue Jackets Creek comme une valeur aberrante plutôt distante des autres. La position de l'échantillon de Bella Bella était ambiguë.

INTRODUCTION

This paper expands upon a previous investigation of the presumptive biological relationships of past human populations on the north coast of British Columbia (Cybulski 1992:112-128). The earlier investigation formed part of a study of a Late Developmental Stage (Late Pacific) burial ground at Greenville, located in the Nass River valley. Morphological data were compared with those of skeletons excavated at Prince Rupert Harbour and Namu on the mainland coast, and Blue Jackets Creek on Haida Gwaii (Queen Charlotte Islands). Greenville and Prince Rupert Harbour proved closest to one another in multivariate assessments of craniometric characters and cranial nonmetric variants. Namu and the two series formed a second level cluster, more tightly knit on the basis of metric than nonmetric characters, whereas Blue Jackets Creek was clearly separate from all three in both sets of data.

Historical explanations were offered to account for the results. The apparent morphological closeness of Greenville and Prince Rupert Harbour may have reflected a common candidacy for Tsimshian ancestry. Greenville is in traditional Nisga'a territory and Prince Rupert Harbour, near the mouth of the Skeena River, is in traditional Coast Tsimshian territory (see Fig. 1). The Nisga'a and Coast Tsimshian have been grouped culturally and linguistically as Tsimshian (Boas 1916, Garfield 1939, Garfield and Wingert 1951).

The unique position of Blue Jackets Creek suggested little if any ancestral connection between Tsimshian and the Queen Charlotte Islands' Haida. Indeed, the ancient Blue Jackets Creek sample was previously shown to differ from recent Haida skeletal samples in univariate assessments of cranial morphology (Murray 1981). Namu, while osteologically close to Greenville and Prince Rupert Harbour, was noted to be removed in time and space, and presumptively ancestral to Bella Bella (Heiltsuk). The latter were ethnolinguistically different from Tsimshian. It may be added here, however, that the apparent morphological nearness of the earlier Namu sample could have indicated that a Tsimshian ancestral element extended at some point in the past to the central coast of British Columbia.

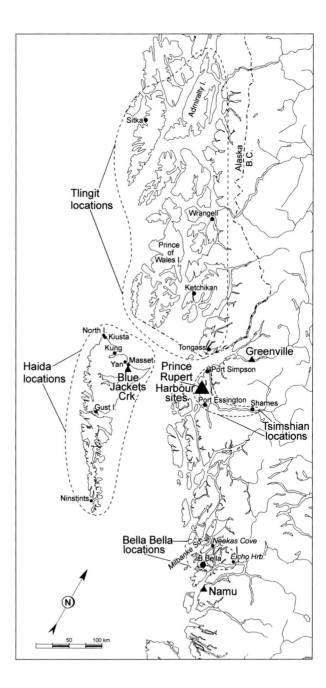

Fig. 1. Northern Northwest Coast with locations of skeletal samples reported in the text. Not all local collection points are named here (see Table 1). Triangles denote ancient sites. Broken outlines encompass ethnographic areas where recent skulls were collected, not necessarily ethnolinguistic boundaries or traditional territories.

The present paper attempts to test these interpretations and enliven the debate by considering additional skeletal series. The added samples include Tsimshian, Tlingit, Haida, and Bella Bella as principally defined by skulls in museum collections. My comparisons largely rest on multivariate techniques of distance analysis based on cranial nonmetric variation and cranial measurements, but other information is considered in the discussion of the results. There are limitations in the skeletal data used and in the samples themselves, as will be explained, but I was interested in the following questions. Is the original pattern of relationships among the four prehistoric series maintained with the addition of new samples? Can the ancient Greenville and earlier Prince Rupert Harbour series indeed be shown to have been ancestral to the ethnographically known Tsimshian? Is there a connection of ethnic origin between Tsimshian and the central British Columbia coast as has been proposed by some investigators based on evidence from mythology and the archaeology of culture (e.g., Coupland 1989)? Are there osteological indications for Bella Bella ancestry in the Namu sample? Is there a biological correlate to the so-called North Coast interaction sphere or area co-tradition concept of cultural development among the Tsimshian, Haida, and Tlingit (MacDonald 1969; Patricia Sutherland, this volume), or did the investigation inspired by the Greenville excavation effectively dispel notions along those lines? Does the Blue Jackets Creek series maintain its morphological or biological uniqueness when compared with other skeletal series, including, and especially, those labeled Haida? As will be shown, the potential answers to these questions are tempered by the data at hand.

MATERIALS AND METHODS

THE SAMPLES

Aside from occasional isolated finds (e.g., Simonsen 1973; Skinner 1984), the skeletal remains of Blue Jackets Creek, Greenville, and Prince Rupert Harbour constitute the only human population samples from the north coast of British Columbia known to date from ancient (pre-European contact) times. Together with those excavated at Namu, they are the only feasibly studiable ancient population samples from the whole of the northern Northwest Coast, that portion which ranges from Yakutat Bay in Alaska to the northern tip of Vancouver Island (Matson and Coupland 1995:3).

As discussed at length elsewhere (Cybulski 1992), the skeletal samples from Blue Jackets Creek and Namu are roughly contemporaneous, assignable for the most part to an Early Developmental Stage of British Columbia coast prehistory, 5500 to 3500 years B.P., as defined by Knut Fladmark (1986). The Prince Rupert Harbour series is later, from a Middle Developmental Stage of about 3500 to 1500 years B.P., and the Greenville series is still later, having been radiocarbon dated from about 1500 to 500 years ago. Kenneth Ames and Herbert Maschner (1999:66, 87-96) have recently used the terms Early, Middle, and Late Pacific to identify these periods for the Northwest Coast as a whole.

The site of Blue Jackets Creek (FlUa-4) is located just south of Masset on the east side of Masset Sound, Queen Charlotte Islands (Fig. 1). The archaeology has been described by Patricia Sutherland (Severs, 1974; Fladmark, Sutherland and Ames, 1990) and the human osteology of 28 individuals by Jeffrey Murray (1981). I later studied the collection specifically for elements of skull pathology, age at death and sex composition, and the statistical occurrence of cranial nonmetric variants (Cybulski, 1990, 1992, 1994). The collection has since been repatriated and reburied.

Namu (ElSx-1) is a deeply stratified site on the central mainland coast of British Columbia which was excavated in the 1960's and 1970's, and as recently as 1994 (Hester and Nelson 1978; Carlson 1979, 1996). A sample of 42 skeletal individuals was identified and studied in its entirety by A. Joanne Curtin (1984) and cranial nonmetric variants were additionally investigated by Nancy S. Ossenberg (1994). While a few of the individuals are from the Middle and Late Pacific periods, the cranial data, for all intents and purposes, pertain to the Early period.

Remains representing 282 skeletal individuals were collected from eight midden sites in the Prince Rupert Harbour region between 1966 and 1987 (MacDonald 1969; MacDonald and Inglis 1981; Simonsen 1988). They are well dated and have been osteologically reported elsewhere (Cybulski 1974, 1978, 1988, 1990, 1991, 1992, 1994, 1996a, 1999). The sites include Boardwalk (GbTo-31) with 120 individuals, Lachane (GbTo-33) with 73, Garden Island (GbTo-23) with 29, Baldwin (GbTo-36) with 22, Dodge Island (GbTo-18) with 20, Parizeau Point (GbTo-30) with 12, Ridley Island (GbTn-19) with five, and Grassy Bay (GbTn-1) with one. The numbers for most of the sites are minimum estimates. Not all individuals were represented by intact burials. Some were represented by disturbed burials in varying states of completeness or by isolated bones.

A 1981-1983 excavation at Greenville (GgTj-6) yielded 57 skeletal individuals. Two others, collected by Laxgalts'ap Band officials during a 1984 excavation for a water line, were added to the published sample (Cybulski 1992). Five additional individuals are represented in the present study. They were located in 1995 while workers were digging a trench for a sewer connection to a private home about 80 m southeast of the originally demarcated site (Cybulski 1996b). All of the remains were subsequently reburied.

Sampling details about the ancient series are provided in Table 1 as are comparable details about the other, recent series. The latter represent the European contact period from the eighteenth to the late nineteenth centuries A.D. General and specific locations of both the recent and ancient samples are shown in Figure 1 (see also Fig. 2 of MacDonald and Cybulski in this volume for the locations of specific Prince Rupert Harbour sites).

The recent series were assembled from museum labeled skulls which were mostly collected late in the nineteenth or early part of the twentieth centuries, but in some cases as recently as the 1960's. As may be seen in Table 1, accuracy of provenience varied. Towns or abandoned villages were identified in museum records in a number of instances as were two archaeological sites. Some locations of collection were simply identified by variably sized geographical features such as islands, bays, coves, or harbours. In a couple of cases, only broad territorial identifications or presumed ethnic affiliations were mentioned in the catalogues.

METHOD

This study essentially follows the approach used in the earlier investigation of the four ancient series. The samples were compared by means of separate multivariate assessments of cranial nonmetric and metric variables and resultant pairwise distances. Two data reduction techniques, cluster analysis and multidimensional scaling, were variably used to view the results and to try to make sense of them.

The selection of variables for analysis was limited by data available for the Namu and Tlingit series. Due to restrictions related to repatriation issues, I did not directly study these samples. In the case of Namu, I used the frequency data for nonmetric variants reported by Joanne Curtin (1984) in her Master's thesis and some direct observations provided by Nancy Ossenberg (pers. comm. 1990). Dr. Ossenberg also provided me with a set of raw nonmetric observations she made on Tlingit skulls in the United States National Museum (pers. comm. 1996). For metric comparisons, I used the summary cranial measurement data reported by Joanne Curtin for Namu and the individual measurements for the same Tlingit skulls as published by Ales Hrdlicka (1924, 1944).

Table 1. Details of cranial samples and sample data used in the present study

Series	Individuals studied for nonmetric variants[1]	Measured male skulls[1]	No. of sites or known localities	Represented sites or localities of collection	Sources of collections (n)[2]
Tlingit	40 (34-78)	18 (16-18)	11	Admiralty, Heceta, Japonski, Pennock and Prince of Wales Islands; Bobs Bay, Sitka, Staney Creek, Tongass and Wrangell; SE Alaska and unspecified	USNM (38),[3] FMNH (1), USGS (1)
Tsimshian	9 (4-16)	5 (3-4)	5	Port Simpson, Port Essington, Seal Cove, Prince Rupert, Shames area, and unspecified	FMNH (4), CMC (3), AMNH (2)
Haida	80 (44-156)	41 (36-41)	10	North Coast (North Island, Kiusta), Kung, Masset (Yan, New and Old Masset, Kayung), Gust Island (FhUb-1), Cumshewa, and Ninstints	FMNH (57), CMC (17), AMNH (5), RBCM (1)
Bella Bella	29 (16-58)	12 (9-12)	6	Bella Bella, Clatse Bay (FcSx-1), Elcho Harbour, Johnson Channel, Milbanke Sound, Neekas Cove, and unspecified	AMNH (10), FMNH (9), CMC (7), RBCM (3)
Prince Rupert Harbour	211 (52-322)	102 (23-77)	9	Dodge Island (GbTo-18), Garden Island (GbTo-23), Parizeau Point (GbTo 30), Boardwalk (GbTo-31), Lachane (GbTo-33), Baldwin (GbTo-36), Grassy Bay (GbTn-1), and Ridley Island (GbTn-19)	CMC (282)
Greenville	48 (4-72)	15 (5-9)	1	Greenville (GgTj-6)	Reburied
Blue Jackets Creek	17 (2-33)	12 (3-10)	1	Blue Jackets Creek (FlUa-4)	Reburied
Namu	26 (5-49)	8?(2-8)	1	Namu (ElSx-1)	SFU (42)[4]

[1] The first integer in these columns is the total of skulls (individuals) available for observation. The parentheses give the sample size ranges for specific nonmetric variants or measurements. Many nonmetric observations were based on combined side occurrences, accounting for the larger numbers in the ranges, and included adults of both sexes and subadults. Compared measurements were based solely on males due to consistent sex differences and reduced sample sizes for females.

[2] AMNH=American Museum of Natural History; CMC=Canadian Museum of Civilization; FMNH=Field Museum of Natural History; RBCM=Royal British Columbia Museum; SFU=Simon Fraser University Department of Archaeology; USGS=U.S. Geological Survey; USNM=U.S. National Museum. The Greenville, Blue Jackets Creek, and CMC Haida remains have been reburied. In parentheses, n is the number of skeletal individuals represented from each institution.

[3] The nonmetric data used from the USNM were provided by N.S. Ossenberg (pers. comm. 1996) and the metric data were collected by Ales Hrdlicka (1924, 1944). I added my data on two individuals from the Field Museum and the U.S. Geological Survey.

[4] The nonmetric data used from SFU were collected by A.J. Curtin (1984) and, in part, by N.S. Ossenberg (pers. comm. 1990). The metric data are those reported by A.J. Curtin (1984).

Table 2. Cranial nonmetric variants used in distance analyses

Variant	17-trait set[1]	21-trait set[2]
Metopism (full expression)	—	xx
Coronal suture bones	xx	—
Lambdic (apical) bone	xx	xx
Lambdoidal suture (Wormian) bones	xx	—
Asterionic bone	xx	xx
Occipitomastoid bone	—	xx
Parietal notch bone	xx	xx
Os Inca (variant expressions excluding trace)	xx	xx
Supraorbital foramen (single or multiple expressions)	—	xx
Parietal foramen absent	xx	—
Tympanic dehiscence	xx	xx
Pterygobasal bridge	—	xx
Spinobasal bridge	xx	—
Divided hypoglossal canal	xx	xx
Condyloid canal absent	—	xx
Auditory exostosis	xx	—
Posterior zygomatic fissure (trace of os Japonicum)	xx	xx
Supraorbital grooves	xx	xx
Infraorbital suture	—	xx
Palatine torus	xx	—
Foramen spinosum anomalous	—	xx
Paracondylar process	—	xx
Pharyngeal fossa	—	xx
Precondylar anomaly	—	xx
Sagittal sinus turns left	xx	—
Clinoid process bridging	—	xx
Mylohyoid bridge	xx	xx
Multiple mental foramina	xx	xx

[1]This data set was previously used by J.S. Cybulski (1992).
[2]This trait set is based on data provided by N.S. Ossenberg for the Tlingit series (pers. comm. 1996).

Nonmetric variants

Minor anatomical variants of the skull, usually identified as nonmetric cranial variants or discrete traits, have been used over the last five decades to investigate the biological affinities of past human populations, particularly effectively through methods of multivariate distance analysis (e.g., Laughlin and Jørgensen 1956; Szathmary and Ossenberg 1978; Ishida and Dodo 1993). Stimulated, in part, by the results of studies on inbred laboratory mice (Grüneberg 1963) and because some of the traits show familial tendencies in humans, researchers have concluded that the expression of nonmetric traits, usually recorded as present or absent, is under some form of genetic control (see Prowse and Lovell 1995 for a review). The presumed underlying genetic influence may thus account for varying frequencies in the occurrence of traits between human populations.

Whether discrete traits are more or less valuable for biological inferences than metric, or continuously measurable characters of the skull is debatable (ibid.; Saunders 1989). In either case, osteological traits are unlike blood and other serum protein types in living populations for which actual gene (allele) frequencies may be calculated (e.g., Cybulski 1990). Discrete as well as metrical traits may suggest biological affinities but neither offer unobstructed views of a population's gene pool. The manifestations of these traits are almost certainly influenced by other internal and external factors which bear on an individual's growth and development.

Upwards of 45 nonmetric variants have been described for the human skull (e.g., Prowse and Lovell 1995; Hauser and De Stefano 1989). Rarely, however, have all been used to define a particular set of population relationships. Subsets have been favoured by most investigators depending on the availability of data for the samples being tested (e.g., Cybulski 1992), specific problem orientation or interobserver reliability (Konigsberg and Buikstra 1995), and arguments or perceptions, either theoretically or empirically based, that certain traits are more biologically acceptable or "racially" valid than others (Kozintsev 1992; Ossenberg 1994).

Here I investigate two subsets of traits as reported in Table 2. One subset consists of 21 traits which Dr. Ossenberg and I recorded in common. The other consists of 17 traits which were used in my published 1992 assessment of the four ancient series. Given the questions outlined in the introduction, it is appropriate to consider this subset with the addition of the new samples. Unfortunately, the Tlingit sample cannot be fully assessed because only ten traits were recorded in common between the two subsets. My initial conservative inclination was to use only those ten traits. Other investigators have used as few as seven traits in their attempts to define ancient population relationships or structural demographics (Laughlin and Jorgensen 1956; Konigsberg and Buikstra 1995). It appears, however, that the use of only a few or several traits reduces the possibility of adequately characterizing a cranial sample's total morphological pattern which might be considered essential to properly evaluate its underlying biological structure. Preliminary tests indicated that the 10-trait subset was inadequate for evaluating the northern coast samples and, therefore, I chose to test all samples by the 17-trait set. Data for the missing seven traits were substituted for the Tlingit by calculations derived from the unweighted mean percentages of the other samples.

For each subset, the frequencies for all samples were appropriately standardized and reduced to a single mean measure of divergence (MMD) between each pair of samples using C.A.B. Smith's method as refined by Torstein Sjøvold (1977). The statistical significance of each MMD was tested by calculating its variance and standard deviation (ibid.). Results were accepted as significant at the 0.05 level of probability when an MMD was more than twice its standard deviation (Ishida and Dodo 1993).

Cranial Measurements

Fourteen absolute cranial measurements were used in the original assessment of the four ancient samples (Cybulski 1992). For this paper, I used 13 measurements as identified in the footnote to Table 8, eliminating minimum frontal breadth which was not available for the published Tlingit data. These measurements were entered into pairwise sample comparisons using L.S. Penrose's "mean square distance," a viable mathematical alternative to the more complex "generalized distance" or D^2 technique of P.C. Mahalanobis (Penrose 1954; Giles and Bleibtreu 1961).

Data Reduction

To help make sense of the resultant distance matrices, cluster analyses were generated and dendrograms (tree diagrams) constructed using the personal computer program SYSTAT for Windows, Version 6.1.2.[2] Several clustering methods were investigated as explained in the following sections of this paper though not all of the results are presented here.

Some clustering methods require use of a dissimilarity matrix wherein all values are positive. The distance matrices computed from the data included a few negative MMD values which are reported here. Since negative MMD values effectively mean no difference between the paired groups, I converted the values to zero for the purposes of cluster analysis. Multidimensional scaling of the dissimilarity matrices was also completed using SYSTAT.

---

[2] ©1996, SPSS Inc., 444 North Michigan Ave., Chicago, Ill, USA 60611.

RESULTS AND DISCUSSION

Results of the matrix analyses are displayed in Tables 3 through 6, Table 8, Figures 2 through 6, and Figure 8. Additional, related information is provided in Table 7 and Figure 7.

For the nonmetric assessments, the paper I read at the 1996 North Coast Prehistory symposium in Halifax investigated local group and site samples of the Haida and Prince Rupert Harbour series rather than each series as a whole. Likewise, the analysis of nonmetric variation in the 1992 Greenville study was site oriented, utilizing data from only one Prince Rupert Harbour site, albeit the largest, Boardwalk. It is useful here to initially view the data in like fashion in order to examine the relative homogeneity of the two series. At the same time, the assessment allows for partial investigation of the biological (genetic) validity of the trait subsets. The local group assessment has been done only for the nonmetric cranial variants. Because of significantly reduced sample sizes as a result of sex differences, it was not feasible to investigate local samples metrically.

LOCAL GROUP ASSESSMENTS

The subset matrices of the 17 and 21-trait mean measures of divergence among 14 cranial samples are reported in Tables 3 and 4 respectively. Resulting dendrograms are shown in Figures 2 and 3. Only the four largest Prince Rupert Harbour site samples were considered for local analysis but they account for 86 per cent of the total series structure. Similarly, the entire Haida sample was not used to investigate local group variation. Following an earlier examination of local group cranial variation among the Haida (Cybulski 1975), the collection localities represented here from Kiusta and North (Langara) Island were combined into a Haida Gwaii "North Coast" sample and those of Kayung, Yan, Old Masset, and New Masset were combined into a "Masset" sample by virtue of their proximity. Ninstints, much farther to the south, and Gust Island, at an intermediate location in Skidegate Inlet, were treated as separate third and fourth local groups (see Fig. 1).

Cluster analysis has been identified as "the art of finding groups in data" (Kaufman and Rousseeuw 1990:1). Accordingly, many different clustering methods have been developed to achieve what might be termed satisfying results. Here I have considered only heirarchical agglomerative methods of which eight are commonly recognized. Mathematicians and statisticians have argued for the validity of certain of these methods over others though not necessarily in agreement. Biological anthropologists tend to rely on the group average clustering algorithm or unweighted pair group linkage method (e.g., Ishida and Dodo 1993; Pietrusewsky 1999). Although generally not stated, this technique appears to be preferred because it is "space conserving." It affords compromise between the more extreme space contracting and space dilating characteristics of the single (nearest neighbour) and complete (furthest neighbour) linkage methods which, although often employed in taxonomic studies, usually produce too few clusters (in the first instance) or too many (in the second) (Kaufmann and Rousseeuw 1990:225-227).

Other clustering algorithms may, however, produce useful results and are worth testing if for no other reason than to investigate the consistency of patterning as a potential indicator of meaningfulness. Here I report results from the average linkage method because of its space conserving quality and its common use in biological anthropology. As well, there were elements of common sense in the relationships shown by the method in this study. The single linkage method, used in my original test of the four ancient samples, generally did not differentiate the samples of this study well, tending to pull most of them into a single cluster.[3]

A run using the complete linkage method had the expected opposite effect but also displayed some interesting groupings. The Ward linkage method, the results of which are reproduced here, retained or clarified some of those groupings, thereby implying consistency and, hence, acceptability to the data. Like the average linkage method, the Ward method is space conserving. A possible drawback may be that the method emphasizes homogeneity in its clustering algorithm (v. Shennan 1988:217), thus having a tendency to over-join samples. Some of the other clustering algorithms (median, centroid) were tried but the results they produced neither added to nor detracted from the patterns already evident.

There are two general aspects of the nonmetric variant results apparent in Figures 2 and 3. On the one hand, site or local group samples cluster or tend to cluster within each of the larger series where sample breakdowns were possible. On the other hand, the two subsets of nonmetric variants produce different overall results, a potentially important finding which is retained and made clearer in the series assessments shown in Figures 4 and 5.

---

[3] The SYSTAT manual (preceding footnote citation, p. 350) reports that its single linkage algorithm produces hierarchical clustering via the "min method" when dissimilarity matrices are used as in the present study. Likewise, SYSTAT's complete linkage algorithm produces hierarchical clustering via "Johnson's max method."

Table 3. Mean measures of divergence (MMD) for 14 skull samples based on 17 discrete traits[1]

Sample	Baldwin	Bella Bella	Blue Jackets	Garden Island	Greenville	Gust Island	Lachane	Masset	Namu	North Coast	Ninstints	Tlingit	Tsimshian	Boardwalk
Baldwin	0	–	–	–	–	–	–	–	–	–	–	–	–	–
Bella Bella	0.0963*	0	–	–	–	–	–	–	–	–	–	–	–	–
Blue Jackets	0.0756*	0.2284*	0	–	–	–	–	–	–	–	–	–	–	–
Garden Island	-0.0165	0.0142	0.1880*	0	–	–	–	–	–	–	–	–	–	–
Greenville	0.0831*	0.0635*	0.3027*	0.0103	0	–	–	–	–	–	–	–	–	–
Gust Island	0.0860*	0.1453*	0.1465*	0.0884*	0.0500	0	–	–	–	–	–	–	–	–
Lachane	0.0113	0.0096	0.2256*	-0.0236	0.0151	0.0850*	0	–	–	–	–	–	–	–
Masset	0.1539*	0.1580*	0.3987*	0.0554	0.0190	0.1025*	0.0843*	0	–	–	–	–	–	–
Namu	0.0608	0.0577*	0.2451*	0.0050	0.0702*	0.1720*	0.0229	0.0977*	0	–	–	–	–	–
North Coast	0.1131*	0.1234*	0.3675*	0.0120	0.0103	0.1310*	0.0416	0.0308	0.0782*	0	–	–	–	–
Ninstints	0.1040*	0.1241*	0.2563*	0.0308	-0.0048	0.0604*	0.0760*	0.0193	0.0941*	0.0049	0	–	–	–
Tlingit	0.0414	0.0477*	0.2120*	-0.0112	0.0480*	0.0790*	0.0287*	0.0790*	0.0046	0.0493*	0.0672*	0	–	–
Tsimshian	0.1497*	0.0987*	0.3113*	0.0263	-0.0102	0.0369	0.0484	-0.0212	0.0218	0.0177	-0.0122	0.0056	0	–
Boardwalk	0.0353	0.0754*	0.2749*	-0.0246	0.0284*	0.1019*	-0.0029	0.0686*	0.0435*	0.0272	0.0537*	0.0389*	0.0170	0

[1] The 17 traits are those used in Cybulski 1992 and identified in Table 2. Statistically significant MMD's (p 0.05) are marked with an asterisk. For the Tlingit series, the frequencies of seven traits were unavailable (see Table 2) and, therefore, calculated from unweighted mean percentages derived from the other series. The distances in this case are to be considered with caution if not suspicion.

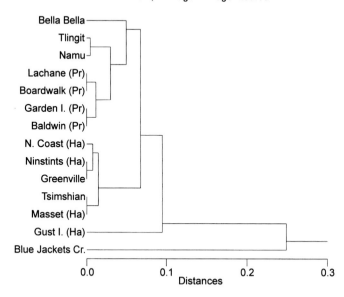

a. 17-Trait Set, Average Linkage Method

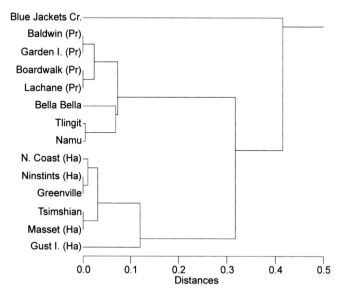

b. 17-Trait Set, Ward Linkage Method

Fig. 2. Diagram of relationships among 14 cranial samples based on cluster analysis of MMD's derived from 17-trait subset of nonmetric variants: (a) average linkage method; (b) Ward linkage method.

a. 21-Trait Set, Average Linkage Method

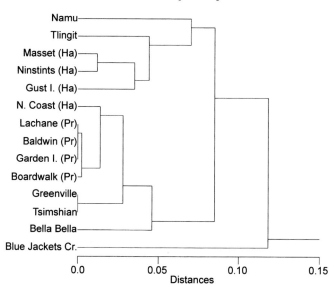

b. 21-Trait Set, Ward Linkage Method

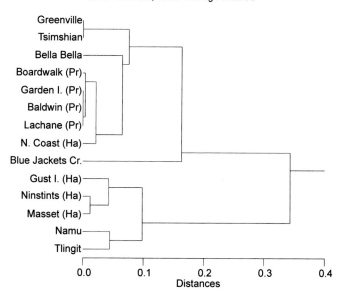

Fig. 3. Diagram of relationships among 14 cranial samples based on cluster analysis of MMD's derived from 21-trait subset of nonmetric variants: (a) average linkage method; (b) Ward linkage method.

Table 4. Mean measures of divergence (MMD) for 14 skull samples based on 21 discrete traits[1]

Sample	Baldwin	Bella Bella	Blue Jackets	Garden Island	Greenville	Gust Island	Lachane	Masset	Namu	North Coast	Ninstints	Tlingit	Tsimshian	Boardwalk
Baldwin	0	–	–	–	–	–	–	–	–	–	–	–	–	–
Bella Bella	0.0579	0	–	–	–	–	–	–	–	–	–	–	–	–
Blue Jackets	0.0568	0.0954*	0	–	–	–	–	–	–	–	–	–	–	–
Garden Island	-0.0624	-0.0243	0.0907	0	–	–	–	–	–	–	–	–	–	–
Greenville	0.0420	0.0589*	0.1781*	-0.0194	0	–	–	–	–	–	–	–	–	–
Gust Island	0.0864	0.0860*	0.0900	0.0172	0.1060*	0	–	–	–	–	–	–	–	–
Lachane	-0.0402	0.0232	0.0685	-0.0387	0.0485	0.0721*	0	–	–	–	–	–	–	–
Masset	0.0830	0.0966*	0.1799*	0.0708	0.1784*	0.0500	0.0563*	0	–	–	–	–	–	–
Namu	0.0763	0.0895*	0.1748*	0.1079*	0.1915*	0.0991*	0.0803*	0.0332	0	–	–	–	–	–
North Coast	0.0019	0.0830*	0.1267*	-0.0167	0.0834*	0.0481	0.0126	0.0184	0.1136*	0	–	–	–	–
Ninstints	0.1228*	0.1283*	0.1578*	0.0635	0.1652*	0.0204	0.0940*	0.0119	0.1035*	0.0433	0	–	–	–
Tlingit	0.0803*	0.0691*	0.1167*	0.0386	0.1341*	0.0438	0.0448*	0.0424	0.0448	0.0497*	0.0461*	0	–	–
Tsimshian	0.0349	0.0547	0.0900	-0.0039	-0.0155	-0.0178	-0.0183	0.0382	0.0737	0.0576	0.0544	-0.0037	0	–
Boardwalk	0.0116	0.0439*	0.1124*	-0.0450	0.0034	0.0826*	0.0072	0.1236*	0.1700*	0.0408	0.1381*	0.1050*	0.0109	0

[1] Trait selection (see Table 2) was determined by data available for the Tlingit series as supplied by N.S. Ossenberg (pers. comm. 1996). Statistically significant MMD's (p (0.05) are marked with an asterisk.

The four Prince Rupert Harbour sites were persistently closely associated in all tests based on cluster analysis regardless of linkage method used. For the 21-trait subset (Table 4), five of the six possible pair groupings ranked #1 and the sixth ranked #4 of 76 possible pair-group rankings when negative MMD's were treated as zero (rank = 1). In the 17-trait subset (Table 3), four of the site pair groupings ranked #1, one ranked #9, and the sixth ranked #25 of 83 possible rankings. One may conclude that the Prince Rupert Harbour sites form a tightly knit population unit relative to all other cranial samples considered in this paper, also giving justification to treating the series as a unit in further, external comparisons.

The four Haida subsamples also tend to cluster in the dendrograms but not as well or as persistently as the Prince Rupert sites. In the 21-trait MMD analysis, the Haida sample pair-groups ranked 6th through 10th and 19th through 28th, and in the 17-trait subset analysis, they ranked 3rd, 16th through 23rd, 39th, and 61st through 66th.

The fact that the Prince Rupert and Haida subsample pair-groups rank lower in the 21-trait than 17-trait analyses – i.e., the subsamples are respectively closer together in each series – suggests that the 21-trait set may be more biologically (or genetically) reflective, or at least more meaningfully discriminating for comparison with external groups. This is borne out by the cluster analysis, especially in the case of the Haida where three of the four groups cluster before tying to other, external samples (Fig. 3).

The strong association of the Prince Rupert sites makes perfectly good sense biologically given their proximity to one another. As well, there is little reason to conclude that the historic Haida would not have formed a cohesive biological population unit by virtue of their sharing a common and distinct language and a common archipelago habitat which may have promoted a relative degree of isolation from other Northwest Coast groups. That is, one might expect a greater sharing of genes between and among local population centres within the archipelago than between those centres and any external population. Earlier studies of cranial morphology which tested local groups from around the Queen Charlotte's identified the Haida as a distinctive unit relative to contemporary mainland groups such as the Southern Kwakiutl, Nootka, and Coast Salish (Cybulski 1975). Possibly also indicating a certain genetic distinctiveness is that the Haida have been shown to exhibit high incidences of skeletal or related conditions which may be strongly influenced by heredity (Gofton et al. 1966; Cybulski 1977).

Be that as it may, the Haida subsamples are not as closely knit as the Prince Rupert site samples. This may be because the Haida samples are more geographically dispersed or because of differences in local group sampling structure. The Prince Rupert cranial samples may be more structurally equal because each is known to come from a single archaeological site. Each site appears to represent a semi-permanent "winter" village used over a significant period of time (MacDonald and Inglis 1981). Hence, each sample may be more phenotypically and genetically representative of the population from whence it was derived.

Table 5. Mean measures of divergence (MMD) for eight skull samples based on 17 discrete traits[1]

Sample	Bella Bella	Blue Jackets	Tsimshian	Greenville	Haida	Namu	Prince Rupert	Tlingit
Bella Bella	0	-	-	-	-	-	-	-
Blue Jackets	0.2284*	0	-	-	-	-	-	-
Tsimshian	0.0987*	0.3113*	0	-	-	-	-	-
Greenville	0.0635*	0.3027*	-0.0102	0	-	-	-	-
Haida	0.1241*	0.2698*	-0.0117	-0.0003	0	-	-	-
Namu	0.0577*	0.2451*	0.0218	0.0702*	0.0936*	0	-	-
Pr. Rupert	0.0570*	0.2358*	0.0413	0.0297*	0.0512*	0.0372*	0	-
Tlingit	0.0477*	0.2120*	0.0056	0.0480*	0.0560*	0.0046	0.0318*	0

[1] The 17 traits are those used in Cybulski 1992 and identified in Table 2. Statistically significant MMD's (p ≤ 0.05) are marked with an asterisk. For the Tlingit series, the frequencies of seven traits (see Table 2) were calculated from unweighted mean percentages derived from the other samples. The distances in this case are to be considered with caution if not suspicion.

With one exception, there is less known or less than might be inferred about the population structure of each Haida sample. Except for Gust Island which was archaeologically investigated in 1967 (MacDonald 1973), the Haida samples were assembled from early museum-collected skulls for which sampling details were sparse. Just how representative they are of the populations they are presumed to represent is unknown or difficult to infer. The local group subsamples, North Coast and Masset, though comprised of skulls from localities within 5 km of one another, may, in fact, be artificial population constructs or not otherwise fully genetically representative of the local populations from which they were drawn. Ninstints, comprised of skulls presumably collected from a single Haida village location (though not necessarily a single cemetery) may be better representative of its parent population.

The Gust Island sample, known to have been collected from a single rock shelter, may represent a lineage. Small in size, it features an age and sex distribution that implies two or three generations of family members, and lineage deposition in a single repository appears to have been the norm in Haida burial practices (MacDonald 1973). Six Gust Island individuals exhibited bridging of the atlas vertebra (Cybulski 1973:75), a skeletal anomaly more apt to be shared by family members than non-relatives (Saunders and Popovich 1978). The sample may, therefore, give a skewed representation of the genetic and resultant phenotypic structure of the general or local Haida population.

Table 6. Mean measures of divergence (MMD) for eight skull samples based on 21 discrete traits[1]

Sample	Bella Bella	Blue Jackets	Tsimshian	Greenville	Haida	Namu	Prince Rupert	Tlingit
Bella Bella	0	-	-	-	-	-	-	-
Blue Jackets	0.0954*	0	-	-	-	-	-	-
Tsimshian	0.0547	0.0900	0	-	-	-	-	-
Greenville	0.0589*	0.1781*	-0.0155	0	-	-	-	-
Haida	0.0799*	0.1183*	0.0210	0.1094*	0	-	-	-
Namu	0.0895*	0.1748*	0.0737	0.1915*	0.0839*	0	-	-
Pr. Rupert	0.0453*	0.0932*	0.0061	0.0213	0.0621*	0.1518*	0	-
Tlingit	0.0691*	0.1167*	-0.0037	0.1341*	0.0405*	0.0448	0.0803*	0

[1] Trait selection (see Table 2) was determined by data available for the Tlingit series as supplied by N.S. Ossenberg (pers. comm. 1996). Statistically significant MMD's are marked with an asterisk.

Regardless of possible reasons, the Haida subsamples do not cluster as tightly as the Prince Rupert samples. But at the same time, they are not dispersed to the extent that the Haida could not be considered a reasonably cohesive biological population unit. It may be noted as well that there is no apparent patterning of the local dispersion which might be interpreted in terms of geographic distance or historic dialect variation within Haida (Thompson and Kinkade 1990).

SERIES ASSESSMENTS

In the local group 21-trait assessment of Figure 3, the Greenville and Tsimshian cranial samples form a tight unitary cluster of a distance equal to the cluster formed by three, or even all four of the Prince Rupert Harbour sites. There is little reason to doubt such an association which is not immediately apparent in the 17-trait local group assessment. In previous study, available biological, archaeological, cultural, and ethnohistorical evidence pointed to a clear relationship between the Late Stage Greenville burial ground and historic Nisga'a (Tsimshian) (Cybulski 1992). The analysis and representation here, in the midst of many other samples, appears to confirm or even solidify that conclusion.

The singular Greenville-Tsimshian cluster is also present in the 21-trait eight-sample series comparisons shown in Figure 5. Here, the cluster is joined by Prince Rupert Harbour and the resultant three-group cluster is then joined by the Bella Bella sample. The relationship is evident in the dendrograms produced by both the average linkage clustering algorithm and the Ward method. Both methods also cluster Haida and Tlingit, and then Namu, into a roughly equivalent overall cluster which, however, is not as tightly knit.

An association between Haida and Tlingit was proffered in the 1970's by Emöke Szathmary and Nancy Ossenberg (1978). Their work employed nonmetric cranial variants as well as the blood group distributions of living populations in an investigation of "Indian-Eskimo" biological differences. While the Haida and Tlingit association was close in their larger context, it could not be considered primary and no other Northwest Coast population samples were included to properly assess the significance of the association with that reported in the present study.

Haida and Tlingit cranial samples were further investigated by Nancy Ossenberg (1994) who also included Namu in a general study of Circum-Pacific (Asian and American) cranial samples and North American samples more deeply set in the continent. While the Haida and Tlingit did not, again, form a primary cluster, they were considered close enough to be interpreted as part of a "Na-Dene" grouping by virtue of their presumed, albeit controversial membership in a common language phylum.[4] The Namu sample was linked to the "Na-Dene" and "Aleut" groupings (Ossenberg 1994:97).

Many of the 21 traits used to produce Table 6 and the resulting dendrograms of Figure 5, c and d, are those which have been employed by Nancy Ossenberg in her studies. Perhaps, it is not surprising then that the Haida, Tlingit, and Namu

---

[4] It is common for many students of population biology to identify and group Haida and Tlingit as "Na-Dene speakers," often automatically, for comparisons with Asian and other native American samples. In fact, 1990's studies of similarities and differences in mtDNA variation have relied heavily on the presumed Haida component rather than Tlingit where only two individuals have been tested (e.g., Lorenz and Smith 1996) despite the fact that it is Haida that is in dispute as a member of the Na-Dene language phylum (see later text and following footnote).

cluster in the present assessment. It is difficult, however, to gauge the closeness or, even, the accuracy of the association. Figure 6a shows the results of multidimensional scaling on the eight samples of this study based on the subset of 21 nonmetric variants. I used the Young loss function in the SYSTAT application which is the loss function featured in ALSCAL, a more widely used computer program for multidimensional scaling (Takane, Young and de Leeuw 1977). The authors of the SYSTAT manual caution that the Young loss function tends to favour large distances over smaller ones. The results here, however, are essentially the same as those given by the more conventional and conservative Kruskal loss function which is also employed in SYSTAT.

The two dimensional scaling effectively produces results similar to those of the cluster analysis based on the average linkage method. Three groupings are produced: (1) Greenville-Tsimshian-Prince Rupert-Bella Bella; (2) Haida-Tlingit-Namu; (3) Blue Jackets Creek.

Blue Jackets Creek is an outlier in virtually every data reduction technique regardless of trait lists (see, also, Table 8 and Fig. 8a) It is only in the 21- trait cluster analysis utilizing the Ward linkage method (Figs. 3b and 5b) that Blue Jackets Creek joins an existing cluster. The sample is noticeably removed from its apparent brethren, however, the joining possibly forced by the linkage method. Seven pair-group comparisons involving Blue Jackets Creek ranked 17-19, 21-22, and 25-26 out of 27 pair-group rankings involving the eight cranial samples.

Outliers may skew the graphical relationships of other samples and it is permissible, with caution, to delete them and view the remaining data (Kaufman and Rousseeuw 1990:219; see also Shennan 1988). No relative change could be detected when the seven remaining sample MMD's alone were subjected to cluster analysis. Though the distances varied, the relative associations were identical in the average and Ward linkage methods. Multidimensional scaling, however, produced some interesting new results.

As shown in Figure 6b, the only persisting association is among Tsimshian, Prince Rupert, and Greenville. Whereas the Tlingit and Haida samples were quite closely situated in Figure 6a, they are now at opposite ends of dimension-2 and Namu is removed from each sample in both dimensions. The apparent threefold "Na-Dene" association seen by N.S. Ossenberg (1994) is not borne out here. It may also be noted that Bella Bella associates with Tlingit in this view rather than with the Tsimshian-Prince Rupert-Greenville assemblage of Figure 6a, lending a measure of ambiguity to its position in the overall scheme.

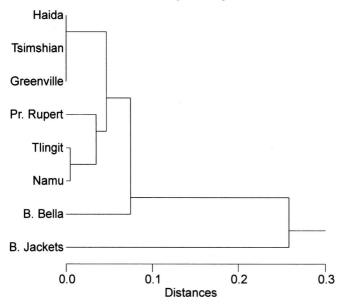

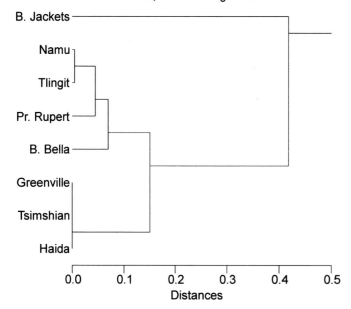

Fig. 4. Diagram of
relationships among
8 cranial samples based
on cluster analysis of
MMD's derived from
17-trait subset of
nonmetric variants:
(a) average linkage
method; (b) Ward
linkage method.

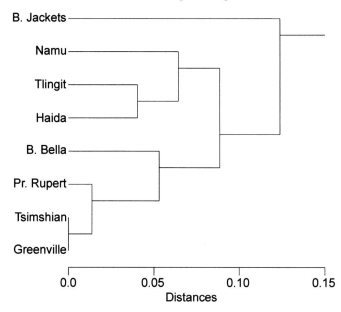

a. 21-Trait Set, Average Linkage Method

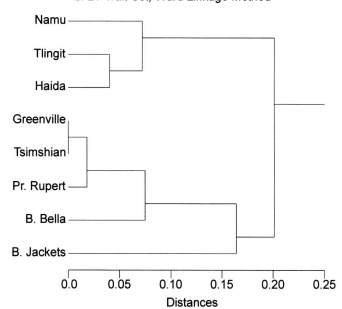

b. 21-Trait Set, Ward Linkage Method

Fig. 5. Diagram of relationships among 8 cranial samples based on cluster analysis of MMD's derived from 21-trait subset of nonmetric variants: (a) average linkage method; (b) Ward linkage method.

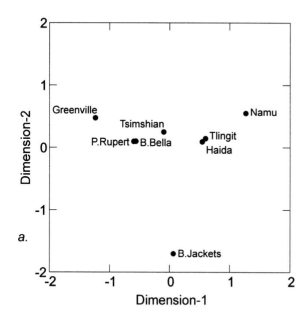

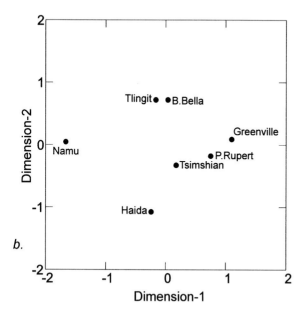

Fig. 6. Multidimensional scaling of MMD's for cranial series based on a subset of 21 nonmetric variants: (a) scales 8 samples; (b) scales 7 samples, eliminating Blue Jackets Creek. Scaling method uses Young loss function.

If the Tlingit and Haida do associate biologically, the relationship might more readily be argued on the basis of geographic proximity and resultant long-term accessibility for the exchange of genes than on the basis of language and, therefore, an inferred distant ancestral relationship. There is no unanimity on the subject, but some linguists treat Haida as a language isolate outside of the Na-Dene phylum and, therefore, quite separate from Tlingit which is treated as a language isolate within the phylum (Thompson and Kinkade 1990).[5]

The Namu crania are separated from the recent Haida and Tlingit by 4000 years. One might, therefore, question an association between the former and the latter two groups unless it is a distant ancestral one. In fact, if there were any association between Namu and a recent group, a more obvious candidate might be Bella Bella given their proximate locations on the central B.C. coast (see Fig. 1) and the fact that modern Bella Bella (Heiltsuk) regard the Namu archaeological site as ancestral (J. Carpenter, pers. comm., 1999). Indeed, an early 1970's study of nonmetric cranial variation among Northwest Coast Indian, Aleut, and Coast, Yukon, and St. Lawrence Eskimo samples associated "ancient Bella Bella" with "recent Bella Bella" in a singular cluster, the "ancient" skulls coming from the site of Namu (Finnegan 1974). For both series, however, the sample sizes were significantly smaller than in the present study, the local composition of the recent series differed, and the MMD method of analysis used then was less mathematically refined. Forty-two variants were used in the analysis, all apparently equally considered biologically relevant. It may also be noted that a much closer association was portrayed for samples of Haida and "Coast Eskimo" than for the "ancient" and "recent" Bella Bella samples. Based on a sample of 13 skulls, Tlingit, the only other group in common with the present study, was shown to be distantly removed from the Haida sample.

Here, the Namu and Tlingit samples are very closely associated in the 17-trait nonmetric MMD analysis of which little has yet been said outside of the local group assessment detailed above. They do not group with the Haida, as in the 21-trait series assessment, but with Prince Rupert Harbour. The Haida sample is, in fact, synonymously clustered with Tsimshian and Greenville, the three series essentially indistinct. In the dendrogram generated by the Ward linkage method (Fig. 4b), there is a hint of association between Bella Bella and Namu but only secondarily through Prince Rupert. Any inferential association would have to

---

[5] To add to the confusion, a recent paper on linguistic origins treats Haida and Tlingit as single language "branches" of Na-Dene which in this case is identified as a "family" rather than a phylum (Ruhlen 1998) apparently following the work of Joseph Greenberg (1987).

be considered distant in the 17-trait cluster analysis derived from the average linkage method.

Table 7. Frequencies of auditory exostosis in Northwest Coast cranial samples[1]

Sample	Number present	Number of observations	Percent occurrence
Blue Jackets Creek	13	33	39.4
Namu	13	48	27.1
Prince Rupert Harbour	54	322	16.8
(Tlingit[2]	~11	~76	~14.0)
Bella Bella	8	58	13.8
Haida	1	155	0.6
Greenville	0	72	0.0
Tsimshian	0	16	0.0

[1] The numbers reported are based on observations per side.

[2] The actual occurrence in this Tlingit sample is unknown. The figures here are substitute calculations derived from the unweighted percentages of the other samples as explained in the Materials and Methods, and Results and Discussion sections of the text.

While a close biological association between Tsimshian and Haida might be expected on the basis of contemporaneity and geographic accessibility, as discussed for the apparent Haida and Tlingit association in the 21-trait analysis, why aren't the three groups then shown together in either setting? If Prince Rupert Harbour were ancestral to Tsimshian, as has been proposed and virtually accepted on the basis of archaeological context (MacDonald and Inglis 1981; Dale Croes, this volume) and as well might be inferred from the 21-trait analysis, why does Prince Rupert Harbour stand separate from the Tsimshian - Greenville association in the 17-trait analysis?

The position of Tlingit is, of course, suspect in the 17-trait analysis since frequency data for seven traits (41 percent of the list) were missing and derived from calculations of the other sample frequencies. This treatment, however, may also be revealing other influences in the 17-trait assessment. As possibly exemplified by one of the variants used in the analysis, those influences may involve developmental elements of functional or behavioral morphology rather than morphology largely reflective of genetics.

Auditory exostosis is a bony eminence or pea-shaped growth in the floor of the external auditory meatus or ear hole. Its occurrence has been causatively associated with habitual diving in cold water (Kennedy 1986; Katayama 1998). Colleagues have been critical of my previously treating this nonmetric variant as a biological indicator, regarding it as a "functional" trait strongly influenced by mechanical factors (N.S. Ossenberg, pers. comm. 1999; J.E. Molto, pers. comm. 2000). My argument for including the trait in study of the Greenville site arose from its inconstant representation in Northwest Coast skulls (Cybulski 1992:123-124). Some sample data appeared to fit the so-called "thermal aquatic hypothesis," while others didn't, leaving a genetic interpretation plausible by default.

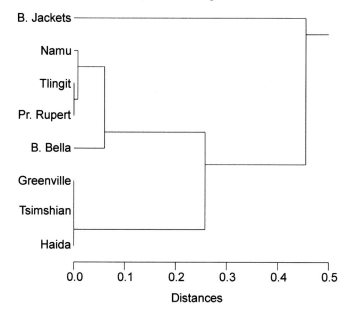

7-Trait Set, Ward Linkage Method

Fig. 7. Diagram of relationships among 8 cranial samples based on cluster analysis of MMD's derived from 7 nonmetric variants used in the 17-trait set but not in the 21-trait set (see Table 2).

It is useful to have a detailed look at the distribution in the current samples, shown in Table 7. The frequency is quite high in Blue Jackets Creek, notably high in the Namu sample, and clearly represented in the Prince Rupert Harbour and Bella Bella crania. Auditory exostosis is non-existent in the Greenville and Tsimshian samples and virtually non-existent in the Haida. The Tlingit data represent an average occurrence based on the other sample data. The actual occurrence in this particular sample of skulls is unknown.

Of interest is that the haves and have-nots tend to cluster accordingly in the 17-trait analyses shown in Fig. 4, especially Fig. 4b, with the exception of Blue Jackets Creek.[6] This may well indicate a functional or behavioral influence in this cluster pattern. When I re-ran the clustering program using only the seven traits *not* included in the 21 trait list, an almost identical three-cluster pattern emerged with the Ward technique, only with less distance within the Namu-Tlingit-Prince Rupert-Bella Bella cluster and somewhat less separation of Blue Jackets Creek (Fig. 7). As well, the same pattern emerged using the average linkage and complete linkage methods.

Table 8. *Penrose distances (MSD) among eight male cranial samples based on 13 measurements[1]*

Sample	Bella Bella	Blue Jackets	Tsimshian	Greenville	Haida	Namu	Prince Rupert	Tlingit
Bella Bella	0	-	-	-	-	-	-	-
Blue Jackets	44.7893	0	-	-	-	-	-	-
Tsimshian	4.5568	41.5382	0	-	-	-	-	-
Greenville	4.5227	31.5660	2.8170	0	-	-	-	-
Haida	6.6613	33.9342	3.4526	4.2720	0	-	-	-
Namu	10.5542	37.4774	6.5758	7.7388	4.4447	0	-	-
Pr. Rupert	10.6431	25.8568	4.2357	3.6760	2.3880	4.2355	0	-
Tlingit	9.7503	33.0760	6.8070	6.4382	2.9529	5.6665	5.3459	0

[1] MSD = mean square distance. The measurements used were cranial length, cranial breadth, bizygomatic diameter, basion-bregma height, basion-nasion length, basion-prosthion length, upper facial height, orbital height, orbital breadth, nasal height, nasal breadth, alveolar length, and alveolar breadth.

There is no attempt here to promote all seven traits as functional through a form of guilt by association. As well, other factors are obviously influencing the uniqueness of Blue Jackets Creek. The overall implication, however, is that the 21-trait list is more reflective of biological influences than the 17-trait list, a situation also seemingly apparent in the assessment of local groups or site samples. The seven traits not shared by the two sets are likely having greater influence in the patterns shown in Fig. 4 than those shared. Given this perspective, it may be that the Prince Rupert sites clustered in the 17-trait analysis of Figure 2 not so much because they were genetically close but because they also were functionally or behaviorally similar.

---

[6] The Haida may be considered a have-not sample. The single occurrence is suspect and possibly anomalous since auditory exostosis is usually expressed bilaterally. It is more likely to be expressed unilaterally if bilateral occurrences also are present in a sample. Interestingly, if the thermal aquatic hypothesis is accepted for Table 7, one would have to conclude that the Blue Jackets Creek, Namu, Prince Rupert Harbour, and Bella Bella populations favoured diving for the exploitation of marine resources while the Haida, Tsimshian, and Greenville populations did not.

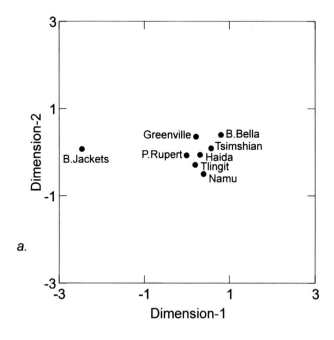

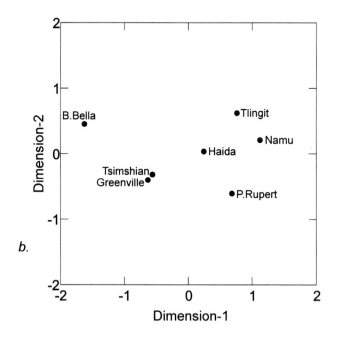

Fig. 8. Multidimensional scaling of Penrose distances (MSD) for male series based on 13 cranial measurements: (a) scales 8 samples; (b) scales 7 samples, eliminating Blue Jackets Creek. Scaling method uses Young loss function.

CRANIOMETRIC ASSESSMENT

The results of the analysis based on male cranial measurements are shown in Table 8 and in Figure 8. The refinement apparent in the analysis based on nonmetric variants is not duplicated in the assessment based on measurements. It may be because, technically, only part of the data is being tested here, given the restrictions derived from sex differences in measurements. It may also be because of the dominant uniqueness of Blue Jackets Creek, leaving little separation among the other samples. When the outlier is removed, the only apparently clear result is that multidimensional scaling reveals a notably close association between Greenville and Tsimshian, duplicating that particular finding in the 21-trait nonmetric variant cluster analyses.

SUMMARY AND CONCLUSIONS

Three sets of cranial morphological data have been used in this paper to assess distance relationships among four ancient and four recent northern Northwest Coast population samples. Two data sets were composed of variably different subsets of nonmetric (present or absent) variants used to calculate mean measures of divergence, while the third was formed of cranial measurements used to produce mean square distances. In combination with the data reduction techniques of cluster analysis and multidimensional scaling, it appears that one of the nonmetric data sets, made up of 21 variants, provides more relevant information about genetic relationships among the samples than the other, made up of 17 variants. One piece of potential evidence is that the 21-trait subset logically promotes closer associations than the 17-trait subset among local group or site samples within two cranial series which could be tested, Haida and Prince Rupert Harbour. Opposing the acceptance of the 17-trait set is the inclusion of a variant with an apparent behavioral or mechanical component whose pattern of frequency distribution among the eight series mimics the pattern of MMD relationships shown by the 17-trait set.[7]

Virtually all of the data point to Blue Jackets Creek as an outlier, or a sample quite distantly removed from the other groups. The 21-trait subset of nonmetric variants also promotes a notably close association among Prince Rupert Harbour,

---

[7] It is unlikely that each of the 21 variants is equally genetically relevant, just as it is unlikely that each of the seven variants in the 17-trait set are equivalently functional. There are other factors in both cases that likely have bearing on the relationships shown and it is the big picture that is important rather than variable details which might be explained ad infinitum.

Greenville, and Tsimshian, and a separate, notably looser association among Haida, Tlingit, and Namu. The latter association tends to come apart when the outlier is removed from the equation, while the former association is maintained. The position of Bella Bella is ambiguous under these circumstances. In terms of distance based on cranial measurements a very close association is shown between Tsimshian and Greenville.

Several questions were put forth at the beginning of this treatise on the presumptive biological relationships of northern Northwest Coast populations. Perhaps, the simplest one to answer involves Blue Jackets Creek. The cranial sample from this 4000-year-old archaeological site on the Queen Charlotte Islands maintains a uniqueness and separation from other north coast samples as first put forth in study of the Greenville site (Cybulski 1992). Possibly the most significant finding here involves the clear separation between Blue Jackets Creek and recent (historic) Haida, confirming previous suspicion based on the investigation of individual morphological characteristics (Murray 1981).

One might be quick to conclude that Blue Jackets Creek is not ancestral to the historic Haida and that, logically, the Haida cannot trace their archipelago roots back 4000 years. Sample size and sampling, however, are clearly at issue. For the 4000-year component, we are dealing with 17 skulls at best, from a single archaeological site. We have no idea how representative the Blue Jackets Creek cranial sample is of the general islands population of that time. As explained for the recent Gust Island rock shelter skeletal sample, Blue Jackets Creek may represent a lineage burial whose biological profile was different from that of the general population. The only way this can be tested, however, is to excavate and study contemporaneous human burials from other sites and other locations on Haida Gwaii. It is also necessary to investigate temporally intermediate burial sites and skeletal samples to demonstrate ancestral connections or the lack of them with the historic period.

In terms of a possible North Coast co-tradition concept of cultural development, there does not appear to be a close biological association of the Haida, Tlingit, and Tsimshian in this study. Nor can any ancestral connections be identified through, say, Prince Rupert Harbour and Blue Jackets Creek. An association of sorts has been identified between historic Haida and Tlingit but it is loose and ephemeral depending on how the data are investigated. Ancestral connections between Haida and Tlingit have commonly been assumed by students of human biology on the basis of presumed shared linguistic origins (i.e., the Na-Dene phylum or family). The jury of linguists is still out on this presumption and the associative biological data in the current arena of mitochondrial DNA variation are suspect (see footnote 4). While other investigators of skeletal morphology have shown "Na-Dene" associations in much larger contexts than presented here, finer inspection suggests those associations could also be interpreted as loose.

Only two of the four ancient cranial population samples previously analyzed (Cybulski 1992) maintain their association here, and those are Prince Rupert Harbour and Greenville. In fact, the association appears enhanced by this study and its larger population context. Interestingly, there doesn't appear to be any genetic or biological association with Namu. Namu's closest affiliation is with Haida and Tlingit although like the Haida-Tlingit association, the relationship here is less than secure (Fig. 6).

From the available data, an ancestral-descendant relationship appears to have been demonstrated for the Middle Pacific Prince Rupert Harbour, Late Pacific Greenville, and historic Tsimshian populations. This conclusion is tempered, however, by the small sample size for the Tsimshian. Nine skulls clearly leave something to be desired for the acceptance of data representation, though a possible saving grace is that at least five different Tsimshian localities are included. Notwithstanding, the diminished sample size may also be influencing other Tsimshian relationships reported in this study.

ACKNOWLEDGEMENTS

I am indebted to Dr. Nancy S. Ossenberg, Professor Emeritus, Queen's University, for the loan of her unabridged cranial nonmetric data for the Tlingit series. I thank both Dr. Ossenberg and Dr. J.E. Molto, Lakehead University, for sharing and discussing their ideas on methodology in the application of nonmetric morphological variation to questions of biological affinity in past populations. Stephanie McGill and Janet Young kindly reviewed an earlier draft of the manuscript, and I am grateful for their comments. Much of the original data on which this paper is based was collected through the courtesy of various First Nations groups. I extend my appreciation to the people of Greenville, Metlakatla, Waglisla, and Haida Gwaii.

REFERENCES CITED

Ames, K.M., and H.D.G. Maschner (1999). *Peoples of the Northwest Coast; Their Archaeology and Prehistory*. Thames and Hudson, London.

Boas, F. (1916). Tsimshian mythology. In *Thirty-first Annual Report of the Bureau of American Ethnology, 1909-1910*, U.S. Government Printing Office, Washington, pp. 29-1037.

Carlson, R.L. (1979). The early period on the central coast of British Columbia. *Canadian Journal of Archaeology* 3:211-228.

Carlson, R.L. (1996). Early Namu. In *Early Human Occupation in British Columbia*, edited by R.L. Carlson and L.R. Dalla Bona, University of British Columbia Press, Vancouver, pp. 83-102.

Coupland, G. (1989). Evolution of the Lower Skeena Cultural System. In *Circum-Pacific Prehistory Conference Reprint Proceedings*, Seattle, pp. 1-27.

Curtin, A.J. (1984). Human Skeletal Remains from Namu (ElSx 1): A Descriptive Analysis. Master's Thesis, Department of Archaeology, Simon Fraser University, Burnaby.

Cybulski, J.S. (1973). The Gust Island Burial Shelter: Physical Anthropology. In *Archaeological Survey of Canada Mercury Series Paper 9*, Canadian Museum of Civilization, Hull, pp. 60-113.

Cybulski, J.S. (1974). Tooth wear and material culture: precontact patterns in the Tsimshian area, British Columbia. *Syesis* 7:31-35.

Cybulski, J.S. (1975). Skeletal Variability in British Columbia Coastal Populations: A Descriptive and Comparative Assessment of Cranial Morphology. Archaeological Survey of Canada Mercury Series Paper 30. Canadian Museum of Civilization, Hull.

Cybulski, J.S. (1977). Cribra orbitalia, a possible sign of anemia in early historic native populations of the British Columbia coast. *American Journal of Physical Anthropology* 47:31-40.

Cybulski, J.S. (1978). Modified human bones and skulls from Prince Rupert Harbour, British Columbia. *Canadian Journal of Archaeology* 2:15-32.

Cybulski, J.S. (1988). Brachydactyly, a possible inherited anomaly at prehistoric Prince Rupert Harbour. In *American Journal of Physical Anthropology*, vol. 76 pp. 363 376.

Cybulski, J.S. (1990). Human biology. In *Handbook of North American Indians, Vol. 7, Northwest Coast*, edited by W. Suttles, Smithsonian Institution, Washington, pp. 52-59.

Cybulski, J.S. (1991). Observations on Dental Labret Wear at Crescent Beach, Pender Canal, and Other Northwest Coast Prehistoric Sites. Unpublished manuscript (Ms. No. 3409), Information Management Services (Archaeological Records), Canadian Museum of Civilization, Hull.

Cybulski, J.S. (1992). *A Greenville Burial Ground: Human Remains and Mortuary Elements in British Columbia Coast Prehistory*. Archaeological Survey of Canada Mercury Series Paper 146. Canadian Museum of Civilization, Hull.

Cybulski, J.S. (1994). Culture change, demographic history, and health and disease on the Northwest Coast. In *In the Wake of Contact: Biological Responses to Conquest*, edited by C.S. Larsen and G.R. Milner, Wiley-Liss, New York, pp. 75-85.

Cybulski, J.S. (1996a). Context of Human Remains from the Lachane Site, GbTo 33 (Including Evidence for Decapitation). Unpublished manuscript (Ms. 3973), Information Management Services (Archaeological Records), Canadian Museum of Civilization, Hull, Québec.

Cybulski, J.S. (1996b). Archaeological Human Remains and Associated Cultural Materials from Greenville, B.C., October, 1995. Unpublished manuscript (Ms. No. 3947), Information Management Services (Archaeological Records), Canadian Museum of Civilization, Hull.

Cybulski, J.S. (1999). Trauma and warfare at Prince Rupert Harbour. *The Midden* 31 (2):5-7.

Finnegan, M.J. (1974). A migration model for Northwest North America. In *International Conference on the Prehistory and Paleoecology of Western North American Arctic and Subarctic*, edited by S. Raymond and P. Schledermann, University of Calgary Archaeological Association, Calgary, pp. 57-73.

Fladmark, K.R. (1986). *British Columbia Prehistory*. Canadian Museum of Civilization, Hull.

Fladmark, K.R., K.M. Ames, and P.D. Sutherland (1990). Prehistory of the northern coast of British Columbia. In *Handbook of North American Indians, Vol. 7, Northwest Coast*, edited by W. Suttles, Smithsonian Institution, Washington, pp. 229-239.

Garfield, V.E. (1939). Tsimshian clan and society. *University of Washington Publications in Anthropology* 7 (3):167-340.

Garfield, V.E., and P.S. Wingert (1951). *The Tsimshian Indians and Their Arts.* 1979 reprint edition. Douglas and McIntyre, Vancouver.

Giles, E., and H.K. Bleibtreu (1961). Cranial evidence in archeological reconstruction: a trial of multivariate techniques for the Southwest. *American Anthropologist* 63:48-61.

Gofton, J.P., J.S. Lawrence, P.H. Bennett, and T.A. Burch (1966). Sacro-iliitis in eight populations. *Annals of the Rheumatic Diseases* 25 (6):528-533.

Greenberg, J.H. (1987). *Language in the Americas.* Stanford University Press, Stanford.

Grüneberg, H. (1963). The Pathology of Development; A Study of Inherited Skeletal Disorders in Animals. John Wiley and Sons, New York.

Hauser, G., and G.F. De Stefano (1989). *Epigenetic Variants of the Human Skull.* E. Schweizerbart'sche Verlagsbuchhandlung (Nägele u. Obermiller), Stuttgart.

Hester, J.J., and S.M. Nelson, eds. (1978). *Studies in Bella Bella Prehistory.* Department of Archaeology Publication 5. Simon Fraser University, Burnaby.

Hrdlicka, A. (1924). Catalogue of human crania in the United States National Museum collections. *Proceedings of the U.S. National Museum* 63 (Article 12): 1-51.

Hrdlicka, A. (1944). Catalog of human crania in the United States National Museum collections: Non-Eskimo people of the Northwest Coast, Alaska, and Siberia. *Proceedings of the U.S. National Museum* 94 (3171):1-xx.

Ishida, H., and Y. Dodo (1993). Nonmetric cranial variation and the populational affinities of the Pacific peoples. *American Journal of Physical Anthropology* 90:49-57.

Katayama, K. (1998). Auditory exostoses among ancient human populations in the Circum-Pacific area: Regional variations in the occurrence and its implications. *Anthropological Science* 106 (4):285-296.

Kaufman, L., and P.J. Rousseeuw (1990). *Finding Groups in Data: An Introduction to Cluster Analysis.* John Wiley & Sons, Inc., New York.

Kennedy, G.E. (1986). The relationship between auditory exostoses and cold water: a latitudinal analysis. *American Journal of Physical Anthropology* 71:401-415.

Konigsberg, L.W., and J.E. Buikstra (1995). Regional approaches to the investigation of past human biocultural structure. In *Regional Approaches to Mortuary Analysis,* edited by L.A. Beck, Plenum Press, New York, pp. 191-219.

Kozintsev, A.G. (1992). Ethnic epigenetics: a new approach. *Homo* 43 (3):213-244.

Laughlin, W.S., and J.B. Jørgensen (1956). Isolate variation in Greenlandic Eskimo crania. *Acta Genetica et Statistica Medica* 6:3-12.

Lorenz, J.G., and D.G. Smith (1996). Distribution of four founding mtDNA haplogroups among Native North Americans. *American Journal of Physical Anthropology* 101:307-323.

MacDonald, G.F. (1969). Preliminary culture sequence from the Coast Tsimshian area, British Columbia. *Northwest Anthropological Research Notes* 3 (2):240-254.

MacDonald, G.F. (1973). Haida Burial Practices: Three Archaeological Examples. In *Archaeological Survey of Canada Mercury Series Paper 9,* Canadian Museum of Civilization, Hull, pp. 1-59.

MacDonald, G.F., and R.I. Inglis (1981). An overview of the North Coast Prehistory Project (1966-1980). *BC Studies* 48:37-63.

Matson, R.G., and G. Coupland (1995). *The Prehistory of the Northwest Coast.* Academic Press, San Diego and London.

Murray, J.S. (1981). Prehistoric skeletons from Blue Jackets Creek (FlUa 4), Queen Charlotte Islands, British Columbia. In *Contributions to Physical Anthropology, 1978-1980,* edited by J.S. Cybulski, Archaeological Survey of Canada Mercury Series Paper 106, Canadian Museum of Civilization, Hull, pp. 127-175.

Ossenberg, N.S. (1994). Origins and affinities of the native peoples of northwestern North America: The evidence of cranial nonmetric traits. In *Method and Theory for Investigating the Peopling of the Americas*, edited by R. Bonnichsen and D.G. Steele, Peopling of the Americas Publications, Center for the Study of the First Americans, Oregon State University, Corvallis, pp. 79-115.

Penrose, L.S. (1954). Distance, size and shape. *Annals of Eugenics* 18:337-343.

Pietrusewsky, M. (1999). A multivariate craniometric study of the inhabitants of the Ryukyu Islands and comparisons with cranial series from Japan, Asia, and the Pacific. *Anthropological Science* 107 (4):255-281.

Prowse, T.L., and N.C. Lovell (1995). Biological continuity between the A- and C-Groups in Lower Nubia: Evidence from cranial non-metric traits. *International Journal of Osteoarchaeology* 5:103-114.

Saunders, S.R. (1989). Nonmetric skeletal variation. In *Reconstruction of Life from the Skeleton*, edited by M.Y. Iscan and K.A.R. Kennedy, Alan R. Liss, Inc., New York, pp. 95-108.

Saunders, S.R., and F. Popovich (1978). A family study of two skeletal variants: Atlas bridging and clinoid bridging. *American Journal of Physical Anthropology* 49:193-204.

Severs, P.D.S. (1974). Archaeological investigations at Blue Jackets Creek, FlUa-4, Queen Charlotte Islands, British Columbia, 1973. *Canadian Archaeological Association Bulletin* 6:165-205.

Shennan, S. (1988). *Quantifying Archaeology*. (Reprinted with minor corrections 1990). Edinburgh University Press; Academic Press, Inc., Edinburgh; San Diego.

Simonsen, B.O. (1973). Archaeological Investigations in the Hecate Strait-Milbanke Sound Area of British Columbia. National Museum of Man, National Museums of Canada, Ottawa.

Simonsen, B.O. (1988). Final Report on Archaeological Salvage Excavations and Construction Monitoring at the Lachane Site (GbTo-33) Prince Rupert, B.C. Unpublished manuscript (Ms. No. 3033), Information Management Services (Archaeological Records), Canadian Museum of Civilization, Hull.

Sjøvold, T. (1977). Non-Metrical Divergence between Skeletal Populations. *Ossa* 4 (Supplement 1):1-133.

Skinner, M.F. (1984). Ancient Native Human Remains Discovered at Masset Trailer Court (Dec. 8, 1983) Masset, Queen Charlotte Islands, B.C. Unpublished manuscript (Permit 1983-46), Resource Information Centre, Heritage Conservation Branch, Government of British Columbia, Victoria.

Szathmary, E.J.E., and N.S. Ossenberg (1978). Are the biological differences between North American Indians and Eskimos truly profound? *Current Anthropology* 19 (4):673-701.

Takane, Y., F.W. Young, and J. de Leeuw (1977). Nonmetric individual differences multidimensional scaling: An alternating least squares method with optimal scaling features. *Psychometrika* 42 (1):7-67.

Thompson, L.C., and M.D. Kinkade (1990). Languages. In *Handbook of North American Indians, Vol. 7, Northwest Coast*, edited by W. Suttles, Smithsonian Institution, Washington, pp. 30-51.

North Coast Prehistory – Reflections From Northwest Coast Wet Site Research

Dale R. Croes

ABSTRACT

By their very nature, Northwest Coast wet (waterlogged) sites offer substantially more material culture information then typical shell-midden sites. Wet sites on the North Coast hold the oldest examples to date of perishable artifacts and provide significant time depth for *in situ* ethnographic cultural continuity. A 6000-year-old basket from Alaska has been shown to be statistically Tlingit in style, while distinctively Tsimshian styles of basketry and cordage have been reported from a ca. 2000 B.P. wet component of the Lachane site, Prince Rupert Harbour. Two major wooden shanked fish hook types common in 3000 to 1000 B.P. wet site levels of the Central Coast, but subsequently unknown there, were also common to the ethnographic North Coast. This suggests North Coast cultural continuity of procurement artifact types and related subsistence practices that were apparently discontinued on the Central Coast.

RÉSUMÉ

Par leur nature, les sites saturés d'eau de la Côte Nord-Ouest offrent substantiellement plus d'information sur la culture matérielle que les amas de coquillages typiques. Les sites saturés d'eau situés dans le nord de la Côte ont livré les échantillons les plus anciens à date d'objets en matière périssable et *in situ*. On a démontré qu'un panier de l'Alaska remontant à 6000 ans était statistiquement de style tlingit, même si les styles de panier et de cordage distinctement tsimhans remontent à environ 2000 A.A. et proviennent des couches saturées d'eau du site Lachance, Prince Rupert Harbour. Deux grandes tiges en bois appartenant à des types de corps d'hameçon communs dans les couches saturées d'eau du centre de la

In *Perspectives on Northern Northwest Coast Prehistory*, edited by Jerome S. Cybulski. Hull: Canadian Museum of Civilization, Archaeological Survey of Canada, Mercury Series Paper 160, pp. 145-171, © 2001.

Côte de 3000 à 1000 A.A. , mais inconnus par la suite, étaient également généralisés en enthnographie dans le nord de la Côte. Ceci suggère une continuité culturelle dans le nord de la Côte eu égard à l'usage de ce type d'objets et aux activités de subsistance qui avaient été abandonnées dans le centre de la Côte.

INTRODUCTION

Waterlogged or wet sites as they are sometimes called have been actively investigated over the past thirty years along the Northwest Coast of North America. Though the most extensively investigated wet sites have been on the Central Coast, initial and recent explorations on the North Coast show many intriguing findings.[1] Also, Central Coast wet site investigations involving prehistoric wood and fiber artifact styles and functions provide interesting comparisons with ethnographic North Coast wood and fiber artifacts (Croes 1997). The North Coast also provides the earliest example of basketry, the approximately 6000 years old Silver Hole Site basket, showing us the first example of textiles from the earliest known archaeological occupation of this region, the North Coast Microblade Tradition.

This study will explore how wet site research throughout the Northwest Coast might reflect cultural evolution trends on the North Coast in terms of understanding the cultural dichotomy between the North and Central Coast and the diffusion of wood and fiber technologies between the two regions. The main areas of consideration that appear to be the most productive in wet site research are: (1) style continuities reflected in basketry and cordage investigations, and (2) the spread of perishable subsistence related artifacts, especially wooden fish hook types. Also, I will explore how this kind of research might be expanded from the North Coast into a broader look at Pacific Rim prehistory trends.

A unique aspect of Northwest Coast wet site research is how it opens the door to a far broader view of the rich material culture of this overall region's past. Across all substantially excavated Northwest Coast wet sites, over 95 percent of the prehistoric material culture recovered is of wood and fiber, with only 5 percent comprising stone, bone, and shell artifacts (Croes 1976a, 1992a, 1992b, 1995, 1997).

---

[1] As used in this paper, the Central Coast includes that segment of the Northwest Coast defined by Matson and Coupland (1995:3) plus the central coast of British Columbia reported by Hobler (1990). The North Coast includes the B.C. mainland north of Douglas Channel, the Queen Charlotte Islands, and southeast Alaska (see Fig. 2).

With at least 95 percent of the material culture preserved in these sites, several new dimensions of Pacific Northwest Coast cultural evolution have been explored. I will summarize the results of this work in reference to North Coast prehistory.

With increasing wet site perishable data, especially with abundant and complex basketry and cordage artifacts, one is able to better explore the longevity and, possibly, origins of distinct cultural ethnicities all along the coast. Additionally, Northwest Coast wet sites produce frequent examples of perishable fishing equipment, allowing us to better examine the evolution of Northwest Coast fishing economies. At this time over 1300 prehistoric wooden shanked fish hooks have been recovered from Central Coast wet sites, representing fishing practices for at least three millennia (Croes 1997). These subsistence related artifacts may be less sensitive for ethnicity studies (in comparison to basketry and cordage), but probably reflect the evolution of broader economic trends along the entire coast.

Terrestrial environments and resources vary considerably throughout the Northwest Coast of North America and the entire Pacific Rim. However, the availability and abundance of general maritime aquatic resources would be, relatively speaking, more consistent throughout the region (Schalk 1981). This pattern adds to the overall likelihood that aquatic procurement artifacts, especially fish hooks, may spread broadly by diffusion throughout the Pacific Rim.

BASKETRY AND CORDAGE STUDIES

A particularly common container characteristic of wet sites along the entire Northwest Coast for at least 6000 years is the presence of baskets (Fig. 1). Often hundreds of examples of basketry and cordage artifacts are found in extensively investigated Northwest Coast wet sites, as well as a few examples of containers made from wood.[2] Of particular note here, the numerous basketry and cordage artifacts, of any Northwest Coast artifact categories (including those of stone, bone, and shell), have proven to be the most stylistically sensitive and complex for comparative studies through time and space along the entire Northwest Coast and in many other parts of the world (Adovasio 1980; Bernick 1988, 1989, 1998; Croes 1977, 1980, 1988, 1989a, 1989b, 1993, 1995, 1997).

---

[2] Good examples of prehistoric wooden containers on the North Coast are the kerfed bentwood box fragments, carved wooden bowls, and trays recovered from the 1600-2500-year-old component at the Lachane site, Prince Rupert Harbour (Inglis 1976:158-185).

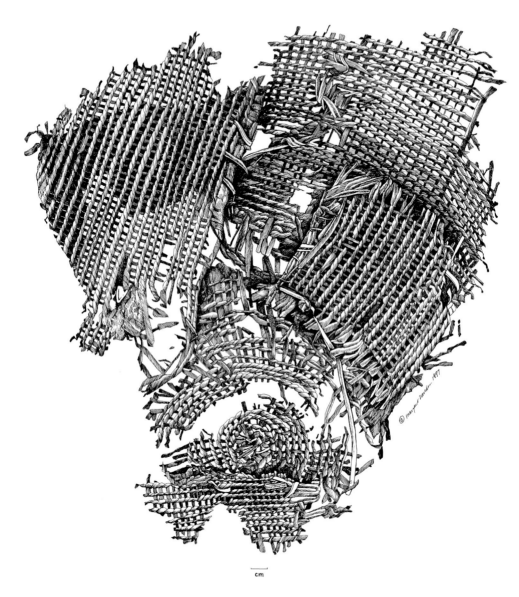

Fig. 1. *North Coast Microblade Tradition basket recovered from the Silver Hole site (49CRG433), Prince of Wales Island, Alaska, and calibrated at 5945 ^{14}C years B.P. (Fifield 1995). This early basket is in the heart of historic Tlingit-Haida territory (illustration by Margaret Davidson).*

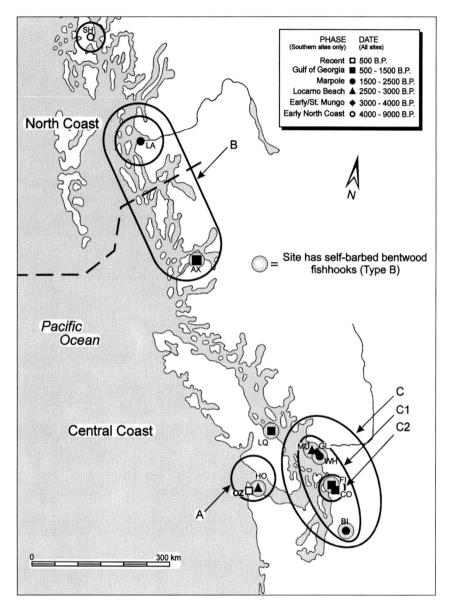

Fig. 2. *Regional continuity of basketry and cordage styles. Also noted are sites with the self-barbed bentwood fish hooks (Type B). Discussed wet sites are abbreviated as follows: SH= Silver Hole, LA= Lachane, AX= Axeti, LQ= Little Qualicum River, MU= Musqueam Northeast, GL= Glenrose Cannery, WH= Water Hazard, FI= Fishtown, CO= Conway, BI= Biederbost, OZ= Ozette Village, HO= Hoko River.*

The frequent basketry (baskets, hats, and mats) and cordage (twisted and braided) artifacts are "additive" in construction, in contrast to lithics, shell and bone, which are "subtractive." A wide array of construction materials, base and body construction techniques, selvages, forms, and attachments are used in combination to form basketry artifact types, providing a particularly complex artifact for comparisons. Cordage artifacts, though less complex, have also been shown to be very complementary to studies of basketry styles (Croes 1980, 1989a, 1993, 1995).

Probably the single most outstanding pattern, derived by comparing basketry artifacts from all presently investigated Northwest Coast wet sites, is their deep-rooted regional style continuity in distinct coastal areas for thousands of years (Fig. 2). This pattern is best demonstrated from wet sites in Central Coast regions, where nine of the ten main village or camp wet sites have been most extensively investigated (Lachane is the main extensively excavated wet site on the North Coast [Fig. 2; Croes 1989b, 1995]).

In this actively studied Central Coast area, regional phases are well defined by the stone, bone, and shell artifacts found in shell midden sites. In surprising contrast to the phases defined by those artifacts on the Central Coast, prehistoric basketry and cordage styles demonstrate distinct sub-regional continuity, crosscutting phases, in at least two areas, the outer coast of Washington (Hoko and Ozette wet sites) and the Gulf of Georgia – Puget Sound region (Musqueam, Water Hazard, Biederbost, Fishtown, and Conway wet sites) (Fig. 3).

It has been proposed that basketry and cordage artifacts appear to be much more sensitive for the identification of ethnicity than procurement related stone, bone, and shell artifacts. The tested 4000 to 4500-year-old wet site of Glenrose Cannery in the Gulf of Georgia region suggests, from a very small sample of basketry, an interesting mix of distinctive regional styles which foreshadow later style divergences on the Central Coast (Eldridge 1991; see also Fig. 3).

On the North Coast, wet sites have been less numerous, no doubt a result of only recent extensive archaeological investigations in this region, but the sensitivity to style continuity studies can be predicted from the Central Coast results. A good hint of the potential in Northwest Coast wet site archaeology to the North was the recent discovery of the oldest wet site basketry from the Silver Hole site, Thorne River Estuary, Prince of Wales Island, Alaska, with a calibrated ^{14}C date of 5945 years B.P. (Fifield 1995; Fig. 1 and 2). This discovery gives a first look at the basketry from the earliest known postglacial colonizing traditions on the North Coast, the North Coast Microblade Tradition (as defined by Matson and Coupland 1995). Previously, archaeologists have seen the well-developed microblade and pebble tool industries dating from at least 9000 to, perhaps, 4500 B.P., but never their basketry industries. Since basketry appears to reflect ethnicity more closely than stone and bone artifacts (Adovasio 1980; Bernick 1988; Croes 1989a), our first look at a North Coast Microblade Tradition basket is intriguing.

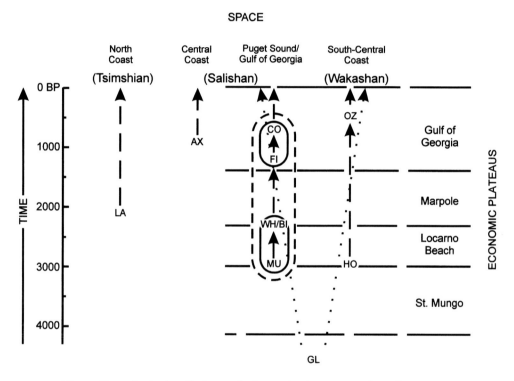

Fig. 3. Hypothetical stylistic or ethnic continuity patterns based on basketry and cordage artifact analyses. For full site names see Figure 2.

Of particular note, the basket in many ways closely resembles the ethnographic Tlingit and Haida basketry of this northern area. In particular, it has most of the distinct Tlingit and Haida ethnographic basketry modes (attributes) as defined by Jones (1976) and Croes (1989b:187; 1997; see below). Therefore, the oldest basket so far found on the Northwest Coast, from the North Coast Microblade Tradition, appears in most characteristics to reflect a continuity of ethnic style in the traditional Tlingit and Haida regions of the Northwest Coast for up to 6000 years and supports other data, suggesting that a proposed dichotomy between the North Coast and Central Coast is deeply rooted (see also Matson and Coupland 1995:65-66; Croes 1999).

Another wet site in the North Coast area traditionally defined by cultural similarities among the Tlingit, Haida, and Tsimshian is a component of Lachane, primarily a shell midden (GbTo-33) in the city limits of Prince Rupert, British Columbia, the heart of historic Tsimshian territory (Inglis 1976). At present, this component represents the most extensively investigated wet site on the North Coast.

Basketry and cordage artifacts, as well as the other organic items preserved in this site, are demonstrably a part of George F. MacDonald's "middle horizon" as preliminarily assigned to the prehistory of Prince Rupert Harbour (MacDonald 1969:250). The artifacts in the waterlogged portion of Lachane were recovered in deposits having ^{14}C calculations ranging from 2500 to 1600 B.P. (Inglis 1976). These preserved perishable artifacts provide entirely new information about the middle horizon time period, and add significantly to our understanding of the prehistory in the North Coast region.

With numerous examples of basketry and cordage artifacts, a detailed analysis of this aspect of the Lachane site was conducted and reported in the *Canadian Journal of Archaeology* (Croes 1989b). Besides comparing the results of these stylistic and functional studies to Central Coast analyses, a comparison was also made between prehistoric and historic basketry of the Lachane area, including Tsimshian, Tlingit and Haida basketry. These comparative data were used to test some aspects of the hypothetical model suggested by George MacDonald (1969:243) for the prehistory of the Coast Tsimshian area. He proposed that proto-Tsimshian were "occupying the lower Skeena . . . for a minimum of 3,000 years. All three horizons of the Prince Rupert middens then represent continuous Tsimshian cultural development." If this cultural continuity model is correct, then the prehistoric Lachane basketry and cordage, from the heart of this Coast Tsimshian area, should show some degree of stylistic and technological continuity with historic Tsimshian basketry and cordage.

In terms of the historic and prehistoric basketry of this area, Tsimshian differs considerably from Tlingit and Haida basketry. This is somewhat surprising since these three groups closely interacted historically and have been interpreted to define a co-tradition (MacDonald 1969:244). Since Tsimshian basketry is distinct from that of the other two groups (which were very similar to each other), basketry may be an important prehistoric cultural marker. If prehistoric Lachane basketry is very similar to historic Tsimshian basketry, this may indicate an in situ techno-cultural continuity. Therefore, technological similarities between Lachane, Tsimshian, and Tlingit-Haida basketry, as well as the Silver Hole site basket in the heart of Tlingit-Haida territory, may be considered here. For this particular study, I regard historic Tlingit and Haida basketry essentially equivalent since major differences, except for decoration techniques (cf. Jones 1976), are not evident.

For these comparisons, all available Tsimshian baskets from the Canadian Museum of Civilization (n=42) and an equivalent sample of Tlingit-Haida baskets (n=55) from the Thomas Burke Museum, University of Washington, and the Anthropology Museum, Washington State University, were carefully analyzed according to the same attributes and basket classification framework used in analyzing the Lachane prehistoric baskets (Croes 1989b).

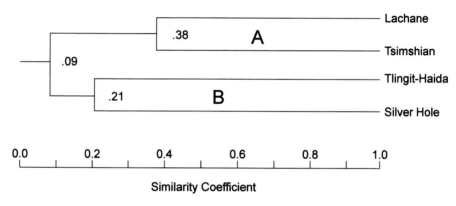

Fig. 4. Dendrogram representing an average linkage cluster analysis of Lachane, historic Tsimshian, historic Tlingit-Haida, and Silver Hole site basketry modes on a matrix of Jaccard's coefficients. Degrees of similarity: 0= complete similarity to 1= no similarity. (Number of basketry examples and basketry attributes (modes) compared from each collection: Lachane 27 basketry examples/12 modes; historic Tsimshian: 42/17; historic Tlingit-Haida 55/12; Silver Hole: 1/5 (see Croes 1989b for complete analysis.).

Additionally, the prehistoric basket recovered from the Silver Hole site in Tlingit-Haida territory (49CRG433) can now be compared according to the same attributes (modes).

Comparison of most basketry characteristics demonstrated a close correlation between prehistoric Lachane and historic Tsimshian basketry, and both were shown to be dissimilar to historic Tlingit-Haida basketry (Croes 1989b). The latter are surprisingly similar to the approximately 6000-year-old Prince of Wales Island Silver Hole site basket. To further summarize and verify these statements, the combination of all basketry modes from these collections was tested in an average linkage cluster analysis on a matrix of Jaccard's coefficients (including the attributes of the Silver Hole site basket, recognizing this is a sample of one basket). This test considers the presence or absence of each basketry mode from the collections and creates a dendrogram indicating the degrees of similarity between the collections. For this test, the following attribute categories or dimensions were used: (1) basketry construction materials, (2) basket base construction techniques, (3) basket body construction techniques, (4) lean of the twining, and (5) basket shape (see Croes 1989b for definitions). Combining these categories yields a total of 31 basketry modes for comparison. Of these, the Lachane collection demonstrated 12 basketry modes, the Tsimshian collection 17, the Tlingit-Haida collection 12, and the Silver Hole site basket five. The resulting dendrogram is shown in Figure 4.

As may be seen, the combined test of basketry modes closely associates the prehistoric Lachane and historic Tsimshian basketry (Fig. 4A). Lachane-Tsimshian basketry is associated with Tlingit-Haida basketry at a very distant coefficient. The Silver Hole site basket links most with the historic Tlingit-Haida (Fig. 4B, even with only one basket example existing). The general pattern emerging from this test and the previous close-proximity tests (with the double-link method; see Croes 1989b) indicates a close technological similarity between the prehistoric and historic basketry from the Tsimshian area, and a distinct difference between both and the "co-tradition" Tlingit-Haida historic and prehistoric basketry. This pattern of basketry mode similarity between Lachane and Tsimshian collections provides a basis for suggesting a Tsimshian techno-cultural continuity model in this Coast Tsimshian regional area for at least 2000 years and, more hypothetically, suggests up to 6000 years of cultural continuity in the Tlingit-Haida region. In the following section, the combination of basketry modes into classes (types) of baskets from these areas will be further examined to determine if basketry classes (or types) from these areas additionally support these conclusions.

Lachane baskets and mats were often recovered in a complete enough condition to reconstruct their original composition. However some were too fragmentary and only certain aspects of their original composition can be hypothetically reconstructed (see Croes 1989b for complete data). The Lachane basket and mat modes, as analyzed above, were synthesized into hypothetical basketry classes, and these basket classes are defined and illustrated in Figure 5. These illustrated reconstructions are based on all the available information. Specifically, the basket and mat classes are defined paradigmatically by the combination of the following basketry features: (1) construction material, (2) shape, (3) base construction, (4) body construction, (5) base reinforcement technique, and (6) miscellaneous (size, selvage, attachments, etc.). This classification combines the major attributes (modes) of Lachane basketry and provides a basis for discussion and comparison of Lachane basketry.

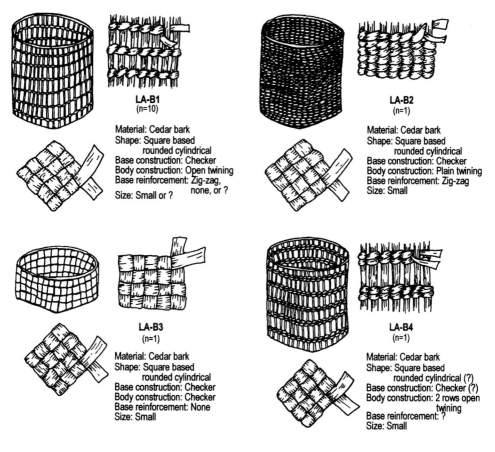

LA-B1
(n=10)

Material: Cedar bark
Shape: Square based
rounded cylindrical
Base construction: Checker
Body construction: Open twining
Base reinforcement: Zig-zag,
Size: Small or ? none, or ?

LA-B2
(n=1)

Material: Cedar bark
Shape: Square based
rounded cylindrical
Base construction: Checker
Body construction: Plain twining
Base reinforcement: Zig-zag
Size: Small

LA-B3
(n=1)

Material: Cedar bark
Shape: Square based
rounded cylindrical
Base construction: Checker
Body construction: Checker
Base reinforcement: None
Size: Small

LA-B4
(n=1)

Material: Cedar bark
Shape: Square based
rounded cylindrical (?)
Base construction: Checker (?)
Body construction: 2 rows open
twining
Base reinforcement: ?
Size: Small

Fig. 5. Lachane basket functional class (type) definitions (from Croes 1989b, illustrations by Kathryn Bernick (Matson and Coupland 1995:232))

These basketry type definitions can be considered technological or stylistic definitions. When the resulting technological types in Figure 5 are examined it appears that the basket classes are quite similar except in one feature, the body weave category. If either this feature is eliminated or one considers all the baskets as composed of plaiting and twining body weave techniques, then a single class of basket is the result, comprised of small, cedar bark, checker plaited base, twined or plaited body, square-based rounded cylindrical baskets (see example, Fig. 6). This would be a "functional" class definition of the common Lachane baskets. Since they are all basically the same kind of basket, they probably, at a general level, functioned in similar ways. Lachane mats were also generally and "functionally" checker plaited, cedar bark mats (Croes 1989b).

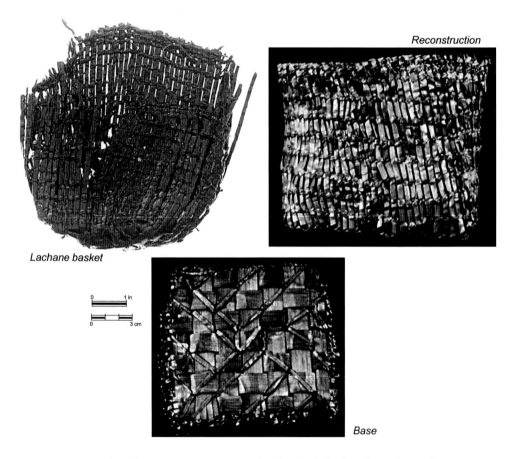

Fig. 6. Examples of a common open twined cedar bark basket from the Lachane site and a reconstruction of this type of basket by the author (both side and base views).

Table 1. *Frequency of basket 'functional' classes recorded from Lachane, Tsimshian and Tlingit/Haida collections*

'Functional' classes	Lachane		Tsimshian		Tlingit-Haida	
Cedar bark, square-based rounded cylindrical, checker plaited base, twined or plaited body weave, basket	16	100%	28	67%	—	—
(Plaited body weave)	(4)	—	(23)	—	—	—
(Twined body weave)	(12)	—	(5)	—	—	—
Other and distinctive Tsimshian basket classes	—	—	14	33%	—	—
Other and distinctive Tlingit-Haida basket classes	—	—	—	—	55	100%
Other and equivalent Tsimshian and Tlingit-Haida basket classes	—	—	—	—	—	—
Total	*16*	*100%*	*42*	*100%*	*55*	*100%*

In comparing Lachane with historic Tsimshian and Tlingit-Haida basket types, the "functional" general classes of basket probably provide the most meaningful units for comparison. These general basket classes to be compared are defined as follows: (1) cedar bark, square-based rounded cylindrical, checker plaited base, twined or plaited body weave, baskets (typical of Lachane baskets), (2) other and distinctive Tsimshian basket classes, (3) other and distinctive Tlingit-Haida historic and prehistoric basket classes (including the Silver Hole site basket: small, spruce root, spiral-base twined, open twined, rounded cylindrical basket), and (4) other and equivalent Tsimshian and Tlingit-Haida basket classes (Table 1). A close-proximity analysis utilizing these general "functional" classes of baskets creates a chain-series that again strongly clusters Lachane-Tsimshian basket classes (Fig. 7A). Tlingit-Haida historic and prehistoric basket classes do not correlate with the others to any degree. The correlation coefficient between Lachane and Tsimshian basket classes is 135, 0 for these two and Tlingit-Haida historic and prehistoric basket classes.[3] If the type (1) definition above is altered to separate classes of (1a) twined or (1b) plaited body weave on Lachane and Tsimshian basket classes, the chain-series is less strongly clustered, but still clusters with a correlation coefficient of 70 (Table 1, Fig. 7B). The fact that there is a strong correlation of similarity of the combination of basketry modes into basket types from both Lachane and

---

[3] In this close-proximity analysis, using a double-link method (after Renfrew and Sterud 1969:265-277) and employing Robinson's (1951) method to construct the correlation matrix, a coefficient of 0 equates to no similarity and 200 equates to complete similarity.

Tsimshian groups is significant. These data certainly suggest strongly some form of techno-cultural continuity in this Coast Tsimshian area that does not correlate to any degree with the historic and single prehistoric Tlingit-Haida basketry from groups adjacent to the area and considered a cultural co-tradition to the Coast Tsimshian groups. Certainly the sample sizes in each case considered here are limited, but the emerging patterns are significant for future testing.

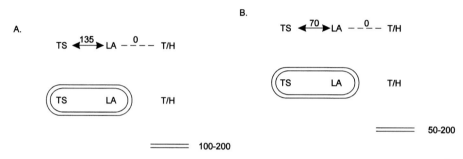

Fig. 7. Close-proximity analysis (double-link method) concerning (A) general basket functional classes, and (B) twined or plaited basket functional classes. Degrees of similarity: 0= no similarity to 200= complete similarity (test following Renfrew and Sterud 1969, Robinson 1951). Legend: TS=Tsimshian basketry; LA=Lachane basketry; T/H=Tlingit-Haida basketry.

Lachane basketry has been analyzed considering several attributes (modes) and these attributes have been synthesized into hypothetical basketry classes (types). This study has been particularly concerned with the comparison of these data to historic Tsimshian and Tlingit-Haida basketry data. Since the Lachane site was in the center of the historic Coast Tsimshian area, any basketry technological similarities or distinctions between Lachane and historic Tsimshian can be considered significant for testing models of cultural continuity in the area. Since Tlingit-Haida groups were adjacent to and considered co-tradition groups with the Coast Tsimshian, the historic and prehistoric basketry technologies from their region were also compared. The comparison of the basketry attributes (modes) are summarized in Table 2.

In each case, Lachane and Tsimshian basketry attributes were strongly correlated, and the Tlingit-Haida basketry attributes were in strong contrast (cf. Fig. 7). Also of interest, the approximately 6000-year-old basket found in the heart of Tlingit-Haida territory demonstrated considerable style continuity with historic Tlingit-Haida baskets in considerable contrast to the Lachane and historic Tsimshian basketry.

Table 2. *Comparison of basketry attributes (modes) common to Lachane-Tsimshian basketry and Tlingit-Haida / Silver Hole basketry*

Basketry characteristic	Lachane-Tsimshian	Tlingit-Haida / Silver Hole (SH)
Basketry construction materials	Mostly cedar bark	Spruce root
Basket base construction techniques	Mostly checker plaiting	Spiral based twining
Basket base outlines	Mostly square	Round
Basket body construction techniques	Plaiting and twining	Mostly twining
Lean of the twining	Up to the right	Up to the left (SH is up to the right)
Gauge of twining	Medium gauge	Fine gauge
Basket shape	Square based rounded cylindrical	Round based cylindrical

In summary, these differences accentuate the strong patterns of correlation and separation considered in both the Central Coast and the North Coast wet sites of Lachane and Silver Hole. These data respectively support and suggest the following hypotheses:

1) The Tsimshian cultural continuity model proposed by MacDonald (1969:243) for the Coast Tsimshian area is well supported by these basketry data for at least the last 2000 years.

2) This form of Lachane/Tsimshian basketry can be considered a technological cultural marker, separating the Tsimshian cultural continuity model from adjacent and co-tradition Tlingit-Haida cultural styles.

3) The first recorded example of prehistoric basketry in Tlingit-Haida territory, the Silver Hole site basket, suggests potentially 6000 years of cultural style continuity in this northern region.[4]

---

[4] Since this discovery, additional basketry has been reported from the heart of Tlingit traditional territory, South Baranof Island, Alaska, dating to approximately 5000 B.P. (Bernick 1999:6-7). From detailed analysis, Bernick concluded that the basketry items (n=11) "are highly sophisticated artistic constructions that are stylistically like 19th century Tlingit manufactures" (ibid. p. 32) and "techno-stylistic characteristics of the Lanaak basketry confirm considerable similarity to Tlingit basketry" (ibid. p. iii-iv). Also, a twined "spruce root" hat found with a partial corpse (Kwaday Dan Sinchi) preserved in a glacier in Tatshenshini-Alsek Wilderness Park, British Columbia, may add to this pattern of continuity (Al Mackie, pers. comm. 1999).

The Lachane basketry artifacts provide a strong and sensitive data base for testing a Tsimshian cultural continuity model. Similar basketry artifacts from other extensively excavated Northwest Coast wet sites also have been very useful in demonstrating cultural continuity patterns for up to 3000 years in distinct regions of the Central Coast (Croes 1977, 1980a, 1988, 1989a, 1995). In terms of the solid patterns emerging with the Lachane and regional Tsimshian materials, the ideal test would be to investigate further and locate other prehistoric wet sites in the Tlingit-Haida cultural area of similar time periods (see footnote 4 above). Much more research can be done concerning Northwest Coast prehistoric and historic basketry, and studies of these artifacts will provide invaluable new information and hypotheses concerning the prehistory of the entire Northwest Coast area and beyond (Bernick 1983, 1988, 1989, 1998; Croes 1989a, 1993, 1995, 1997).

WET SITE PROCUREMENT RELATED ARTIFACTS – WOODEN FISH HOOKS

Fish hooks have not been recorded in North Coast wet sites yet, but with 1300 recorded from Central Coast wet sites, one might certainly expect high frequencies of fish hooks when North Coast wet sites are further explored. In the Central Coast, three main types of fish hooks have been recovered (Fig. 8), two of which are well represented in historic ethnographic collections on the North Coast and, therefore, warrant discussion here:

Type A. Composite three-piece V-shaped hooks (consisting of two wooden shanks and bone barb) of which over 200 have been recovered from the early Hoko River wet site (Hoff 1980; Croes 1995, 1997). The Type A composite fish hook is the common ethnographic halibut hook of the Northern co-tradition Tlingit-Haida-Tsimshian (Stewart 1977, 1987; Croes 1997).

Type B. Self-barbed bentwood fish hooks with a carved knob (tab) end for leader attachment of which over 135 were recovered from the early Hoko River wet site (Croes 1995, 1997), over 90 from the Axeti site (Phil Hobler 1976; pers. comm. 1999), some (one to seven) from Musqueam Northeast, Water Hazard, Biederbost and Little Qualicum River sites (see distribution in Fig. 2). The Type B bentwood fish hook is the common ethnographic cod fishing hook of the northern co-tradition Tlingit-Haida-Tsimshian (Stewart 1977; Croes 1997).

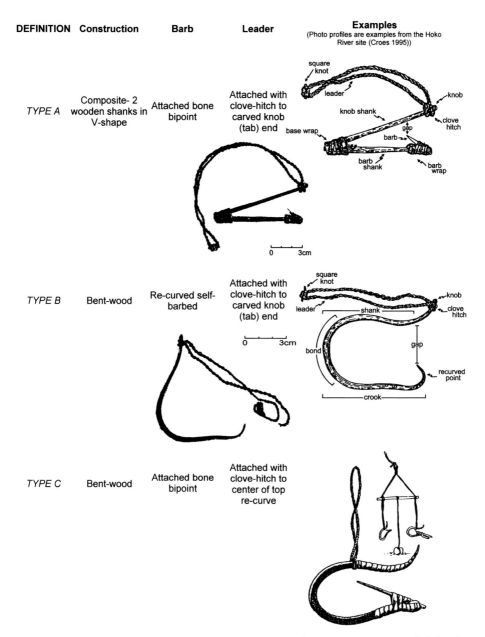

DEFINITION	Construction	Barb	Leader	Examples (Photo profiles are examples from the Hoko River site (Croes 1995))
TYPE A	Composite- 2 wooden shanks in V-shape	Attached bone bipoint	Attached with clove-hitch to carved knob (tab) end	
TYPE B	Bent-wood	Re-curved self-barbed	Attached with clove-hitch to carved knob (tab) end	
TYPE C	Bent-wood	Attached bone bipoint	Attached with clove-hitch to center of top re-curve	

Fig. 8. Definitions and illustrations of three major Northwest Coast wet site fish hook types so far recovered (Type A and B illustrated by Ricky Hoff (1980:160-187) and Type C illustrated by Hilary Stewart (1987:89)).

Type C. Bentwood fish hook with a bone barb bound into a slot at one end and pointing into the inside concave curve, with the leader attached midway into the bend at the other "top" end (Stewart 1977, 1987; Croes 1997). As the most abundant prehistoric hook, over 850 were recovered at the late prehistoric Ozette Village wet site (Draper 1989).

With available data, the common Central Coast wet site Type A and B fish hooks do not seem to continue into the historic ethnographic Central Coast region. However, they are the most common ethnographically recorded fish hook types on the North Coast. The Type C halibut hook appears to replace the early Hoko River Type A halibut hook, though the Type A hook is the common halibut hook into the historic period on the North Coast, often highly decorated with zoomorphic carvings.

If the hypothesis that procurement related artifacts, especially those of stone, bone, and shell which define phases, might be shared between prehistoric ethnic groups with distinct basketry styles is valid (Croes and Hackenberger 1988; Croes 1992b, 1997), the procurement related wooden fish hook types from Hoko River should potentially be found in other early Central Coast wet sites, especially in the Gulf of Georgia – Puget Sound region. In fact the same Type B self-barbed, bentwood fish hook appears to be at the contemporary Locarno Beach site of Musqueam Northeast (two tip fragments were found according to Archer and Bernick 1990:24-25), and exactly the same type was found in the Marpole phase Water Hazard site (n=7 according to Bernick 1989) and Biederbost (n=4; Nordquist 1976:191, 199) site in the Gulf of Georgia - Puget Sound region. To the north, the later site of Little Qualicum River has one example (Bernick 1983) and the Axeti site has over ninety (Philip Hobler 1970, 1976, 1990; pers. comm. 1996) (see Fig. 2 for the distribution of Type B fish hooks).

Thus, this procurement artifact type, the self-barbed bentwood fish hook with a knob leader attachment (Type B), appears to cross-cut basketry style areas as do the stone, bone, and shell artifacts that define phase designations. This hook type does not extend into the historic period on the Central Coast. Of importance here, however, this fish hook type appears on the historic North Coast as the main cod fishing hook (Fig. 8; Stewart 1977:40).

In ethnographic times, cod fishing was emphasized by the northern co-tradition groups of the Tlingit, Haida, and Tsimshian. Numerous examples of bentwood hooks were collected by early explorers and ethnographers and they are essentially the same fish hook type seen from several of the prehistoric Central Coast wet sites from at least 3000 to 1000 years ago (Fig. 8, Stewart 1977:40).[5] However this fish hook style was abandoned in the Central Coast region by the historic period.

Curiously, the West Coast Makah used a new form of bentwood fish hook (Type C, known as Chibood in the Makah language) with a bone barb in a slot at one end and leader attached midway in the bend on the other for the heavily emphasized historic halibut fisheries (Fig. 8). This style of bentwood hook is very abundant at the late prehistoric Ozette Village wet site (131 complete hooks, 607 shanks, and 117 shank blanks according to Draper 1989), but is not seen at earlier Central Coast wet sites.

The most numerous fish hook type found at Hoko River prehistoric site is the three piece, V-shaped composite fish hook (Type A, n=207, 59 percent). Through replication experiments involving actual use of this type of hook for fishing off the Hoko River and in the Seattle Aquarium, we concluded that this Type A hook was the deep sea hook used to capture the most emphasized fisheries at Hoko River, the flatfish and halibut (Croes 1995:99-107; 1997:603-613). The cod in the Seattle Aquarium often struck and broke this type of composite hook (in a manner similar to those found in the prehistoric site [Croes 1997:603-613]) and, therefore, we believe the bentwood (spring-loaded) hooks (Type B) were probably used for the cod fisheries at Hoko River as they continued to be used on the historic ethnographic North Coast (Croes 1995, 1997).

This Hoko River V-shaped, composite shanked fish hook Type A is not recorded in this form in any other Central Coast wet site. The closest analogy, both in hook composition and its use in deep sea fishing for flatfish and halibut, are the three piece, V-shaped composite fish hooks used into the historic period in northern areas, such as among the Tlingit, Haida, and Tsimshian co-tradition groups. Often these historic wooden shanked Type A examples are highly decorated through surface carving and those collected for museums tend to be larger (for a larger size flatfish) (Stewart 1977:52). However some illustrated northern examples are very similar to the 3000-year-old types so common at Hoko River.

---

[5] I recorded 98 ethnographic fish hooks of this type at the Royal British Columbia Museum, Victoria, in 1996.

The evolution of these fish hook procurement artifacts, both the self-barbed and knobbed bentwood Type B and the V-shaped composite shanked hook Type A, appears to be well developed on the prehistoric Central Coast and continued in general style into the historic ethnographic period in the North Coast, while being replaced by different styles in the Central Coast late prehistoric and historic periods.

SUMMARY AND CONCLUSIONS

This brief overview of available data on North and Central Coast wet sites suggests a general set of hypotheses:

1) The style dichotomy represented from the earliest time periods in the North and Central Coasts appear supported, with a North Coastal Microblade Tradition basket dating to about 6000 B.P. associating well with the general Tlingit-Haida styles into the historic period.

2) The northern Lachane basketry reveals a distinct Tsimshian culture marker by 2000 B.P., effectively distinguishing their basketry from other northern co-tradition members, the Tlingit and Haida.

3) A distinct style of self-barbed bentwood fish hooks (Type B) from prehistoric wet sites on the central coast distribute broadly across these regions and through Locarno and Marpole phases to be replaced by a bone barbed bentwood with a leader attached to the top of the bend (Type C) by the historic period. The ethnographic self-barbed bentwood cod fish hooks on the North Coast appear to be analogous to those (Type B) found prehistorically from at least 3000 to 1000 years ago in the Central Coast.

4) The V-shaped composite bone-barbed fish hooks (Type A) so common to the flatfish and halibut fisheries at Hoko River are not seen at contemporary and later wet sites on the Central Coast. The closest analogy in fish hook type and function appears to exist in the historic period in the northern areas, where V-shaped composite bone-barbed fish hooks for deep-sea fishing for halibut is common.

In a general economic evolutionary sequence, some of these fisheries technologies appear to have developed earliest in the Central Coast to be continued as an effective technology into the historic ethnographic period on the North Coast. If the phase sequence on the Central Coast actually represents economic stages or plateaus they passed through regardless of ethnicities, and as solutions to growing population and environmental pressures (Croes and Hackenberger 1988; Croes 1992a, b), then possibly the economies represented by the Central Coast Locarno Beach and Marpole phases are partly represented by the historic northern co-tradition with smaller sized populations, who have not passed through to the later economic stages of "Gulf of Georgia" or "Late" phase as represented on the Central Coast. Note further that the northern co-tradition (MacDonald 1969) is really an economic co-tradition, cross-cutting a very distinct difference in linguistic ethnicity at least between the Tsimshian and Tlingit-Haida (see also Jorgensen 1980).

This hypothesis is not necessarily contrary to the common view of complexity to the north, but implies they, in economic stage, are still in a formative period of Northwest Coast economic development better represented by Locarno Beach and (or) Marpole phases in earlier stages on the Central Coast. The "Gulf of Georgia" or "Late" phase may represent, in economic stage, how these potentially post-formative groups adjusted to support larger populations on the Central Coast. Many scholars have noted the marked emphasis on riverine salmon fishing in the Marpole phase as an emphasis "never seen before or again" (Mitchell 1971:52). Also the complexities in Marpole art, and other cultural patterns, are seen earlier on the Central Coast, to change direction into the historic period (e.g., some of the elaborate styles seen in stone bowl sculptures, which tend to reflect styles seen later in the northern regions).

Other apparent shifts in the Central Coast region through time that do not seem to disappear in the North Coast is the use of labrets as probable status markers, which ended between 500 B.C. and A.D. 1 in the Central Coast (Cybulski 1996). Again the Central Coast groups appear to change directions and supplant the use of labrets with head shaping to mark status.

An additional example would again potentially involve general basketry techniques on the Central Coast. In the early wet sites, a distinct emphasis on finer gauge twining and wrapping techniques is well demonstrated in Locarno Beach and Marpole wet sites to be less emphasized in later Gulf of Georgia wet sites (Croes 1995:111-117; 1997:611-613). On the North Coast, the continued emphasis on finer gauge twining (especially Tlingit-Haida basketry) is well known.

Considering the Central Coast as representing a "post-formative" tradition should not be read as a lessening of cultural complexity, but mainly a shift in new directions for social complexity, religion, art and economy. In fact, the Central Coast groups appear to have moved into an economic stage including an add-on emphasis on sea mammal hunting (as especially developed in the fur seal and whaling traditions on the West Coast) and increased emphasis on trolling in open waters for fresh salmon and herring as reflected by the dramatic increase in bone points in the Gulf of Georgia phase or economic stage (up to 60 percent bone bi-points in sites of this late phase versus 5 percent or less in earlier phases (Mitchell 1971:47; Croes 1992b:358)).

In a broader sense, one might explore how some of these procurement trends may have even diffused throughout the Pacific Rim through the exploration of future Pacific Basin wet sites. As a conduit of economic practices, the coast no doubt provides a relatively easy avenue for maritime subsistence strategies to pass. On the other hand, and probably a more exciting possibility, the basketry and cordage artifacts will undoubtedly be the best means to not only look for continuity of ethnicities in the North and Central Coast dichotomy (Croes 1997), but also between the proposed North Coast Microblade Tradition (considered a slightly later movement of a Pacific Rim culture onto the Northwest Coast) and other Denali Complex or Paleoarctic Traditions (Matson and Coupland 1995: 65-66). As wet sites are located throughout the Pacific Rim, many of the proposed migration routes of earliest people will be much better defined through their basketry and cordage styles. Early wet sites in Japan are beginning to reveal some of the basketry and cordage from early Jomon time periods. If these peoples represent a remnant of an earlier pan Continental Shelf Maritime tradition, then their affiliations may be best tracked through the basketry and cordage artifacts (Croes 1999).

Preliminary results of wet site research on the Northwest Coast indicate a potential for tracing both ethnicity and economic evolution. As more extensive investigations occur on the North Coast, this region may be visualized as the major link in the broader perspective of Circum-Pacific prehistory.

ACKNOWLEDGEMENTS

I thank Jerome Cybulski for inviting my addition to this volume and for his editorial assistance. Research on the Lachane basketry and cordage was supported by the Canadian Museum of Civilization through Dr. George F. MacDonald and the assistance of Richard Inglis, excavator of the site. The analysis of the Thorne River basket from the Silver Hole site was assisted and encouraged by Terry Fifield, Archaeologist, U.S.D.A. Forest Service, Craig, Alaska. The beautiful illustration of the Thorne River basket was done by Margaret Davidson. Much of my basketry, cordage and fish hook research was conducted as an outcome of the Hoko River Project, co-sponsored by the Makah Tribal Nation, and was made possible through support of the M.J. Murdock Charitable Trust, the National Endowment for the Humanities, and Ray and Jean Auel. Numerous project researchers, tribal community members, field personnel, and students contributed to data recovery, analysis and reporting. Though this research owes its existence to these and many previous and current researchers, the summary and conclusions remain the responsibility of the author.

REFERENCES CITED

Adovasio, J.M. (1980). Fremont: An artifactual perspective. In *Fremont Perspectives*, edited by D.B. Madsen, Antiquities Section, Selected Papers, Vol. 7, No. 16, Division of State History, Salt Lake City, pp. 35-40.

Archer, D.J.W., and K. Bernick (1990). Perishable Artifacts from the Musqueam Northeast Site. Unpublished manuscript, Resource Information Centre, Heritage Conservation Branch, Government of British Columbia, Victoria.

Bernick, K. (1983). *A Site Catchment Analysis of the Little Qualicum River Site, DiSc 1: A Wet Site on the East Coast of Vancouver Island, B.C.* Archaeological Survey of Canada Mercury Series Paper 118. Canadian Museum of Civilization, Hull.

Bernick, K. (1988). The potential of basketry for reconstructing cultural diversity on the Northwest Coast. In *Ethnicity and Culture*, edited by R. Auger, M.F. Glass, S. MacEachern, and P. McCartney, The University of Calgary Archaeological Association, Calgary, pp. 251-257.

Bernick, K. (1989). Water Hazard (DgRs30) Artifact Recovery Project Report. Unpublished manuscript (Permit 1988-55), Resource Information Centre, Heritage Conservation Branch, Government of British Columbia, Victoria.

Bernick, K. (1998). Stylistic characteristics of basketry from Coast Salish area wet sites. In *Hidden Dimensions: The Cultural Significance of Wetland Archaeology*, edited by K. Bernick, University of British Columbia Press, Vancouver, pp. 139-156.

Bernick, K. (1999). Lanaak (49XPA78), A Wet Site on Baranof Island, Southeastern Alaska. Report of June 1999 Archaeological Investigations, State of Alaska Field Archaeology Permit 99-10. Alaska Office of History and Archaeology, Division of Parks and Outdoor Recreation, Anchorage.

Croes, D.R., ed. (1976). *The Excavation of Water-Saturated Archaeological Sites (Wet Sites) on the Northwest Coast of North America.* Archaeological Survey of Canada Mercury Series Paper 50. Canadian Museum of Civilization, Hull.

Croes, D.R. (1977). *Basketry from the Ozette Village Archaeological Site: A Technological, Functional and Comparative Study.* Ph.D. Dissertation, Washington State University. University Microfilms 77-25, 762, Ann Arbor.

Croes, D.R. (1980). *Cordage from the Ozette Village Archaeological Site: A Technological, Functional and Comparative Study.* Laboratory of Archaeology and History, Project Report 9. Washington State University, Pullman.

Croes, D.R. (1988). The significance of the 3,000 BP Hoko River waterlogged fishing camp in our overall understanding of southern Northwest Coast cultural evolution. In *Wet Site Archaeology*, edited by B. Purdy, Telford Press, Caldwell, pp. 131-152.

Croes, D.R. (1989a). Prehistoric ethnicity on the Northwest Coast of North America: An evaluation of style in basketry and lithics. In *Research in Anthropological Archaeology*, vol. 8, edited by R. Whallon, Academic Press, New York, pp. 101-130.

Croes, D.R. (1989b). Lachane basketry and cordage: A technological, functional and comparative study. *Canadian Journal of Archaeology* 13:165-205.

Croes, D.R. (1992a). An evolving revolution in wet site research on the Northwest Coast of North America. In *The Wetland Revolution in Prehistory*, edited by B. Coles, Wetlands Archaeological Research Project Occasional Paper 6, University of Exeter Department of History and Archaeology, Exeter, pp. 99-111.

Croes, D.R. (1992b). Exploring prehistoric subsistence change on the Northwest Coast. In *Long-term Subsistence Change in Prehistoric North America*, edited by D.R. Croes, R.A. Hawkins, and B.L. Isaac, Research in Economic Anthropology, Special Supplement 6, JAI Press, Greenwich, pp. 337-366.

Croes, D.R. (1993). Prehistoric Hoko River cordage, a new line on Northwest Coast prehistory. In *A Spirit of Enquiry, Essays for Ted Wright*, edited by J. Coles, V. Fenwick, and G. Hutchinson, Wetlands Archaeology Research Project Occasional Paper 7, University of Exeter Department of History and Archaeology, Exeter, pp. 32-36.

Croes, D.R. (1995). *The Hoko River Archaeological Site Complex, The Wet/Dry Site (45CA213), 3,000-1,700 B.P.* Washington State University Press, Pullman.

Croes, D.R. (1997). The north-central cultural dichotomy on the Northwest Coast of North America: Its evolution as suggested by wet site basketry and wooden fish-hooks. *Antiquity* 71:594-615.

Croes, D.R. (1999). Waterlogged Site Research on the Northwest Coast of North America, Hoko River: A Circum-Pacific Comparative Case Study. Paper read at Conference on Bones and Woods as Human Resource, Revealed by Archaeological Scientific Analysis, Center of Excellence (COE) Project, Nara National Cultural Properties Research Institute, Nara, Japan.

Croes, D.R., and S. Hackenberger (1988). Hoko River archaeological complex: Modeling prehistoric Northwest Coast economic evolution. In *Prehistoric Economies of the Pacific Northwest Coast*, edited by B.L. Isaac, Research in Economic Anthropology, Special Supplement 3, JAI Press, Inc., Greenwich, pp. 19-85.

Cybulski, J.S. (1996). Conflict and Complexity on the Northwest Coast: Skeletal and Mortuary Evidence. Paper Read at the 61st Annual Meeting of the Society for American Archaeology, New Orleans.

Draper, J.A. (1989). Ozette Lithic Analysis (with an introduction by R.D. Daugherty and contributions by A.L. Stanfill). Unpublished contract report, Department of Anthropology, Washington State University, Pullman.

Eldridge, M. (1991). The Glenrose Cannery Wet Component: A Significance Assessment. Unpublished manuscript (Permit 1990-24), Resource Information Centre, Heritage Conservation Branch, Government of British Columbia, Victoria.

Fifield, T. (1995). Thorne River Basket: Benefits through Cooperation. Paper read at Conference on Hidden Dimensions, The Cultural Significance of Wetland Archaeology, University of British Columbia, Vancouver.

Hobler, P.M. (1970). Survey and excavation in the vicinity of Bella Coola. *B.C. Studies* 6-7:77-94.

Hobler, P.M. (1976). Wet site archaeology at Kwatna. In *The Excavation of Water-Saturated Archaeological Sites (Wet Sites) on the Northwest Coast of North America*, edited by D.R. Croes, Archaeological Survey of Canada Mercury Series Paper 50, Canadian Museum of Civilization, Hull, pp. 146-157.

Hobler, P.M. (1990). Prehistory of the central coast of British Columbia. In *Handbook of North American Indians, Vol. 7, Northwest Coast*, edited by W. Suttles, Smithsonian Institution, Washington, pp. 30-51.

Hoff, R. (1980). Fishhooks. In *Hoko River: A 2,500 Year Old Fishing Camp on the Northwest Coast of North America*, edited by D.R. Croes and E. Blinman, Laboratory of Anthropology Reports of Investigations 58, Washington State University, Pullman, pp. 160-188.

Inglis, R.I. (1976). 'Wet' site distribution – the northern case, GbTo-33 – the Lachane site. In *The Excavation of Water-Saturated Archaeological Sites (Wet Sites) on the Northwest Coast of North America*, edited by D.R. Croes, Archaeological Survey of Canada Mercury Series Paper 50, Canadian Museum of Civilization, Hull, pp. 158-185.

Jones, J.M. (1976). Northwest Coast Indian Basketry: A Stylistic Analysis. Ph.D. Dissertation, Department of Anthropology, University of Washington, Seattle.

Jorgensen, J. (1980). *Western Indians*. W.H. Freeman and Co., San Francisco.

MacDonald, G.F. (1969). Preliminary culture sequence from the Coast Tsimshian area, British Columbia. *Northwest Anthropological Research Notes* 3 (2):240-254.

Matson, R.G., and G. Coupland (1995). *The Prehistory of the Northwest Coast*. Academic Press, San Diego and London.

Mitchell, D.H. (1971). Archaeology of the Gulf of Georgia Area, a Natural Region and Its Culture Types. *Syesis* 4 (Supplement 1):1-228.

Nordquist, D. (1976). 45SN100 – The Biederbost site, Kidd's Duvall site. In *The Excavation of Water-Saturated Archaeological Sites (Wet Sites) on the Northwest Coast of North America*, edited by D.R. Croes, Archaeological Survey of Canada Mercury Series Paper 50, Canadian Museum of Civilization, Hull, pp. 186-200.

Renfrew, C., and G. Sterud (1969). Close-proximity analysis: A rapid method for the ordering of archaeological materials. *American Antiquity* 34 (3):265-277.

Robinson, W.S. (1951). A method for chronologically ordering archaeological deposits. *American Antiquity* 16 (4):293-301.

Schalk, R. (1981). Land use and organizational complexity among foragers of northwestern North America. In *Affluent Foragers*, edited by S. Koyama and D.H. Thomas, Senri Ethnological Studies 9, National Museum of Ethnology, Osaka, pp. 53-75.

Stewart, H. (1977). *Indian Fishing: Early Methods on the Northwest Coast.* J.J. Douglas, Vancouver.

Stewart, H. (1987). *The Adventures and Suffering of John R. Jewitt, Captive of Maquinna.* Annotated and illustrated edition. Douglas and McIntyre, Vancouver and Toronto.

Prehistoric Subsistence and Seasonality at Prince Rupert Harbour: History and Synthesis of Zooarchaeological Research

Kathlyn M. Stewart & Frances L. Stewart

ABSTRACT

Recent excavations combined with re-analyses of previously excavated material from prehistoric sites in Prince Rupert Harbour provide a detailed picture of diet and subsistence of this area. The data derive from the Boardwalk, Grassy Bay, Dodge Island, Co-op, McNichol Creek and GbTn-19 sites. The span of time in which some or all of these sites were occupied ranges from about 4000 B.P. to about 350 B.P. Variations in the fauna from the sites suggest considerable change in reliance on food resources, and probable change in seasonal population movements during this time. A population increase around 1600-1900 B.P. appears to be the motivating factor in changing the seasonal pattern in the area. Coordination of faunal data from these sites provides a model against which subsistence patterns in other Northwest Coast localities can be examined.

RÉSUMÉ

Des fouilles récentes de concert avec une nouvelle analyse des objets provenant de fouilles préhistoriques antérieures a fourni, à Prince Rupert Harbour, un portrait détaillé du régime alimentaire et des activités de subsistance dans cette région. Les données proviennent des sites Boardwalk, Grassy Bay, Dodge Island, Co-op, McNichol Creek et GbTn-19. La période de temps pendant laquelle quelques-uns ou tous ces sites ont été occupés varie de 4000 A.A. à environ 350 A.A. La variation faunique révélée par ces sites permet de croire à un changement considérable eu égard à la dépendance envers les ressources alimentaires, et

In *Perspectives on Northern Northwest Coast Prehistory*, edited by Jerome S. Cybulski. Hull: Canadian Museum of Civilization, Archaeological Survey of Canada, Mercury Series Paper 160, pp. 173-202, © 2001.

à un changement probable quand aux mouvements saisonniers des populations au cours de cette période. Un accroissement de la population vers 1600-1900 A.A. semble avoir été le facteur qui a provoqué le changement du mode de vie saisonnier dans la région. La coordination des données fauniques provenant de ces sites fournissent un modèle auquel on compare le mode de subsistance des autres régions de la Côte-Ouest.

HISTORY

When Europeans first came to the Northwest coast in the mid-eighteenth century, they encountered groups of indigenous people who had inhabited the area for centuries and who were skilled in trading. From Vitus Bering's 1741 trip to the Gulf of Alaska, through Russian and Spanish visits, to that of Cook in 1778 on the west coast of Vancouver Island, trading of sea otter pelts was the prime attraction. Cook's publication of his voyages (Cook and King 1784) increased commercial interest in the British Columbia coast and its fur-bearing mammals, an interest which continued beyond the establishment of a Hudson Bay Company post at Fort Simpson on the Nass River in 1831 (Fisher 1996:117-136).

Scientific interest in pre-European culture and subsistence on the Northwest Coast gave rise to archaeological investigations undertaken by members of the Jesup North Pacific Expedition of the American Museum of Natural History, New York (Boas 1898). One member of these expeditions, Harlan I. Smith, described petroglyphs primarily but also mentioned shell midden locations and suggested that midden material is at "the old eulachon fishing ground" on the Nass River (1909:598). In 1915, he made a reconnaissance near the mouth of the Skeena River (Smith 1929:42-43) and thus was the first archaeologist to conduct archaeological research in Prince Rupert Harbour (Fladmark 1975:221-22).

In his initial research, Smith paid little attention to the zooarchaeological remains he must have encountered. Concerning coastal sites, he wrote "palaeontology offers no help. The shells and animal remains found in the heaps all belong to existing species, with no indication that sufficient time has elapsed for noticeable development since they were discarded" (Smith 1929:45). From the middens, he concluded that the same animals were exploited in the same ways over the full span of time represented by the middens.

Between the wars, archaeological work was limited, but in 1943 Philip Drucker published his *Archaeological Survey of the Northern Northwest Coast* based on his 1938 survey of the central and north coasts. It contains a descriptive classification system for artifacts, many of which were made from bones, but little about non-artifactual zooarchaeological remains.

For over 20 years after Drucker's survey, little archaeological research was undertaken in the Prince Rupert Harbour region. In 1954, Charles E. Borden and James Baldwin tested the Co-op site (GbTo-10) and the material they collected, including the zooarchaeological sample, was studied by Gay Frederick (nee Calvert 1968). In 1966, the same year as the Ozette (Daugherty 1973) and Yuquot (Dewhirst 1969) excavations began on the coasts of Washington and Vancouver Island, George F. MacDonald initiated the National Museums of Canada's North Coast Prehistory Project, centred at Prince Rupert Harbour (MacDonald and Inglis 1981). In all three of these projects, local ecological resources and zooarchaeological remains were given prominence in the research objectives, but artifact classifications and cultural chronologies remained the priorities. The ethnohistoric approach to interpreting archaeological materials which began with Smith was also continued.

Based on surveys and excavations from 1966 to 1974 in Prince Rupert Harbour, including those at the large Boardwalk (GbTo-31) and smaller Grassy Bay (GbTn-1) sites, MacDonald established a 5000-year sequence, which he divided into three periods. Period III (3000 B.C. to 1500 B.C.), Period II (1500 B.C. to A.D. 500) and Period I (A.D. 500 to A.D. 1830) were interpreted as parts of a continuous *in situ* development of the historically recorded Tsimshian culture (MacDonald 1969, MacDonald and Inglis 1981). In the earliest horizon, both the artifact and faunal inventories are small. Larger shell middens with larger houses, more burials, more artifacts and many more faunal remains are typical of the middle horizon. By the last horizon the "Northwest Coast pattern is in full stride" (MacDonald and Inglis 1981:52).

Ecological studies were "a prime area of focus" for the North Coast Prehistory Project (MacDonald and Inglis 1981:56). Howard Savage was contracted in 1968 to prepare a comparative zooarchaeological reference collection, to compile a list of the faunal specimens related to west coast archaeology held in Canada and at the Smithsonian Institution in Washington, and to begin analysis of the animal skeletal material collected from the Boardwalk site (GbTo-31) (Savage 1972).

Analysis of the Boardwalk vertebrate material was continued by Frances Stewart from 1973 to 1976 after she had examined small faunal samples from the Co-op site (GbTo-10, now considered to be part of Lachane or GbTo-33 according to MacDonald and Inglis 1981:43) and the Kitandach site (GbTo-34) (Stewart 1972a, b). Her work resulted in preliminary reports on the Boardwalk mammal and bird specimens, on the fish remains (Stewart 1974b, 1975b), and on the artifactual (1973), butchered and burnt remains (1974a). Several of these preliminary studies, copies of which are available at the Canadian Museum of Civilization (Information Management Services, Archaeological Records) were amalgamated in a monograph (F. Stewart 1977) and in conference papers (Stewart 1975a, 1976).

Additional reports with zooarchaeological information for Prince Rupert Harbour exist for the sites of Ridley Island (GbTo-19) (May 1979), McNichol Creek (GcTo-6) (Coupland, Bissel and King 1993), Grassy Bay (GbTn-1) (K. Stewart 1980, with contributions from K. Hull), Co-op (GbTo-10) (Calvert 1968) and Dodge Island (GbTo-18) (Sutherland 1978) (see Fig. 1 for select site locations).

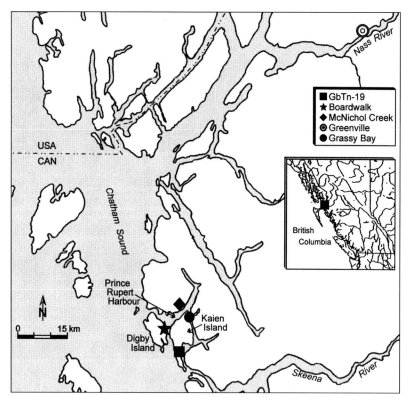

Fig. 1. Locations of archaeologial sites on the North Coast of British Columbia.

Archaeological activities after the National Museum of Canada "megaproject" of the 1960's and 1970's (Coupland 1993:53) were reduced in scale. Gary Coupland (1993) has reviewed archaeological research on the northern coast during the 1980's, while Howard Savage (1973) briefly reviewed coastal faunal changes. Jonathan Driver reviewed zooarchaeological work throughout British Columbia over the past 15 years, but emphasized the southern coast with virtually no mention made of sites in northern B.C., "because very few faunal assemblages have been recovered from that area" (Driver 1995:14). In fact, while considerable fauna had been recovered, the data were primarily contained in unpublished reports as mentioned above.

As Coupland has noted, "termination of the North Coast Prehistory Project . . . left a void which has been filled in the past ten or twelve years by a few 'pure research' projects of more limited scope and by numerous small scale projects of the CRM or salvage variety" (Coupland 1993:53). In the 1980's, Coupland's work on the lower Skeena River at the Paul Mason site (GdTc-16) revealed "the earliest known evidence for a formalized village on the Northwest Coast" (Coupland 1993:56), dating to ca. 3200 B.P. (Coupland 1993:67). Work in the Prince Rupert Harbour area by David Archer (1992) suggested that the region was likely occupied earlier than MacDonald's 5000 B.P. date, with the earliest evidence possibly now underwater. Archer's primary research goal was to study the abandonment of sites in the area, and he did not consider zooarchaeological remains.

In his publication on the Greenville site (GgTj-6) which is located on the lower Nass River, Jerome Cybulski (1992) has given careful consideration to the dating of human remains from the North Coast area, including 120 radiocarbon dates from 11 Prince Rupert Harbour sites. Faunal remains from the Greenville midden burial ground were analyzed in detail by Darlene Balkwill (Balkwill and Cybulski 1992).

Finally, as discussed below, Gary Coupland excavated the McNichol Creek site (GcTo-6), located near the north end of Melville Arm, Prince Rupert Harbour, and analyzed the faunal sample which was mainly comprised of fish (Coupland, Bissel and King 1993). Excavations are continuing at the site (G. Coupland pers. comm. 1996). Thus, although research has continued in the North Coast area, much of the zooarchaeological material available for study has come from the National Museum's megaproject.

The vertebrate faunal remains from two sites, Boardwalk and Grassy Bay, excavated as part of that project, form the basis for this paper. Much of these data also appear in earlier works, particularly in a study previously published by us (Stewart and Stewart 1996). Our purpose here is to discuss our zooarchaeological findings from Boardwalk and Grassy Bay, and then integrate our data into a broader context of subsistence strategies of Prince Rupert Harbour, using data from other reports.

THE BOARDWALK AND GRASSY BAY SITE FAUNAS

As briefly outlined above, northern Northwest coast material culture has been well documented, although only since the mid-1960's have subsistence resources of the North Coast been investigated intensively. Consequently, the subsistence patterns of the Coast Tsimshian for the ethnohistoric period have often been extrapolated backwards for interpretations of prehistoric subsistence. The seasonal cycle typically included people congregating in winter in large villages on the coast while subsisting primarily on shellfish and stored foods, moving to fishing camps on the Nass River for the early spring eulachon (*Thaleichthyes pacificus*) runs, and to the Skeena River fishing camps in summer/fall for the salmon (*Oncorhynchus* spp.) runs (e.g., Mitchell and Donald 1988).

Since exploitation of marine resources underlies most reconstructions of Northwest Coast cultures, it is significant that Prince Rupert Harbour lies between the Skeena and Nass Rivers, both important waterways for the historic Tsimshian as fishing, hunting and trading routes. The two sites emphasized in this paper, Boardwalk and Grassy Bay, are located on Digby and Kaien Islands respectively in Prince Rupert Harbour.

The Boardwalk site is a large shell midden, the excavated portions of which revealed house floor features, over 90 graves and 120 human skeletal individuals (Cybulski 1992; McDonald and Inglis 1981). The total site area was about 180 m by 60 m with deposits reaching a maximum depth of 6.1 m (Fig.2). The excavation units were grouped into six areas, named A to F. There was considerable inter-area diversity and also temporal diversity in terms of faunal representation, presence of human burials, artifact types and numbers, and house forms. Radiocarbon dates indicate aboriginal occupation from about 4000 to 350 years ago (S. Prower and J. Cybulski pers. comm. 1998).

Because of difficult soil conditions, processing of the matrix through quarter inch mesh screen was abandoned. Very small elements were therefore not always collected, probably resulting in under-representation of the smallest taxa, predominantly fish. Nevertheless a complete size range of taxa is present in both the bird and mammal classes, suggesting that no severe biases exist in representation of these classes. However, it should be remembered that it is the macrofaunal sample which is being discussed here.

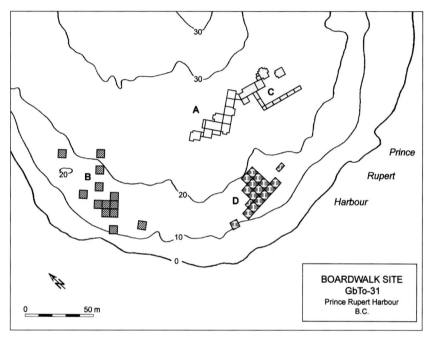

Fig. 2. *Excavation areas A, B, C, and D at the Boardwalk site.*

The Grassy Bay site was much smaller in area than Boardwalk, with only an approximately 24 m by 3 m area being surveyed. The midden deposits were just slightly over 1 m in depth. Radiocarbon dates ranged between 1615 and 620 B.P. (Wilmeth 1978). Collection techniques similar to those used at Boardwalk were utilised at Grassy Bay.

The zooarchaeological samples from each site were analyzed using similar reference collections and the same methodologies. The Boardwalk specimens were collections in Ottawa, the avian reference skeletons in the Department of Ornithology of the Royal Ontario Museum, Toronto, and a few specimens of all classes were further identified with the late Dr. Savage's help in the Howard G. Savage Faunal Archaeo-Osteology Collection in Toronto. Similarly, the Grassy Bay specimens were identified by Kathlyn Stewart and Kim Hull using the Howard G. Savage

Faunal Archaeo-Osteology Collection and rarer specimens were identified by comparison with skeletons in the Royal Ontario Museum collections.

In this chapter we discuss the results of the analyses of these two sites' faunal remains and their implications for prehistoric subsistence in the Prince Rupert Harbour. We believe that any similarities or differences are real considering that similar methods were employed in their retrieval and study.

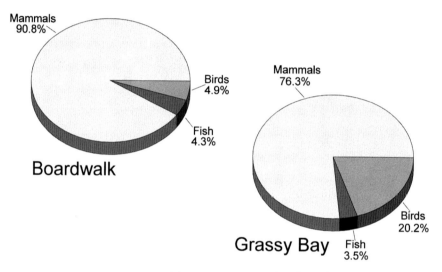

Fig. 3. Represented classes of fauna at the Boardwalk and Grassy Bay sites.

From the Boardwalk site, over 20,000 specimens were identifiable to the level of class (Fig. 3). Mammals were clearly dominant, comprising over 90 percent of the total number of identified specimens. From the Grassy Bay site, approximately 1800 specimens were identifiable to the level of class and, like Boardwalk, mammal remains were dominant, comprising 76 percent of the assemblage. However, bird bones were far better represented at Grassy Bay than at Boardwalk, forming over 20 percent of the Grassy Bay assemblage.

Eight hundred and eighty specimens or 4.3 percent of the total number of vertebrate remains at Boardwalk were fish, although the number may be under-represented due to the collection techniques (Table 1). Perhaps cultural influences also were responsible for the low number. Historically, the Tsimshian discarded most fish skeletons where the fish were caught, not at their main villages (Garfield

1966; Niblack 1870). Flatfish (Pleuronectiformes), salmon (*Oncorhynchus* spp.) and dogfish (*Squalus acanthias*) were the most numerous groups represented zooarchaeologically at Boardwalk (Table 1). While the first two would have been exploited for consumption of their meat, dogfish (*Squalus acanthias*) may have been taken primarily for their liver oil and for their rough skin, which was used like sandpaper, according to ethnographic reports (e.g., Niblack 1890). Of the total specimens collected from Grassy Bay, 3.5 percent were fish and these were not identified beyond class.

Table 1. *Identified fish specimens (NISP) and minimum number of individuals (MNI) by number (n) and percent (%) from the Boardwalk site.*[1]

		Areas A&C				Areas B&D			
		NISP		MNI		NISP		MNI	
Scientific name	Common name	n	%	n	%	n	%	n	%
Chimaeridae:									
Hydrolagus collie	Spotted ratfish	3	5.0	3	12.5	2	6.3	2	7.7
Squalidae:									
Squalus acanthias	Spiny dogfish	—	—	—	—	8	25.0	7	26.8
Salmonidae:									
Onchorhyncus sp.	Salmon sp.	39	65.0	4	16.5	4	12.5	4	15.4
Gadidae:									
Gadus macrocephalus	Pacific cod	3	5.0	2	8.3	1	3.1	1	3.9
Scorpaenidae:									
Sebastes sp.	Rockfish	1	1.7	1	4.2	3	9.4	3	11.5
S. caurinus	Copper rockfish	1	1.7	1	4.2	—	—	—	—
Anoplopomatidae:									
Hexagrammos sp.	Greenling sp.	1	1.7	1	4.2	—	—	—	—
Cottidae:									
Scorpaenichthys marmoratus	Cabezon	1	1.7	1	4.2	—	—	—	—
Pleuronectidae:									
Atheresthes stomias	Arrowtooth flounder	—	—	—	—	1	3.1	1	3.9
Hippoglossus stenolepis	Pacific halibut	1	1.7	1	4.2	6	18.8	2	7.7
Lyopsetta exilis	Slender sole	1	1.7	1	4.2	—	—	—	—
Platichthys stellatus	Starry flounder	1	1.7	1	4.2	—	—	—	—
Pleuronectiformes	Flatfish	8	13.1	8	33.3	7	21.8	6	23.1

[1] Data are from Stewart and Stewart 1996. No fish taxa were represented at Grassy Bay.

The number of identified bird specimens comprised just under five percent of the total Boardwalk faunal assemblage. However, the bird remains were very diverse with over 45 species represented (Fig. 4) (Table 2). The individual species represented most frequently was the bald eagle. In addition to the 54 bones identified as *Haliaeetus leucocephalus*, there were 25 bones identified only as eagle which very probably were from this species. The next most commonly represented birds were various waterfowl, particularly members of the Anatidae family, including the swans (tribe Cygnini), geese (tribe Anserini) and ducks (tribes Anatini, Aythyini, and Mergini), and the loons (Gaviidae). Ethnohistoric accounts of the Tsimshian record a variety of traps and nets for capturing ducks, and by analogy, it can be assumed that some variations of these were likely used by the Boardwalk residents.

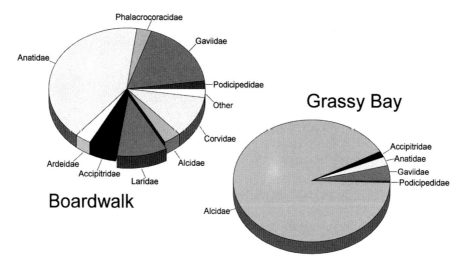

Fig. 4. Represented bird fauna at the Boardwalk and Grassy Bay sites.

Other well-represented birds included the gulls (Laridae), jays and crows (Corvidae), and herons (Ardeidae). While most birds would be captured for food, the feathers and bones of some were likely valued as raw materials for tools and (or) ornaments as well. The zooarchaeological evidence suggests that wings might have been specially selected and/or "curated". Almost 60 percent of the identified bird bones were wing elements, whereas such elements comprise less than 10 percent of the total number of bones in a complete avian skeleton. The long hollow limb bones of birds are excellent preforms for tools such as tubes, whistles, beads or awls. In the historic period, wing bones of the eagle, particularly the radii and ulnae, were used as sucking tubes for the curing of illnesses (Niblack 1890:350).

Table 2. Identified bird specimens (NISP) and minimum number of individuals (MNI) by number (n) and percent (%) from the Boardwalk and Grassy Bay sites

Scientific name	Common name	Areas A&C NISP n	%	MNI n	%	Areas B&D NISP n	%	MNI n	%	Grassy Bay NISP n	%
Gaviidae:											
Gavia stellata	Red-throated loon	4	2.7	2	1.7	5	1.4	4	1.6	—	—
G. arctica	Arctic loon	2	1.3	1	0.9	6	1.6	3	1.2	—	—
G. immer	Common loon	5	3.2	5	4.4	10	2.7	10	4.1	—	—
G. adamsii	Yellow-billed loon	1	0.6	1	0.9	2	0.5	1	0.4	—	—
Gavia sp.	Loon sp.	13	8.3	6	5.2	33	9.0	18	7.3	10	4.0
Podicipedidae:											
Podiceps auritus	Horned grebe	1	0.6	1	0.9	1	0.3	1	0.4	—	—
P. grisegena	Red-necked grebe	1	0.6	1	0.9	3	0.8	3	1.2	1	0.4
Aechmophorus occidentalis	Western grebe	1	0.6	1	0.9	3	0.8	3	1.2	—	—
Podicipedidae	Grebe family	1	0.6	1	0.9	—	—	—	—	—	—
Diomedeidae:											
Diomedia sp.	Albatross	—	—	—	—	2	0.5	2	0.8	—	—
Phalacrocoracidae:											
Phalacrocorax auritus	Double-crested cormorant	1	0.6	1	0.9	6	1.6	6	2.4	—	—
P. sp.	Cormorant sp.	1	0.6	1	0.9	7	1.9	5	2.1	—	—
Phalacrocoracidae	Cormorant family	—	—	—	—	1	0.3	2	0.8	—	—
Ardeidae:											
Ardea herodias	Great blue heron	2	1.3	2	1.7	11	3.0	7	2.9	—	—
Anatidae:											
Olor buccinator	Trumpeter swan	2	1.3	1	0.9	—	—	—	—	—	—
Branta canadensis	Canada goose	16	10.2	11	9.7	23	6.3	20	8.4	3	1.2
Anas carolinensis	Green-winged teal	—	—	—	—	1	0.3	1	0.4	—	—
A. platyrhynchos	Mallard	7	4.5	6	5.2	11	3.0	8	3.3	—	—
A. acuta	Pintail	2	1.3	2	1.7	5	1.4	5	2.1	—	—

(*Table 2. continued*)

	Boardwalk								Grassy Bay	
	Areas A&C				Areas B&D					
	NISP		MNI		NISP		MNI		NISP	
Scientific name	Common name	n	%	n	%	n	%	n	%	n	%
Anatidae (cont'd):											
Anas sp.	Duck sp.	—	—	—	—	1	0.3	1	0.4	—	—
Anas clypeata	Shoveler	1	0.6	1	0.9	1	0.3	1	0.4	—	—
Aythya valisineria	Canvasback	1	0.6	1	0.9	—	—	—	—	—	—
A. marila	Greater scaup	12	7.8	11	9.7	10	2.7	6	2.4	—	—
A. affinis	Lesser scaup	4	2.7	4	3.5	4	1.0	3	1.2	—	—
Aythya sp.	Duck sp.	5	3.2	4	3.5	2	0.5	2	0.8	—	—
Somateria mollissima	Common eider	—	—	—	—	2	0.5	1	0.4	—	—
Clangula hyemalis	Oldsquaw	1	0.6	1	0.9	2	0.5	2	0.8	—	—
Melanitta nigra	Black scoter	2	1.3	2	1.7	9	2.5	6	2.4	—	—
M. perspicillata	Surf scoter	4	2.7	4	3.5	12	3.3	6	2.4	—	—
M. deglandi	White-winged scoter	8	5.1	5	4.4	17	4.6	13	5.3	3	1.2
M. sp.	Scoter sp.	—	—	—	—	4	1.0	2	0.8	—	—
Bucephala clangula	Common goldeneye	4	2.7	4	3.5	2	0.5	2	0.8	—	—
B. islandica	Barrow's goldeneye	1	0.6	1	0.9	—	—	—	—	—	—
Mergus merganser	Common merganser	1	0.1	1	0.9	—	—	—	—	—	—
M. serrator	Red-breasted merganser	—	—	—	—	2	0.5	2	0.8	—	—
Anatidae	Duck family	2	1.3	1	0.9	18	4.9	4	1.6	—	—
Accipitridae:											
Haliaaetus leucocephalus	Bald eagle	5	3.2	4	3.5	54	14.8	31	12.7	3	1.2
Accipiter gentilis	Goshawk	—	—	—	—	—	—	—	—	1	0.4
Buteo jamaicensis	Red-tailed hawk	1	0.6	1	0.9	—	—	—	—	—	—
Accipitridae	Hawks, eagles etc.	3	1.9	—	—	9	2.5	—	—	—	—
Phasianidae:											
Canachites canadensis	Spruce grouse	—	—	—	—	2	0.5	1	0.4	—	—
Lagopus mutus	Rock ptarmigan	2	1.3	2	1.7	—	—	—	—	—	—

(*Table 2. continued*)

Scientific name	Common name	Boardwalk								Grassy Bay	
		Areas A&C				Areas B&D				NISP	
		NISP		MNI		NISP		MNI			
		n	%	n	%	n	%	n	%	n	%
Phasianidae (cont'd):											
Lagopus sp.	Ptarmigan sp.	3	1.9	2	1.7	—	—	—	—	—	—
Bonasa umbellus	Ruffed grouse	—	—	—	—	1	0.3	1	0.4	—	—
Scolopacidae:											
Numenius phaeopus	Whimbrel	1	0.6	1	0.9	—	—	—	—	—	—
Laridae:											
Larus canus	Mew gull	1	0.6	1	0.9	—	—	—	—	—	—
L. argentatus	Herring gull	4	2.7	4	3.5	11	3	7	2.9	—	—
L. glaucescens	Glaucous-winged Gull	2	1.3	2	1.7	9	2.5	6	2.4	—	—
L. hyperboreus	Glaucous gull	4	2.7	1	0.9	1	0.3	1	0.4	—	—
Larus sp.	Gull sp.	2	1.3	—	—	16	4.3	15	6.2	—	—
Alcidae:											
Uria aalge	Common murre	—	—	—	—	6	4.3	5	2.1	—	—
Uria sp.	Murre sp.	—	—	—	—	1	0.3	—	—	—	—
Brachyramphus marmoratus	Marbled murrelet	—	—	—	—	1	0.3	1	0.4	—	—
Cerorhinca monocerata	Rhinoceros auklet	—	—	—	—	6	1.6	3	1.2	229	91.6
Fratercula cirrhata	Tufted puffin	—	—	—	—	3	0.8	2	0.8	—	—
Alcidae	Alcid family	1	0.6	—	—	2	0.5	2	0.8	—	—
Alcedinidae:											
Megaceryle alcyon	Belted kingfisher	—	—	—	—	1	0.3	1	0.4	—	—
Corvidae:											
Cyanocitta stelleri	Stellar's jay	—	—	—	—	1	0.3	1	0.4	—	—
Corvus caurinus	Northwestern crow	2	1.3	1	0.9	—	—	—	—	—	—
C. corax	Common raven	19	12.2	12	10.5	28	7.6	16	6.6	—	—

The use of feathers was common in headdresses in the early historic period and feathers may have been used in featherbeds and pillows (Collison 1981:40-42). The inner body feathers or down were often used as emblems of friendship and peace (Niblack 1890:374).

While the dominance of ducks at a coastal site such as Boardwalk is not surprising, the virtual absence of shorebirds is; only one whimbrel (*Numenius phaeopus*) bone was identified. Similarly, remains of terrestrial birds, such as ruffed grouse (*Bonasa umbellus*) and ptarmigan (*Lagopus* spp.), were extremely infrequent. Based on the avian evidence, it appears that the Boardwalk residents focused their attention on trapping birds while on the water, rather than on land. The Alcidae, including the rhinoceros auklet (*Cerorhinca monocerata*), murres (*Uria aalge* and *Brachyramphus marmoratus*) and puffins (*Fratercula cirrhata*), were relatively common in the later levels of the site, but absent in the earlier levels.

Birds can be excellent seasonal indicators, particularly with the diversity represented at Boardwalk. The most common species represented in the site, including the white-winged scoter (*Melanitta deglandi*), the greater scaup (*Aythya marila*) and the surf scoter (*Melanitta perspicillata*), winter from fall to spring on the coast. In fact, other than year-round residents, winter residents comprised by far the greatest number of species at Boardwalk. However, there were also a small number of spring migrants and summer residents.

A completely different representation of birds occurred at the Grassy Bay site (Table 2; Fig. 4). There, the bird composition was overwhelmingly dominated by auks and puffins (Alcidae). One species in particular, the rhinoceros auklet (*Cerorhinca monocerata*), comprised 91.6 percent of the number of identified bird specimens. Historically, this auklet was important as a food item (Bent 1919:108-109). The habits of the rhinoceros auklet make it easily accessible to hunters, because it nests in colonies in burrows on wooded islands, including those around Prince Rupert Harbour. In addition, some of these colonies were formerly very large, up to 10,000 birds. Bent (1919:108-109) describes group hunting parties raiding these birds' summer breeding grounds.

A very diverse mammalian fauna was recovered at Boardwalk (Fig. 5; Table 3), including 34 species of all size ranges. Most of the represented species are found today on Digby Island or on the adjacent mainland, so were likely easily accessible to the site's inhabitants. Only the moose (*Alces alces*), caribou (*Rangifer tarandus*) and Dall sheep (*Ovis dalli*) are not native to the immediate area. Therefore, these animals, or parts of them, must have been transported or traded to the Boardwalk site. They were rare in the site, however.

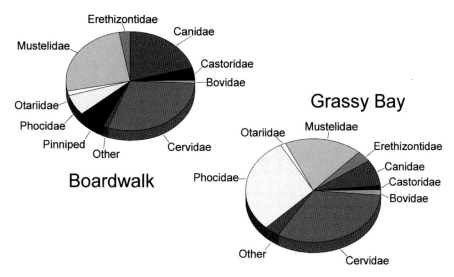

Fig. 5. Represented mammals at the Boardwalk and Grassy Bay sites.

Sea mammals were well represented in the zooarchaeological sample. Sea otters (*Enhydra lutris*), seals (*Phoca* spp.) and less frequently, other pinnipeds comprised 32.7 percent of the total number of identified mammal individuals. Dixon Entrance which is located just north of Prince Rupert Harbour provides a channel to open water, allowing movement of animals between inshore and offshore areas. Thus, Boardwalk villagers would have had access to the animals of both areas.

Sea otter was the most common mammal represented at Boardwalk. Their remains were encountered throughout the site deposits, from the earliest to the most recent levels, contradicting Fladmark's (1975:65) suggestion that they were especially valued after European contact and trading. Their furs were extremely valuable as clothing, and combined with their meat weight value clearly made sea otter a desirable prey. This is evidenced in the butchering marks identified on the bones. Cut marks occurred on limb bones and vertebrae, indicative of sectioning and meat removal, but there were also cuts at the distal ends of lower limb bones, on tarsal bones and on mandibles which suggest skinning (Stewart 1977). Sea otter teeth also appear to have been valued. In Area A of Boardwalk, a total of 209 teeth from at least 26 otters were found associated with a human burial.

Table 3. Identified mammal specimens (NISP) and minimum number of individuals (MNI) by number (n) and percent (%) from the Boardwalk and Grassy Bay sites[1]

Scientific name	Common name	Boardwalk								Grassy Bay	
		Areas A&C				Areas B&D					
		NISP		MNI		NISP		MNI		NISP	
		n	%	n	%	n	%	n	%	n	%
Sciuridae:											
Marmota monax	Woodchuck	3	0.2	2	0.5	6	0.1	4	0.5	—	—
M. caligata	Hoary marmot	1	0.1	1	0.3	1	+	1	0.1	3	0.5
Marmota sp.	Marmot sp.	—	—	—	—	2	+	2	0.2	—	—
Castoridae:											
Castor canadensis	American beaver	76	4.4	37	9.9	228	4.0	83	9.6	8	1.3
Cricetidae:											
Peromyscus sp.	Whitefooted/deer mouse	1	0.1	1	0.3	—	—	—	—	—	—
Clethrionomys gapperi	Boreal redback vole	—	—	—	—	1	+	1	0.1	—	—
Ondatra zibethicus	Muskrat	—	—	—	—	2	+	2	0.2	—	—
Muridae:											
Rattus norvegicus	Norway rat	—	—	—	—	4	+	3	0.3	—	—
Erethizontidae:											
Erethizon dorsatum	Porcupine	36	2.1	22	5.9	159	2.8	59	6.7	22	3.5
Rodentia	Rodents	2	0.1	2	0.5	2	+	2	0.2	—	—
Delphinidae:	Porpoise sp.	—	—	—	—	7	0.1	2	0.2	—	—
Cetacea	Whale	4	0.2	2	0.5	12	0.2	7	0.8	—	—
Canidae:											
Canis lupus	Wolf	1	0.1	1	0.3	—	—	—	—	—	—
C. familiaris	Domestic dog	189	10.8	39	10.4	39	0.7	18	2.1	—	—
Canis sp.	Dog or wolf	685	39.1	75	20.0	618	10.8	80	9.1	51	8.1
Vulpes vulpes	Red fox	—	—	—	—	1	+	1	0.1	—	—
Vulpes sp.	Fox	—	—	—	—	1	+	1	0.1	—	—

(*Table 3. continued*)

Scientific name	Common name	Boardwalk								Grassy Bay	
		Areas A&C				Areas B&D					
		NISP		MNI		NISP		MNI		NISP	
		n	%	n	%	n	%	n	%	n	%
Ursidae:											
Ursus americanus	Black bear	—	—	—	—	21	0.4	8	0.9	18	2.9
U. arctos	Grizzly bear	—	—	—	—	1	+	1	0.1	1	0.2
Ursus sp.	Bear sp.	4	0.2	4	1.0	21	0.4	12	1.4	—	—
Procyonidae:											
Procyon lotor	Raccoon	—	—	—	—	4	+	4	0.5	1	0.2
Mustelidae:											
Martes americana	Marten	9	0.5	3	0.8	20	0.4	8	0.9	—	—
M. pennanti	Fisher	—	—	—	—	1	+	1	0.1	—	—
Mustela vison	Mink	—	—	—	—	11	0.2	8	0.9	1	0.2
Gulo gulo	Wolverine	—	—	—	—	1	+	1	0.1	—	—
Mephitis mephitis	Skunk	1	0.1	1	0.3	2	+	2	0.2	—	—
Lutra canadensis	River otter	11	0.6	4	1.0	29	0.5	14	1.6	3	0.5
Enhydra lutris	Sea otter	257	14.7	53	14.2	1547	27.1	163	18.7	111	17.7
Otariidae:											
Eumetopias jubata	Northern sea lion	7	0.4	5	1.3	49	0.9	26	3.0	3	0.5
Eumetopias/Zalophus	Sea lion sp.	1	0.1	—	—	10	0.2	—	—	—	—
Callorhinus ursinus	Northern fur seal	5	0.3	5	1.3	34	0.6	34	3.9	5	0.8
Odobenidae:											
Odobenus rosmarus	Walrus	—	—	—	—	1	+	1	0.1	—	—
Phocidae:											
Phoca vitulina	Harbour seal	13	0.7	11	2.9	365	6.4	86	9.9	186	29.8
Phoca sp.	Seal sp.	8	0.5	2	0.5	109	1.9	7	0.8	—	—
	Sea mammal sp.	60	3.4	6	1.6	393	6.9	12	1.4	—	—

(*Table 3. continued*)

		Boardwalk								Grassy Bay	
		Areas A&C				Areas B&D					
		NISP		MNI		NISP		MNI		NISP	
Scientific name	Common name	n	%	n	%	n	%	n	%	n	%
Equidae:											
Equus caballus	Domestic horse	—	—	—	—	1	+	1	0.1	—	—
Suidae:											
Sus scrofa	Domestic pig	—	—	—	—	1	+	1	0.1	—	—
Cervidae:											
Rangifer tarandus	Caribou	2	0.1	2	0.5	1	+	1	0.1	—	—
Odocoileus hemionus	Blacktail deer	224	12.7	62	16.6	1368	24.0	144	16.5	—	—
O.h. hemionus	Mule deer	1	0.1	1	0.3	6	0.1	3	0.3	2	0.3
O.h. sitkensis	Sitka deer	3	0.2	1	0.3	136	2.4	26	3.0	198	31.7
Alces alces	Moose	—	—	—	—	1	+	1	0.1	1	0.2
Cervidae	Deer family	131	7.5	27	7.2	340	6.0	14	1.6	—	—
Bovidae:											
Oreamnos americanus	Mountain goat	9	0.5	5	1.3	48	0.8	27	3.1	10	1.6
Ovis dalli	Dall sheep	—	—	—	—	6	0.1	2	0.2	—	—
O. aries	Domestic sheep	—	—	—	—	4	+	2	0.2	—	—
Bos taurus	Domestic cow	1	0.1	1	0.3	—	—	—	—	—	—
Artiodactyla	Cloven-hoofed ungulates	1	0.1	86	1.5	—	—	—	—	—	—

[1] Data are from Stewart and Stewart 1996.

Harbour seal (*Phoca vitulina*) bones were modified in a similar fashion to sea otter bones, suggesting they too were exploited for both their pelts and their food value. Much larger sea mammals, in particular northern fur seals (*Callorhinus ursinus*) and sea lions (*Eumetopias jubata* and, possibly, *Zalophus* sp.), were also reasonably common in the Boardwalk sample. Both represent very large meat sources (male northern sea lions can weigh one ton). Whales (Cetacea) were also represented, but only by very small numbers of specimens. Likely whales were beached or washed up on shore and their bones were scavenged.

Of the land mammals represented, deer (Cervidae) were dominant. Depending on the subspecies, sex and season of exploitation, this animal may have provided considerable nutrition (Speth and Spielman 1983), as well as clothing. In addition, bones and antlers were preferred raw materials for artifacts; of all the animals, deer bones were most utilised for making artifacts. Lower limb bones and antler pieces were the ones most frequently modified by or for use. In the zooarchaeological material, mule deer (*Odocoileus hemionus hemionus*) and sitka deer (*O. h. sitkensis*) limb bones were proportionally more common than trunk elements, suggesting that only the meatiest and most nutritionally valuable sections of the body were transported from the kill sites to the village.

In addition to deer, Canidae (dogs and wolves, but most of the zooarchaeological pieces are presumed to have been from dogs) were also well represented land mammals at Boardwalk. Whether dogs were eaten is unknown, although historic coast Tsimshian reportedly did not eat dog (Drucker 1965). Presumably they had high status, as seven dog skeletons were found buried with humans.

Remains of beaver (*Castor canadensis*) and porcupine (*Erethizon dorsatum*) were also common in the Boardwalk sample. Both were used as meat, and beaver was valued also for its pelt. Incisors of both animals were common artifacts in the assemblage, exhibiting modifications which indicated that they were used as tools. A variety of other mammals were represented in lesser numbers; many were fur-bearers, including bear (*Ursus* sp.), marten (*Martes americana*) and river otter (*Lutra canadensis*). Not unexpectedly, fur-bearers were better represented in the later levels of the site, possibly in response to European contact and the fur trade. Some remains of domestic animals also appeared in the uppermost levels of the site, including cow, horse, sheep and pig, and undoubtedly pertain to a relatively recent occupation of the site. The bones represent only one or two individuals each, and several have saw marks.

The Grassy Bay assemblage also had a very diverse mammalian component (Table 3; Fig. 5). Similar to Boardwalk, deer (Cervidae) and sea otters (*Enhydra lutris*) were dominant, but seals (Phocidae) were proportionally far better represented at Grassy Bay than at Boardwalk. Conversely, canids (likely dogs) were poorly represented at Grassy Bay as compared to Boardwalk, possibly suggesting that Grassy Bay was a seasonal camp, as presumably large numbers of dogs were not taken by boat to seasonal camps.

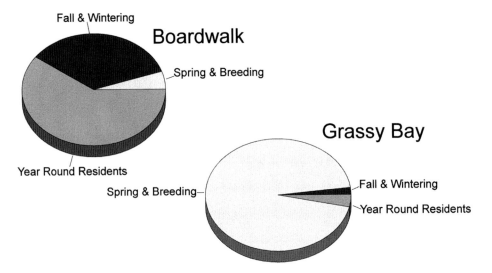

Fig. 6. Seasonality as represented by variant bird species.

There was considerable change in the faunal assemblage through time at Grassy Bay. Both sea mammals and birds are very poorly represented in the lower third of the midden deposits. In the upper two thirds of the site, there is a great increase in the total faunal remains and particularly in the number of sea mammal specimens and bones of the rhinoceros auklet. However, in the two uppermost levels, the quantity of skeletal remains again declines, with virtually only sea mammal remains having been recovered. The great increase in faunal remains in the upper part of the site may reflect a growing human population.

There was considerable difference in seasonality between the Boardwalk and Grassy Bay sites, as inferred from the presence of certain bird species (Fig. 6). While year-round residents can be captured any time, the dominance of fall and wintering species at Boardwalk indicates highest procurement during these seasons. The small number of spring species suggests a lower procurement and smaller population at this time. This interpretation of a predominantly fall and winter occupation at Boardwalk is supported by other evidence. Several deer (*Odocoileus* sp.) frontals with antlers attached were recovered, indicating they were killed during the fall/winter period. Further, terrestrial fur-bearing animals are more valuable in winter, and therefore, usually hunted at that time. Analyses of shellfish remains at Boardwalk also support this interpretation, with heaviest shellfish use occurring during the fall and winter months, especially winter, although there was also evidence for some collection during the spring and summer (Ferguson 1975).

The combined fauna at Boardwalk, therefore, indicates a predominantly fall/winter occupation, with extensions into spring and summer. These data suggest that some people stayed at the Boardwalk village all year, while most moved out in spring to fall, presumably to exploit the eulachon and salmon runs. These seasonal patterns apparently occurred throughout the occupation of the site, since no marked changes were noted in the species representation of the faunal remains within the different levels of the excavation units.

Grassy Bay on the other hand seems to have been occupied during the spring/summer period. As Figure 6 indicates, spring species were overwhelmingly dominant, due mainly to the presence of the rhinocerous auklet. These birds spend their fall and winters offshore (Bent 1919:104), but nest on wooded islands on the coast from April or May to September. Several historic accounts (e.g., Bent 1919: 108-109) tell of hunting parties capturing auklets at night when the females are brooding their eggs, which occurs in June. The young hatch at the end of June or in the first week of July. The only other bird present is the white-winged scoter, which does not support a spring/summer occupation since this scoter is a fall/winter resident on the northern British Columbia coast. However, a total of only three scoter bones was identified. Further support for a spring/summer occupation is found in the large number of harbour seal individuals represented since, historically, these were hunted in spring and summer mainly (e.g., Garfield 1966).

PREHISTORIC SUBSISTENCE AND SEASONALITY AT PRINCE RUPERT HARBOUR

Zooarchaeological data from four sites, in addition to Boardwalk and Grassy Bay, can be used to build a picture of prehistoric subsistence and settlement for Prince Rupert Harbour. These sites are McNichol Creek (GcTo-6), Ridley Island (GhTn-19), Co-op (GbTo-10) and Dodge Island (GbTo-18). The McNichol Creek and Ridley Island sites were excavated by teams led by Gary Coupland (Coupland, Bissel and King 1993) and Joyce May (1979) respectively. These sites were occupied at approximately 1580 and 1990 B.P. respectively. The appearance of these two sites and the Grassy Bay site, as well as increased faunal remains at Boardwalk in the excavation levels attributed to this time period, may suggest a population increase in the Prince Rupert Harbour area. As can be seen in Figure 7, compared with Boardwalk and Grassy Bay, both the McNichol Creek and Ridley Island zooarchaeological samples were almost completely dominated by fish elements (at about 96 percent and 98 percent respectively of the total number of specimens identified at least to family level). Mammals represented only 2.6 percent of this total at McNichol Creek, and less than one percent of the specimens at GbTn-19, while birds represented less than one percent of the totals at both sites. At each, over 90 percent of the fish remains were salmon (*Oncorhynchus* spp.).

Coupland, Bissel and King (1993) have suggested that the salmon bones from McNichol Creek represent stored resources, consumed during the winter at these sites, having been caught and partially processed elsewhere. Coupland's suggestion is largely based on a virtual absence of salmon cranial elements at McNichol Creek. However, fish heads are often removed at the fish catching site, and a lack of skull elements is not in itself evidence of storage. While seasonal indicators are limited at McNichol Creek, shellfish seasonality estimates show by far the greatest exploitation in the early summer, with a lesser peak in spring, and a minor utilization in late summer and fall. Summer occupation is also supported by the most commonly represented bird, the pigeon guillemot (*Cepphus columba*), which could only be taken practically when it comes inland to breed which is in the summer months (Bent 1919: 167, 172). It winters offshore on the ocean. Thus, while McNichol Creek may have been occupied in the winter, there is considerably more evidence for a summer occupation. Because the site is located on a stream, it is possible that the salmon (*Oncorhynchus* spp.) specimens deposited there represent, at least in part, freshly caught fish, taken from the local stream(s) in the summer.

At GbTn-19 on Ridley Island, shellfish seasonality analysis indicates some collection during the winter, but heavy spring collection, and very minor representation during summer and fall (May 1979). The McNichol Creek and GbTn-19 sites therefore had focused subsistence economies, heavily biased towards fishing, with spring and/or summer occupations, and some evidence of winter occupation.

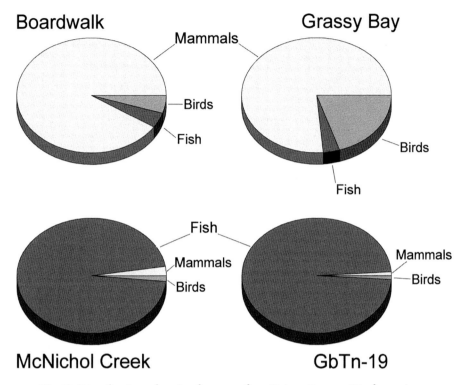

Fig. 7. Distribution of major fauna at four Prince Rupert Harbour sites.

The Co-op/Lachane (GbTo-10) and Dodge Island (GbTo-18) sites, located in Prince Rupert Harbour, were first occupied at about 3000 B.P. and 4800 B.P. respectively, with the most recent dates ranging to around 1000 B.P. for the Co-op site and to around 2000 B.P. for Dodge Island (Wilmeth 1978; Sutherland 1978; J. Cybulski pers. comm. 1998). The Co-op site (GbTo-10) fauna, analyzed by Gay Frederick (nee Calvert 1968), were not quantified, and a lack of good comparative skeletons at the time meant that fish and birds were incompletely identified. Nevertheless, Table 4 indicates that all classes were represented, with considerable diversity among mammals. Frederick stated that deer bones were the most frequently recovered elements, but that sea mammals were also numerous, presenting a pattern similar to the faunal assemblage from Boardwalk. But, unlike Boardwalk, dog remains were infrequent, and fish and bird remains were poorly represented.

The Dodge Island site (GbTo-18) material was studied by Patricia Sutherland (1978). The focus of the study was on artifactual remains. Similar to the Co-op site, there was considerable diversity among mammals (Table 4). Cervid bones were the most common, and sea mammals were well represented. Again due to poor comparative collections, the analysis of bird and fish bones was limited. An increase in fauna is reported for the upper levels of the Dodge Island site (Sutherland 1978:74), which the author suggests may be due to population increase, or change in settlement pattern. This increase presumably dates to about 2000 B.P.; unfortunately, any later evidence from the site would have been destroyed by modern construction activities (J. Cybulski pers. comm. 1998).

Table 4. *Presence (x) or absence (-) of vertebrate fauna at the Co-op and Dodge Island sites[1]*

Vertebrate fauna	Dodge Island	Co-op
Spiny dogfish	x	-
Salmon	x	x
Pacific halibut	-	x
Fish indeterminate	x	x
Bird indeterminate	x	x
American beaver	x	x
Porcupine	x	-
Dog	-	x
Dog or wolf	x	-
Sea otter	x	x
Mustelid indeterminate	-	x
Sea lion	x	x
Harbour seal	x	x
Whale	x	x
Backtail deer	x	x
Mountain goat	x	x

[1] Data are summarized from Calvert (1968) and Sutherland (1978) for each site respectively, and only non-modifed elements are included.

SUMMARY

The varying subsistence and seasonality patterns among the Prince Rupert Harbour sites are both similar and different from the historic coast Tsimshian pattern. The Boardwalk data indicate perennial year-round occupation, suggesting that at least some villages which were occupied throughout the year can be traced back at least to around 5000 B.P., unlike more seasonal occupation in historic times.

The Boardwalk faunal sample was highly diverse and, therefore, non-specialized, with surprising consistency in the overall exploitation patterns over time throughout the site. However some changes in procurement strategy appear from the early to later occupation periods, with ducks, land mammals and non-fur bearing animals being more numerous in later levels. The enormous diversity of birds and mammals, and the abundance of medium to large size mammals throughout the site's deposits suggests that Boardwalk was able to support several families throughout the year, although the greatest population densities likely occurred in the winter months.

The Co-op and Dodge Island sites appear to have subsistence economies similar to that of Boardwalk, although this statement can only be made tentatively due to the lack of quantification of faunal remains from these sites. Certainly, they do not have the apparently focused economies of the McNichol Creek and GbTn-19 sites, given the diversity and abundance of mammal bones at Co-op and Dodge Island, as opposed to the predominance of fish and paucity of mammals at McNichol Creek and GbTn-19.

In contrast to the diversity and abundance of animals represented at Boardwalk is the more focused seasonal subsistence economy at the Grassy Bay encampment. By far the most numerous taxon was the rhinoceros auklet, which must have been exploited by Grassy Bay inhabitants in its breeding grounds between June and September. Other well-represented groups were the sea otter and harbour seal which historically were caught primarily in spring and summer (Garfield 1966).

The patterns at McNichol Creek, Grassy Bay and GbTn19 indicate more seasonal occupations, exploiting specialized resources, such as the rhinoceros auklet at Grassy Bay, and salmon at McNichol and GbTn-19. While the faunal remains suggest that these three later sites were not exclusively seasonal camps, they exhibit a trend towards more seasonal use than does Boardwalk, or probably Dodge Island and Co-op. This trend was apparently intensified into the early historic period.

The appearance between about 1600 and 1900 B.P. of the three sites of McNichol Creek, GbTn-19, and Grassy Bay, combined with possible evidence of an increase of occupation at this time at Boardwalk and Dodge Island, suggests a population increase in the Prince Rupert Harbour area as a whole, and perhaps the beginnings of the establishment of the seasonal exploitation pattern recorded in the historic period.

ACKNOWLEDGEMENTS

The authors would like to thank Patricia Sutherland and Jerome Cybulski for their invitation to participate in the Prince Rupert Harbour session at the Canadian Archaeological Association meetings in Halifax, 1996, and for their invitation to submit a manuscript for this volume. We would also like to thank Dr. George F. MacDonald for giving us the opportunity to study the Boardwalk and Grassy Bay faunal remains. Thanks are due to Dr. Jon Barlow, James Haggarty, Kim Hull, Leslie Moore, Sarah Prower, the late Dr. Stan van Zyll de Jong, and Gordon Watson for their assistance with access to collections and other data needed to put together this paper.

We are grateful for support from the Archaeological Survey of Canada, the Canadian Museum of Nature, the Canadian Museum of Civilization, Social Sciences and Humanities Research Council of Canada (F. Stewart) and the New Brunswick Government Women's Doctoral Fellowship (F. Stewart). Thanks are also due to Dr. Carole Stimmell, editor of the Canadian Journal of Archaeology, for permission to reprint tables.

Both authors would like to express their gratitude to the late Dr. Howard Savage for his support and advice in analysis of these faunas, and many others over the years. We dedicate this paper to his memory.

REFERENCES CITED

Archer, D.J.W. (1992). Results of the Prince Rupert Harbour Radiocarbon Dating Project. Unpublished manuscript, Resource Information Centre, Heritage Conservation Branch, Government of British Columbia, Victoria.

Balkwill, D., and J.S. Cybulski (1992). Faunal Remains. In *A Greenville Burial Ground: Human Remains and Mortuary Elements in British Columbia Coast Prehistory*, by J.S. Cybulski, Archaeological Survey of Canada Mercury Series Paper 146, Canadian Museum of Civilization, Hull, pp. 75-111.

Bent, A.C. (1919). *Life Histories of North American Diving Birds*. Dover Publications Inc., New York.

Boas, F. (1898). The Jesup North Pacific Expedition. *American Museum of Natural History Memoirs* 2 (Publications of the Jesup North Pacific Expedition 1):1-12.

Calvert, S.G. (1968). The Co-Op Site: A Prehistoric Midden Site on the Northern Northwest Coast of British Columbia. Unpublished manuscript (Ms. 175), Information Management Services (Archaeological Records), Canadian Museum of Civilization, Hull.

Cook, J., and J. King (1784). *A Voyage to the Pacific Ocean . . . Performed Under the Direction of Captains Cook, Clarke, and Gore, in His Majesty's Ships the Resolution and Discovery. In the Years 1776, 1777, 1778, 1779 and 1780.* Volume 3, pp. 438-440. G. Nicol and T. Cadell, London.

Coupland, G. (1993). Recent archaeological research on the northern coast. *BC Studies* 99:53-76.

Coupland, G., C. Bissell, and S. King (1993). Prehistoric subsistence and seasonality at Prince Rupert Harbour: Evidence from the McNichol Creek site. *Canadian Journal of Archaeology* 17:59-73.

Cybulski, J.S. (1992). *A Greenville Burial Ground: Human Remains and Mortuary Elements in British Columbia Coast Prehistory.* Archaeological Survey of Canada Mercury Series Paper 146. Canadian Museum of Civilization, Hull.

Daugherty, R.D. (1973). The Ozette Project. Banquet Address, 6th Annual Meeting of the Canadian Archaeological Association, Burnaby.

Dewhirst, J.T. (1969). Yuquot, British Columbia: Prehistory. *Northwest Anthropological Research Notes* 3:232-239.

Driver, J.C. (1995). Zooarchaeology in British Columbia. *Canadian Zooarchaeology* 7:13-22 (Part 1); 8:2-10 (Part 2).

Drucker, P. (1943). Archeological survey on the northern Northwest Coast. *Bureau of American Ethnology Bulletin* 133 (Anthropological Papers No. 20): 1-142.

Drucker, P. (1965). *Cultures of the North Pacific Coast.* Chandler Publishing Company, New York.

Ferguson, R.S.O. (1975). Seasonality of Shellfish Recovered from the Boardwalk Site (GbTo 31), Prince Rupert Harbour, B.C. Unpublished manuscript (Ms. 1117), Information Management Services (Archaeological Records), Canadian Museum of Civilization, Hull.

Fisher, R. (1996). The Northwest from the beginning of the fur trade with Europeans to the 1880s. In *The Cambridge History of The Native Peoples of the Americas. North America, Vol. 1, Part 2*, edited by B.G. Trigger and W.E. Washburn, Cambridge University Press, Cambridge, pp. 117-182.

Fladmark, K.R. (1975). *A Paleoecological Model for Northwest Coast Prehistory*. Archaeological Survey of Canada Mercury Series Paper 43. Canadian Museum of Civilization, Hull.

Garfield, V.E. (1966). The Tsimshian and their neighbors. In *The Tsimshian Indians and Their Arts*, by V.E. Garfield and P.S. Wingert, University of Washington Press, Seattle, pp. 1-55.

MacDonald, G.F. (1969). Preliminary culture sequence from the Coast Tsimshian area, British Columbia. *Northwest Anthropological Research Notes* 3(2):240-254.

MacDonald, G.F., and R.I. Inglis (1981). An overview of the North Coast Prehistory Project (1966-1980). *BC Studies* 48:37-63.

May, J. (1979). Archaeological Investigations at GbTn 19, Ridley Island: A Shell Midden in the Prince Rupert Area, British Columbia. Unpublished manuscript (Ms. No. 1530), Information Management Services (Archaeological Records), Canadian Museum of Civilization, Hull.

Mitchell, D.M., and L. Donald (1988). Archaeology and the study of Northwest Coast economies. In *Prehistoric Economies of the Pacific Northwest Coast*, edited by B.J. Isaac, Research in Economic Anthropology, Supplement 3, JAI Press, Greenwich, pp. 293-251.

Niblack, A.P. (1890). The coast Indians of southern Alaska and northern British Columbia. In *Report of the U.S. National Museum for 1888*, Washington, pp. 225-386.

Savage, H.G. (1972). Faunal Material from the Boardwalk Site (GbTo 31), Prince Rupert, B.C. Unpublished manuscript (Ms. 843), Information Management Services (Archaeological Records), Canadian Museum of Civilization, Hull.

Savage, H.G. (1973). Faunal Changes Through Time in British Columbia Coastal Sites and the Implications Thereof. Paper read at the 6th Annual Meeting of the Canadian Archaeological Association, Burnaby.

Smith, H.I. (1909). Archaeological remains on the coast of northern British Columbia and Alaska. *American Anthropologist, n.s.* 11:595-600.

Smith, H.I. (1929). Kitchen-middens of the Pacific coast of Canada. *National Museum of Canada Bulletin* 56:42-46.

Speth, J.D., and K.A. Spielman (1983). Energy source, protein metabolism and hunter-gatherer subsistence strategies. *Journal of Anthropological Archaeology* 2:1-31.

Stewart, F.L. (1972a). Faunal Analysis of a Sample Collection from the GbTo-33 Site, Prince Rupert Harbour, British Columbia. Unpublished manuscript (Ms. 859), Information Management Services (Archaeological Records), Canadian Museum of Civilization, Hull.

Stewart, F.L. (1972b). Faunal Material Identifications from the British Columbia Site GbTo-34. Unpublished manuscript (Ms. 859), Information Management Services (Archaeological Records), Canadian Museum of Civilization, Hull.

Stewart, F.L. (1973). Faunal artifact identifications: Boardwalk site, GbTo-31, B.C. Unpublished manuscript (Ms. 997), Information Management Services (Archaeological Records), Canadian Museum of Civilization, Hull.

Stewart, F.L. (1974a). Fish Remains from the Boardwalk Site (GbTo-31) of Northern British Columbia. Unpublished manuscript (Ms. 983 verify), Information Management Services (Archaeological Records), Canadian Museum of Civilization, Hull.

Stewart, F.L. (1974b). Faunal Specimens with Butchering Marks and with Evidence of Burning from the Boardwalk Site (GbTo-31). Unpublished manuscript (Ms. 1018), Information Management Services (Archaeological Records), Canadian Museum of Civilization, Hull.

Stewart, F.L. (1975a). The seasonal availability of fish species used by the Coast Tsimshians of northern British Columbia. *Syesis* 8:375-388.

Stewart, F.L. (1975b). Starvation of the West Coast: A Fish Story? Paper read at the 8th Annual Meeting of the Canadian Archaeological Association, Thunder Bay.

Stewart, F.L. (1976). Intra-Site Variability in the Faunal Refuse from the Boardwalk Site (GbTo-31) of Northern British Columbia. Paper read at the 9th Annual Meeting of the Canadian Archaeological Association, Winnipeg.

Stewart, F.L. (1977). Vertebrate Faunal Remains from the Boardwalk Site (GbTo 31) of Northern British Columbia. Unpublished manuscript (Ms. 1263), Information Management Services (Archaeological Records), Canadian Museum of Civilization, Hull.

Stewart, F.L., and K.M. Stewart (1994). Prehistoric Subsistence Patterns in Prince Rupert Harbour, B.C. Paper read at the 27th Annual Meeting of the Canadian Archaeological Association, Edmonton.

Stewart, F.L., and K.M. Stewart (1996). The Boardwalk and Grassy Bay sites: Patterns of seasonality and subsistence on the northern Northwest Coast, B.C. *Canadian Journal of Archaeology* 20:39-60.

Stewart, K.M. (1980). The Grassy Bay Site. Unpublished manuscript, Howard G. Savage Faunal Archaeo-Osteology Collection, Department of Anthropology, University of Toronto, Toronto.

Stewart, K.M., and F.L. Stewart (1996). New Interpretations of Subsistence Patterns in Prince Rupert Harbour, BC. Paper read at the 29th Annual Meeting of the Canadian Archaeological Association, Halifax.

Sutherland, P.D. (1978). Dodge Island: A Prehistoric Coast Tsimshian Settlement Site in Prince Rupert Harbour, British Columbia. Unpublished manuscript (Ms. 1345), Information Management Services (Archaeological Records), Canadian Museum of Civilization, Hull.

Wilmeth, R. (1978). *Canadian Archaeological Radiocarbon Dates (Revised Version)*. Archaeological Survey of Canada Mercury Series Paper 77. Canadian Museum of Civilization, Hull.

Village Patterns and the Emergence of Ranked Society in the Prince Rupert Area

David J.W. Archer

ABSTRACT

An archaeological survey of the Prince Rupert area, conducted between 1982 and 1991, led to the discovery of a number of new, pristine village sites. Analysis of the house depressions at these sites suggests that the idea of inherited rank emerged on the north coast of British Columbia around A.D. 100, which is 600 years later than previous estimates. This paper presents a summary of the new data and examines their implications for the development of cultural complexity on the northern Northwest Coast.

RÉSUMÉ

Une reconnaissance archéologique effectuée dans la région de Prince Rupert, entre 1982 et 1991, a conduit à la découverte de sites de village, nouveaux et à l'état originel. L'analyse des dépressions des maisons dans ces sites permet de croire que l'idée du rang reçu en héritage a émergé dans le nord de la Colombie-Britannique vers 100 ap. J.-C. c'est-à-dire 600 ans plus tard qu'on ne le croyait antérieurement. Cet article présente un résumé des nouvelles données et en dégage les conséquences quant au développement de la complexité culturelle dans le nord de la Côte Ouest.

INTRODUCTION

Over the last twenty years, numerous papers have been written on the origins of social ranking on the Northwest Coast, each drawing attention to a slightly different

In *Perspectives on Northern Northwest Coast Prehistory*, edited by Jerome S. Cybulski. Hull: Canadian Museum of Civilization, Archaeological Survey of Canada, Mercury Series Paper 160, pp. 203-222, © 2001.

set of causal factors. Proposed explanations have included an increase in the abundance and reliability of salmon and other anadromous fish, development of the technology needed to process and preserve the fish, the adoption of a semi-sedentary way of life, population growth and circumscription, the formation of multiple family corporate groups, and the expansion of regional trade and warfare (Ames 1981, 1985; Bishop 1987; Burley 1979, 1980; Cohen 1981; Coupland 1985, 1988a, 1988b; Fladmark 1975; Maschner 1991; Matson 1983, 1985). The differing points of view expressed in those works have generated a vigorous debate on the subject. However, no consensus has yet been reached on the relative importance of the proposed variables.

Attempts to resolve the current impasse have been hindered to some extent by the vagueness of the archaeological record. For the north coast of British Columbia, studies which have focused on the emergence of social ranking have considered three kinds of evidence – artifacts, human burials, and village patterns – none of which has been able to offer a clear indication of when ranked society first appeared in the region. Research conducted in the Prince Rupert area during the 1960's and 1970's suggested that certain important developments were occurring in the period around 500 B.C. (MacDonald 1983:101; MacDonald and Inglis 1981: 45, 52). There was evidence of a growth in regional trade, involving exotic personal ornaments, such as copper bracelets and earrings, and beads of amber, dentalium and jet, items which hinted at wealth and privilege. A degree of status differentiation was also apparent in the human burials from the period. Some graves contained no additions, whereas others included numerous artifacts, both utilitarian and non-utilitarian (Fladmark, Ames, and Sutherland 1990:234).

Warfare also seemed to be on the rise in the period around 500 B.C. Among the new artifact types that appeared at that time were bone and stone clubs, bipointed stone objects and ground slate daggers, all of which have been identified as weapons of war (Fladmark, Ames, and Sutherland 1990:234; MacDonald 1983:101-02). Moreover, the human remains from that era displayed an unusually high rate of trauma to the head, face, forearm and hand, injuries which could well have been caused by interpersonal violence (Cybulski 1990:58). The motivation for the inferred growth in warfare is unknown. However, historically, much of the raiding that occurred among north coast groups was prompted by a desire for wealth and prestige (see also Susan Marsden, this volume). An increase in regional conflict around 500 B.C. would, therefore, be quite consistent with the suggested rise in status differentiation at that time.

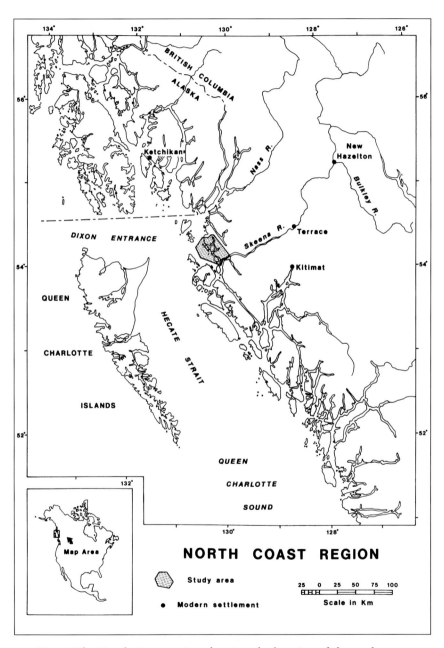

Fig. 1. The North Coast region showing the location of the study area.

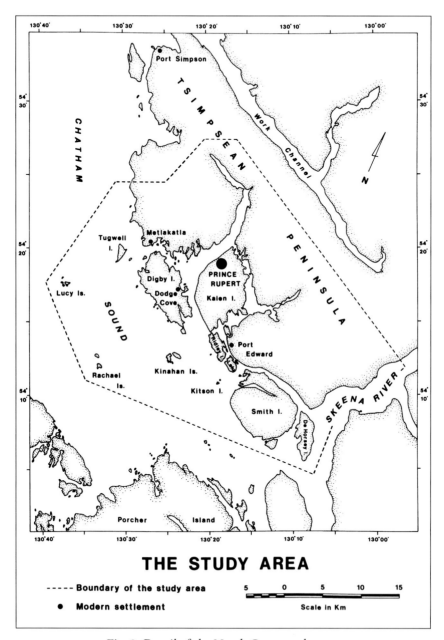

Fig. 2. Detail of the North Coast study area.

The combination of evidence suggested that north coast groups were becoming more affluent in the period around 500 B.C., and that differences in wealth and status were increasing. But were these developments accompanied by a qualitative change in social structure from an egalitarian system to one based on inherited rank? On that issue, the excavated data were largely silent.

In the 1980's, Gary Coupland (1988a) explored an alternative approach to the problem through an analysis of village patterns. The data for his study came from three sites in Kitselas Canyon, about 160 km east of Prince Rupert. Research at the Paul Mason site revealed a small village dating to about 1000 B.C. The house floors at that site were found to be roughly uniform in size, which suggested a society which was egalitarian in structure (Coupland 1988b:233). A very different pattern characterized the nearby sites of Gitsaex and Gitlaxdzawk, both of which dated to the early historic period. There, the houses were of widely varying size, a situation regarded as consistent with a ranked structure (Coupland 1985:48). The contrast between the two patterns was clear. However, no firm conclusions could be drawn due to a lack of comparative data. The excavations conducted in the Prince Rupert area during the 1960's and 1970's produced only scattered, fragmentary evidence on house size and village layout. George MacDonald and Richard Inglis (1981:52) concluded that the first period in the local sequence, which they placed between A.D. 500 and 1830, was characterized by a ranked village structure, similar to that seen at Gitsaex and Gitlaxdzawk, but were unable to provide any specific information as to when the transition had occurred.

In the absence of more definitive data, most researchers have relied on the excavated artifacts and burials from Prince Rupert Harbour to estimate the emergence of ranked society on the north coast. Thus, Kenneth Ames (1981:800-801), Gary Coupland (1988a:115) and George MacDonald (1983:102) have all suggested that the shift from egalitarian to ranked society probably occurred around 500 B.C. One dissenting opinion has recently been expressed by Herbert Maschner (1991:929), who placed the transition 1000 years later, at around A.D. 500. Maschner based his view on the fact that MacDonald and Inglis found no definite signs of a ranked village structure in the Prince Rupert area before A.D. 500.

Some new findings from the Prince Rupert area suggest that both published estimates may be incorrect. The new data consist of village plans from 11 sites, all of which date to the critical period between 500 B.C. and A.D. 500. They suggest that a ranking system appeared quite abruptly around A.D. 100. This paper presents a summary of the new evidence and discusses its implications for further archaeological research in the region.

MATERIALS AND METHODS

DATA COLLECTION

The data reported here were gathered during an intensive shoreline survey of the Prince Rupert area (Figs. 1 and 2). The field work began in 1982-83 as an impact assessment project sponsored by the Canadian Museum of Civilization (Archer 1983, 1984). At that time, the survey was limited to a number of specific localities which were scheduled for development. In 1988, the survey resumed as a research project. The aims were to fill in the gaps left by the earlier survey and to gather more detailed information on local village patterns. Funding for the second project came from the British Columbia Heritage Trust, the British Columbia Ministry of Tourism, Social Services and Housing, the Employment Development Branch of Employment and Immigration Canada, the Metlakatla Indian Band, and the University of Calgary. The field work continued for the next three years and was completed in 1991 (Archer 1989, 1990, 1991).

The methods used on the survey were consistent throughout. Virtually all areas were examined on foot by teams of two to four field workers, walking about 10 m apart. Two sweeps of each area were made, one through the intertidal zone and the other through the forest edge. Each field worker was equipped with an Oakfield soil sampler, used to check for subsurface cultural deposits. In all, 74 new sites were recorded, bringing the total for the study area to 176, including those known prior to 1982 (Table 1).

The present inventory of 60 village sites represents one of the highest concentrations along the entire Northwest Coast. When village sites were recorded, special attention was paid to those with intact house depressions. Two types of house depressions were identified. Plank house depressions with an excavated pit in the centre of the floor were present at a few village sites. However, those sites were all characterized by extensive surface disturbance and were, therefore, excluded from the analysis. The second type was a simple plank house depression. They were shallow and rectangular in outline, with sloping sides and a level floor. In this type of feature, the floor was not deliberately excavated. Instead, the depression resulted from the fact that household refuse accumulated more rapidly outside the house than inside (Fig. 3). House depressions of this type were found at many village sites in the Prince Rupert area, and most were in good condition. As such, they are the features of primary concern here.

Table 1. Inventory of archaeological sites in the study area shown in Figure 2.

Site type	Recorded before 1982	Recorded since 1982	Total
Shell midden:			
Villages	46	14	60
Camps	40	45	85
Isolated find:			
Artifacts	—	6	6
Canoe runs	—	1	1
Rock art:			
Petroglyphs	11	4	15
Pictographs	2	—	2
Petroglyphs & pictographs	1	—	1
Burial:			
Caves	1	—	1
Historic:	1	4	5
Total	*102*	*74*	*176*

The methods used to estimate the length and width of each house floor were based on an inference that the sloping sides of the house depressions resulted from post-occupational slumping of the adjacent midden material (Fig. 3). Hence, the walls of the house would not have stood at the outer edge of the depression but about midway down the slope. Midpoints were, therefore, identified at the four corners of each depression, and the length and width of the house were measured off accordingly. While the figures obtained in this way were only estimates of the original house dimensions, any small errors that may have arisen should have no appreciable impact on the results of the study.

SAMPLING

The choice of sites for detailed analysis was based primarily on their condition. Only those sites believed to be undisturbed were considered, since only they could provide the necessary information on house size and village layout. The exclusion of all damaged sites reduced the total available from 60 to 21. The remaining sites were then screened to eliminate those where the surface features seemed to represent more than one period of occupation. In general, the house depressions at those sites were characterized by a lack of order. Specific irregularities included:

1) important stylistic differences among the house depressions at a site (e.g., square house depressions in one area and rectangular house depressions in another);

2) a clear discontinuity in the village layout indicated by a lack of consistency or coordination in the orientation or positioning of the house depressions at a site;

3) the presence of house features which had been partially filled with refuse from a later occupation.

Five sites were eliminated at this stage in the analysis, leaving a total of 16.

The age of the surface features at each site was determined by radiocarbon dating. Two samples were taken from each site to allow for a check on the consistency of the results. Each radiocarbon sample came from the uppermost layer of midden, and the material collected in each case was marine shell. The assumption was that the uppermost layer of midden would be contemporary with the house depressions, both representing the final period of occupation at the site. The samples were processed by the Radiocarbon Dating Laboratory at Washington State University. Included in the laboratory analysis was a correction for isotopic fractionation, but a further adjustment was made to correct for the marine reservoir effect. Data presented by Stephen Robinson and Gail Thompson (1981:48), Leonard Ham (1990:202), and J.R. Southon, D.E. Nelson and J.S. Vogel (1990:202) suggest that a correction of 650 ± 50 years is appropriate for the north coast of British Columbia, and the laboratory estimates were, therefore, reduced by that amount. The expected level of consistency in the two age estimates from each site was an overlap at the 95 percent confidence level. Five sites failed to meet the standard and were, therefore, dropped from the study. That left a total of 11 village sites to form the basis for the current investigation (Fig. 4). The radiocarbon estimates for the sites are presented in Table 2.

RESULTS

Reference has already been made to the existing body of village data from three sites in Kitselas Canyon including Paul Mason, Gitsaex, and Gitlaxdzawk. Since they provide the context for the current study, a closer examination of the evidence is warranted. The final occupation at the Paul Mason site (GdTc-16) dated to about 1000 B.C. and was represented by ten rectangular house depressions, arranged in two rows running parallel to the riverbank. The average house had a floor area of 61.8 m², and the range of variation for the ten was slight. Based on this information, Coupland (1988:279) inferred an egalitarian pattern of social organization.

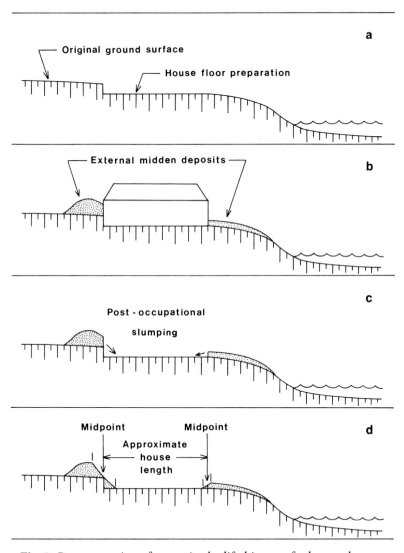

Fig. 3. Reconstruction of stages in the life history of a house plot: (a) house floor preparation, (b) occupation and midden development, (c) house abandonment, and (d) midden slumpage.

Table 2. *Radiocarbon age determinations for selected village sites in the Prince Rupert area.*

Lab No.	Site	Field No.	^{14}C Age in years B.P.	
			Laboratory[1]	Corrected[2]
WSU-4373	GbTo-9	#1	2490 ± 90	1840 ± 105
WSU-4374	GbTo-9	#2	2360 ± 90	1710 ± 105
WSU-4377	GbTo-32	#1	2435 ± 100	1785 ± 110
WSU-4378	GbTo-32	#2	2220 ± 70	1570 ± 90
WSU-4379	GbTo-46	#1	2530 ± 95	1880 ± 110
WSU-4380	GbTo-46	#2	2590 ± 95	1940 ± 110
WSU-4381	GbTo-57	#1	2470 ± 90	1820 ± 105
WSU-4382	GbTo-57	#2	2220 ± 65	1570 ± 85
WSU-4387	GbTo-66	#1	2500 ± 60	1850 ± 80
WSU-4388	GbTo-66	#2	2590 ± 90	1940 ± 105
WSU-4389	GbTo-70	#1	2445 ± 90	1795 ± 105
WSU-4390	GbTo-70	#2	2510 ± 100	1860 ± 110
WSU-4391	GbTo-77	#1	3210 ± 100	2560 ± 110
WSU-4392	GbTo-77	#2	2925 ± 100	2275 ± 110
WSU-4393	GbTo-78	#1	2760 ± 90	2110 ± 105
WSU-4394	GbTo-78	#2	2425 ± 80	1775 ± 95
WSU-4395	GbTo-89	#1	2450 ± 70	1800 ± 85
WSU-4396	GbTo-89	#2	2490 ± 90	1840 ± 105
WSU-4399	GcTo-6	#1	2310 ± 70	1660 ± 85
WSU-4400	GcTo-6	#2	2140 ± 90	1490 ± 105
WSU-4409	GcTo-52	#1	2360 ± 75	1710 ± 90
WSU-4410	GcTo-52	#2	2530 ± 90	1880 ± 105

[1] Value supplied by laboratory includes ^{12}C/^{13}C correction.
[2] Laboratory values were corrected for the marine reservoir effect (see text).

The other two village sites, Gitsaex (GdTc-3) and Gitlaxdrawk (GdTc-1), were both inhabited in early historic times. At Gitsaex, there were 17 houses arranged in two rows running parallel to the riverbank (Coupland 1985:45, 47). The house floors were approximately square with an average area of 101.1 m². At Gitlaxdzawk, the layout was less regular due to the unevenness of the terrain, but in other respects the two villages were alike (Coupland 1985:44, 47). Both sites were characterized by a fairly wide range of house sizes, and in both settlements, the larger houses were situated next to the riverbank. The implication is that they were the houses of the higher ranking chiefs and their families, while the smaller dwellings were those of the lower ranking members of the community (Coupland 1988a:229).

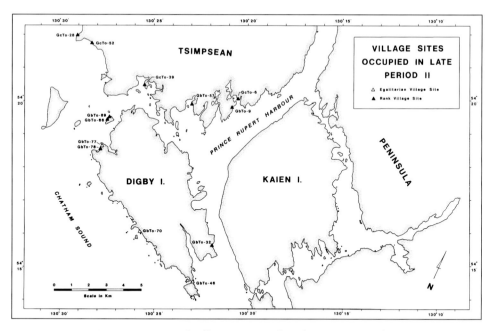

Fig. 4. Location of village sites used in the current analysis.

To quantify the variability in house size within each village, Coupland (1985:48) used the Coefficient of Relative Variation or CRV. This simple index is calculated by dividing the standard deviation by the mean and multiplying by 100 (Mueller, Schussler, and Costner 1970:165-166). The result is an objective, standardized measure of variability, which allows direct comparisons to be made from one site to another. When interpreting CRVs, a higher score indicates more variability. The coefficients obtained for the three Kitselas Canyon sites are presented in Table 3, and the contrasts are clear. The egalitarian village of 1000 B.C. is represented by a coefficient of 16 percent, while the average for the two ranked villages of the early historical period is about 30 percent (Coupland 1985:47).

The same pattern is also evident in the sample of village sites from the Prince Rupert area (Table 3). At three of the 11 sites, the houses were fairly uniform in size, which suggests an egalitarian structure (Fig. 5). As shown in Table 3, the CRVs for those sites range from 9 percent to 16 percent which compares well with the figure of 16 percent quoted for the Paul Mason site. At the other eight sites, the variation in house size was much greater, which suggests a ranked village structure (Fig. 6). The CRVs for seven of those sites range between 22 percent and 35 percent, which is in line with the average of about 30 percent noted for Gitsaex and

Gitlaxdzawk, while the eighth has a high of 59 percent. The disposition of the houses in those villages was also similar to that seen at Gitsaex and Gitlaxdzawk. Typically, the larger houses were located along the shoreline, while the smaller ones were consigned to a second or, even, third row. Priority of position within the villages evidently went to the larger, more powerful households.

Table 3. Variation in house floor areas at village sites in the Kitselas Canyon and Prince Rupert regions.[1]

Site	Range	Mean	Std. dev.	CRV	Sample size
	Egalitarian Village, Kitselas Canyon:				
GdTc-16	45.8 - 72.6	61.8	9.9	16.0	10
	Egalitarian Villages, Prince Rupert:				
GbTo-46	25.2 - 50.0	39.3	6.4	16.3	20
GbTo-70	26.2 - 34.8	30.9	2.8	9.1	11
GbTo-77	17.5 - 25.0	21.5	3.2	14.9	5
	Ranked Villages, Kitselas Canyon:				
GdTc-1	74.6 - 187.7	106.6	36.8	34.5	10
GdTc-3	53.1 - 148.2	101.0	26.5	26.3	17
	Ranked Villages, Prince Rupert:				
GbTo-9	27.7 - 58.7	41.8	9.0	21.5	10
GbTo-32	25.4 - 65.8	43.8	12.6	28.7	21
GbTo-57	13.5 - 62.5	38.1	13.9	36.4	17
GbTo-66	19.6 - 62.2	39.1	13.6	34.7	11
GbTo-78	13.7 - 59.3	34.5	10.3	29.7	34
GbTo-89	15.6 - 67.0	32.7	11.4	35.0	22
GcTo-6	13.3 - 49.0	34.9	9.6	27.5	16
GcTo-52	14.8 - 118.5	46.9	27.5	58.6	11

[1] Data for Kitselas Canyon are from Coupland 1985:47. For both regions, the ranges, means, and standard deviations are reported in m^2. CRV is the coefficient of relative variation and is reported as a percent (see text for explanation).

The radiocarbon estimates obtained on the egalitarian villages from Prince Rupert Harbour indicate that the earliest of the three dated to about 500 B.C., while the other two dated to about A.D. 100. Estimates associated with the presumed eight ranked villages ranged from about A.D. 100 to 400. The evidence suggests that an egalitarian village structure persisted in the Prince Rupert area until around A.D. 100 but was then replaced by one based on social ranking. It also appears that the transition from one system to the other was relatively abrupt. As shown in Figure 7, the emergence of the ranked village structure around A.D. 100 is marked by a sudden doubling of the CRV scores from an average of 15 percent in the egalitarian villages to an average of 30 percent in the ranked villages. The implication is that this was a true turning point in the social history of the region.

Fig. 5. Plan of egalitarian village at GbTo-70.

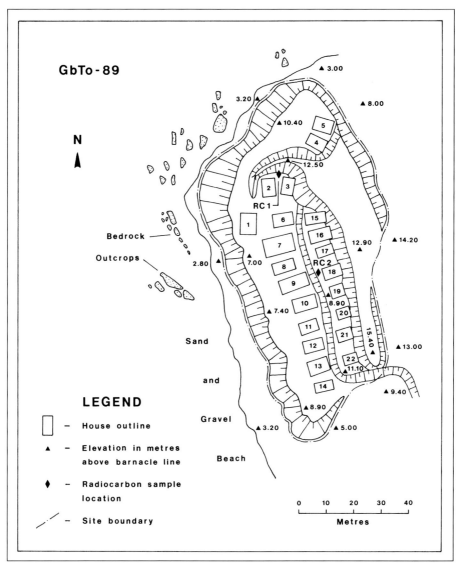

Fig. 6. Plan of ranked village at GbTo-89.

In evaluating the new evidence, it should be noted that there are still significant gaps in the site chronology. Data on village patterns during the first millennium B.C. are sparse, and as yet there is no detailed information on developments between about A.D. 400 and the time of European contact. The operating assumption is that variation in house size remained at a more or less constant level in the period after A.D. 400, but that may be an oversimplification. Further refinement of that and other aspects of the model will obviously require a larger body of settlement data.

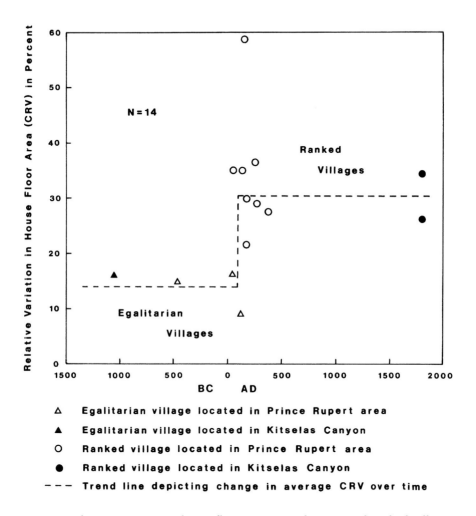

Fig. 7. Relative variation in house floor area in egalitarian and ranked villages.

DISCUSSION

It has long been argued that a system of social ranking evolved on the north coast of British Columbia around 500 B.C. By that time, differences in social status appeared evident in the excavated archaeological record for the Prince

Rupert area, and that was interpreted to signify a shift from egalitarian to ranked society. The information presented in this paper does not support that interpretation. In the one village which dated to about 500 B.C., the houses were still roughly uniform in size, which implies an absence of social ranking. Not until after about A.D. 100 was there evidence of a shift in village patterns. From then on, the villages of the study area seem to have been characterized by a wider range in house size as well as a spatial arrangement that favoured the larger houses. The present data suggest that social ranking appeared in the Prince Rupert area no earlier than A.D. 100.

How, then, can we account for the status differences which are apparent in the period around 500 B.C.? A useful point to consider is the distinction between achieved and ascribed status. In egalitarian societies, there are often some people who are treated with more respect than others in recognition of their special abilities and accomplishments (Fried 1967:33-34). Although status differences of that kind are non-hereditary, they might still be expressed in the kinds of ornaments worn or in the rituals that accompanied death and burial. Perhaps, that was the kind of society which existed in the Prince Rupert area around 500 B.C., a society which acknowledged the contributions made by exceptional individuals, while retaining the leveling mechanisms typical of an egalitarian system. In ranked societies, on the other hand, status positions are basically ascriptive or hereditary in nature (Fried 1967:109). Individual ability continues to play a role, but important positions of respect and authority are regularly passed down from one generation to the next within a single family line. The changes in village patterning that occurred around A.D. 100 in the Prince Rupert area are consistent with the emergence of such a system. The increased variability in house size, together with the distinctive arrangement of the houses, suggest a more stable and predictable social hierarchy, which is the sign of a fully developed ranked society.

Clearly, the dating of a social transition at about A.D. 100 is only a small step towards an understanding of the processes involved, but it is nonetheless an important one. It should now be possible to define more precisely the sequence of events which led to the emergence of ranked society in the Prince Rupert area and to isolate those factors that were most influential in promoting this crucial change.

ACKNOWLEDGEMENTS

The field work on which this paper is based was funded by the Canadian Museum of Civilization, the British Columbia Heritage Trust, the Employment Development Branch of Employment and Immigration Canada, the British

Columbia Ministry of Tourism, Social Services and Housing, the Metlakatla Indian Band, and the University of Calgary. The funds were administered by the Museum of Northern British Columbia in 1982 and 1983, jointly by the Museum of Northern British Columbia and the Archaeology Department at the University of Calgary in 1988 and 1989, and by the Tsimshian Tribal Council in 1990. Logistical support for the project was provided by the Archaeology Department of the University of Calgary and the Anthropology Section of the Royal British Columbia Museum.

During the six seasons of field work, numerous people made important contributions to the project as regular members of the research team. They included Boris Atamanenko, Sidney Bennett, Jennifer Berry, Cairn Crockford, Randy Dundas, Ken Hallett, Paul Hiom, Eric Hotz, Samantha Keely, Rita Koutsodimos, Debi Laughlin, Al Mackie, Godfrey Mason, Pat McFadden, Les McLean, Monty Mitchell, Susan Musgrave, Bill Quackenbush, Sandi Peacock, Malcolm Rewcastle, Calvin Russ, Kristi Salconi, Donald Sankey, Kjerstin Smith, Suzanne Twelker, Wendy Unfreed, Terry Volcano, Paula Watkins, Bennie Williams and Laurie Williamson. There were also a number of volunteers who worked alongside the regular crew members for periods ranging from a day to several weeks. They included Linda Armstrong, Ron Bolton, Lee Boyko, Mary Brown, Jenny Fredrikson, Jacquie Gijssen, Thelma Landon, Diane Peacock, Nannette LaPointe, Susan Marsden, Laurie McArthur, Lynda Millar, Elaine Moore, Dennis Mueller, Allison Neill, Ian Robertson, Sandra Robinson, Kathryn Stewart, Anne Sushames, Teresa Weismiller and Jim Whittome. To one and all, I would like to express my gratitude and best wishes.

In the analysis of the data and preparation of this paper, I benefitted from the advice and guidance of several friends and colleagues, and I would like to take this opportunity to thank Richard Forbis, Teresa Weismiller, Jerome Cybulski, Susan Marsden, and Jay Miller for their help in completing this aspect of the research.

REFERENCES CITED

Ames, K.M. (1981). The evolution of social ranking on the Northwest Coast of North America. *American Antiquity* 46:789-805.

Ames, K.M. (1985). Hierarchies, stress and logistical strategies among hunter-gatherers in northwestern North America. In *Prehistoric Hunter-Gatherers: The Emergence of Cultural Complexity*, edited by T.D. Price and J.A. Brown, Academic Press, Orlando, pp. 155-180.

Archer, D.J.W. (1983). Prince Rupert Harbour Project Preliminary Impact Assessment Report. Unpublished manuscript (Permit 1982-33), Resource Information Centre, Heritage Conservation Branch, Government of British Columbia, Victoria.

Archer, D.J.W. (1984). Prince Rupert Harbour Project, Heritage Site Evaluation and Impact Assessment. Unpublished manuscript (Permit 1983-32), Resource Information Centre, Heritage Conservation Branch, Government of British Columbia, Victoria.

Archer, D.J.W. (1989). The North Coast Heritage Inventory Project – A Report on the 1988 Field Season. Unpublished manuscript (Permit 1988-33), Resource Information Centre, Heritage Conservation Branch, Government of British Columbia, Victoria.

Archer, D.J.W. (1990). The North Coast Heritage Inventory Project – A Report on the 1989 Field Season. Unpublished manuscript (Permit 1989-47), Resource Information Centre, Heritage Conservation Branch, Government of British Columbia, Victoria.

Archer, D.J.W. (1991). The North Coast Heritage Inventory Project – A Report on the 1990 Field Season. Unpublished manuscript (Permit 1990-66), Resource Information Centre, Heritage Conservation Branch, Government of British Columbia, Victoria.

Bishop, C.A. (1987). Coast-interior exchange: the origins of stratification in northwest North America. *Arctic Anthropology* 24:72-83.

Burley, D.V. (1979). Specialization and the evolution of complex society in the Gulf of Georgia region. *Canadian Journal of Archaeology* 3:131-156.

Burley, D.V. (1980). *Marpole: Anthropological Reconstructions of a Prehistoric Northwest Coast Culture Type*. Department of Archaeology, Simon Fraser University, Publication 8. Burnaby.

Cohen, M.N. (1981). Pacific Coast foragers: affluent or overcrowded? In *Affluent Foragers: Pacific Coasts East and West*, edited by S. Koyama and D.H. Thomas, Senri Ethnological Studies 9, National Museum of Ethnology, Osaka, pp. 275-295.

Coupland, G. (1985). Household variability and status differentiation at Kitselas Canyon. *Canadian Journal of Archaeology* 9:39-56.

Coupland, G. (1988a). Prehistoric economic and social change in the Tsimshian area. In *Prehistoric Economies of the Pacific Northwest Coast*, edited by B.J. Isaac, Research in Economic Anthropology, Supplement 3, JAI Press, Greenwich, pp. 211-243.

Coupland, G. (1988b). *Prehistoric Cultural Change at Kitselas Canyon*. Archaeological Survey of Canada Mercury Series Paper 138. Canadian Museum of Civilization, Hull.

Cybulski, J.S. (1990). Human biology. In *Handbook of North American Indians, Vol. 7, Northwest Coast*, edited by W. Suttles, Smithsonian Institution, Washington, pp. 52-59.

Fladmark, K.R. (1975). *A Paleoecological Model for Northwest Coast Prehistory*. Archaeological Survey of Canada Mercury Series Paper 43. Canadian Museum of Civilization, Hull.

Fladmark, K.R., K.M. Ames, and P.D. Sutherland (1990). Prehistory of the northern coast of British Columbia. In *Handbook of North American Indians, Vol. 7, Northwest Coast*, edited by W. Suttles, Smithsonian Institution, Washington, pp. 229-239.

Fried, M.H. (1967). *The Evolution of Political Society*. Random House, New York.

Ham, L.C. (1990). The Cohoe Creek site: A Late Moresby Tradition shell midden. *Canadian Journal of Archaeology* 14:199-221.

Hobler, P.M. (1990). Prehistory of the central coast of British Columbia. In *Handbook of North American Indians, Vol. 7, Northwest Coast*, edited by W. Suttles, Smithsonian Institution, Washington, pp. 30-51.

MacDonald, G.F. (1983). Prehistoric art of the northern Northwest Coast. In *Indian Art Traditions of the Northwest Coast*, edited by R.L. Carlson, Archaeology Press, Simon Fraser University, Burnaby, pp. 99-120.

MacDonald, G.F., and R.I. Inglis (1981). An overview of the North Coast Prehistory Project (1966-1980). *BC Studies* 48:37-63.

Maschner, H.D.G. (1991). The emergence of cultural complexity on the northern Northwest Coast. *Antiquity* 65:924-934.

Matson, R.G. (1983). Intensification and the development of cultural complexity: the northwest versus the northeast coast. In *The Evolution of Maritime Cultures on the Northeast and Northwest Coasts of America*, edited by R.J. Nash, Simon Fraser University Department of Archaeology Publication 11, Burnaby, pp. 125-148.

Matson, R.G. (1985). The relationship between sedentism and status inequalities among hunters and gatherers. In *Status, Structure and Stratification: Current Archaeological Reconstructions*, edited by M. Thompson, M.T. Garcia, and F.J. Kense, The University of Calgary Archaeological Association, Calgary, pp. 245-252.

Mueller, J.H., K.F. Schuessler, and H.L. Costner (1970). *Statistical Reasoning in Sociology*. Houghton Mifflin, Boston.

Robinson, S.W., and G. Thompson (1981). Radiocarbon corrections for marine shell dates with application to southern Pacific Northwest Coast prehistory. *Syesis* 14:45-57.

Southon, J.R., D.E. Nelson, and J.S. Vogel (1990). A record of past ocean-atmosphere radiocarbon differences from the northeast Pacific. *Paleoceanography* 5:197-206.

Does Resource Abundance Explain Local Group Rank Among the Coast Tsimshian?

Gary Coupland, Andrew R.C. Martindale, and Susan Marsden

ABSTRACT

Tsimshian local groups of the late eighteenth and nineteenth centuries owned resource territories and were ranked relative to each other in terms of social preference. This paper explores factors underlying local group rank. We find low, and even negative, correlations among local group rank, population size, and resource abundance, measured in terms of salmon escapement. During the period in question, local group rank was dynamic and mutable, while local group territories and resource abundance were largely static. Evidence indicates that warfare and trade explain the structure of Tsimshian local group rank rather than resource abundance and population.

RÉSUMÉ

Les groupes Tsimshans locaux à la fin des dix-huitière et dix-neuvième siècles possédaient des territoires riches en ressources de telle sorte que la préférence sociale classait ces groupes par ordre d'importance les uns par rapport aux autres. Cet article explore les facteurs qui sous-tendent la hiérarchie des groupes locaux. On trouve une corrélation faible, et même négative, en ce qui concerne le rang des groupes locaux, la taille de leur population et l'abondance des ressources, mesurés par rapport au saumon de remonte. Au cours de cette période à l'étude, le rang des groupes locaux était dynamique et flexible, alors que le territoire des groupes locaux et l'abondance des ressources étaient généralement stables. L'enregistrement indique que les activités guerrières et commerciales, plutôt que l'abondance des ressources et la taille des populations, expliquent la structure qui régissait la position sociale des groupes Tsimshans locaux

In *Perspectives on Northern Northwest Coast Prehistory*, edited by Jerome S. Cybulski. Hull: Canadian Museum of Civilization, Archaeological Survey of Canada, Mercury Series Paper 160, pp. 223-248, © 2001.

INTRODUCTION

This paper addresses an issue that has been of fundamental importance in Northwest Coast anthropology for more than a century: the relationship between aspects of social organization, specifically social rank, and the resource base. To what extent is resource abundance, in particular the abundance of salmon, the traditional subsistence staple of most Northwest Coast societies, a predictor of local group rank? Are any other variables relevant to the determination of rank? In the larger domain, this issue is central to evolutionary and ecological theory in anthropology and to an understanding of the origins of complex societies in general, and of complex hunter-gatherers in particular.

In the 1960's, when the paradigm of cultural ecology gained some prominence in Northwest Coast anthropology, this issue was at the centre of an intense debate. On one side, writers such as Suttles (1960, 1962, 1968), Vayda (1961), and Piddocke (1965) argued that the prestige system, as it existed in various forms among Northwest Coast societies, was a mechanism for adjusting to variations and fluctuations in resource abundance. On the other side, scholars including Drucker and Heizer (1967) and Rosman and Rubel (1971) maintained that while the prestige system may have been allowed by an unusually bountiful natural environment, variations and fluctuations in resource abundance were minor, the possibility of scarcity negligible, and the role of resources in determining rank unimportant. In recent years, this issue seems to have lost some of its urgency for Northwest Coast anthropologists, many of whom have turned their attention to other research problems. However, the problem has not gone away altogether and remains important in archaeological circles.

It has been almost a quarter century since Leland Donald and Donald Mitchell (1975) seemingly laid to rest some of the thorny problems of the "resources and ranking" debate in their seminal essay entitled "Some Correlates of Local Group Rank Among the Southern Kwakiutl." Prior to that article, scholars on both sides of the debate had argued their positions, but had offered little in the way of empirical support. Some arguments even seemed tautological (e.g., Piddocke 1965; see Orans 1975). Through a case study, Donald and Mitchell provided empirical evidence that supported the cultural ecological position. They reasoned that if there was a relationship between resource abundance and local group rank among the Southern Kwakiutl, then groups who had access to the most resources (i.e., those who owned or controlled the most productive territories) would be the highest ranked.

Donald and Mitchell inferred Southern Kwakiutl local group rank from potlatch seating arrangements described in two sources: Boas (1925:83-85; summarized in Codere 1950:66, Table 14) and Ford (1941:16). For measurements of resource productivity, they concentrated entirely on Pacific salmon (*Oncorhynchus* spp.), certainly the most abundant and most important food resource for most Northwest Coast societies including the Southern Kwakiutl. Using detailed escapement figures from the Canadian Department of Fisheries (Aro and Shepard 1967), Donald and Mitchell calculated measures of salmon abundance in the territorial rivers and streams of each Southern Kwakiutl local group for the period from 1950 to 1967. Finally, they obtained local group population estimates for two periods: the 1830's (Tolmie 1963:317-318) and the 1880's (Boas 1887:231). With those data the authors produced rank order correlations for each pair of variables.

The strongest correlation of any two variables used in the Donald and Mitchell study was between the rank orders of Southern Kwakiutl local group size in the 1830's and local group rank (Spearman's *rho*=0.92). Population size explained 84 percent of rank variance ($100*rho^2$). The median salmon escapement in each group's territory correlated with 1830's local group size at *rho*=0.85. Salmon abundance accounted for 72 percent of variance in population size. The *rho* value for median salmon escapement and local group rank was 0.73, or 53 percent of rank variance explained by salmon abundance. The strong correlations led Donald and Mitchell to the unavoidable conclusion " . . . that population in the 1830's will predict local group rank, and that median salmon will predict population in the 1830's" (1975:343). Local group size in the 1880's, although diminished greatly by disease, also correlated strongly with salmon escapement and local group rank (Donald and Mitchell 1975:333). Overall, Donald and Mitchell concluded that a very close connection existed between a Southern Kwakiutl local group's rank and its resource base as measured by salmon abundance.

Donald's and Mitchell's study was the first to rigorously examine the relationship between resource abundance and social rank on the Northwest Coast in terms of empirical evidence. Unfortunately, it was also the last.[1] Our intention here is not to argue, 25 years after the fact, that the study by Donald and Mitchell was flawed.

---

[1] Other studies have used empirical evidence to examine the relationship between resource abundance or resource variability and population size. For example, Sneed (1971) found a strong positive correlation between salmon abundance and population size among early historic groups in the Plateau region of the middle Fraser River drainage. Schalk (1981) showed evidence of a south-to-north gradient along the coast of increasing resource patchiness and increasing local group size (but decreasing numbers of local groups).

Indeed, we would suggest quite the opposite. Their assumptions were made clear, the data carefully gathered, the analytical methods appropriate, the results reproducible, and their conclusions entirely reasonable and well-supported. The problem with the Donald and Mitchell paper is that for the past two decades it has been regularly and frequently cited by many other Northwest Coast scholars (including the senior author of the present paper) as a clear demonstration of the importance of resource structure in determining aspects of social organization over the entire Northwest Coast. Donald and Mitchell can hardly be faulted for that. They make it quite clear that theirs was a case study of the Southern Kwakiutl only, and only applied to a relatively brief period of time. Our purpose here is to show through another case study that the results obtained by Donald and Mitchell do not hold over the entire Northwest Coast, and that salmon, undeniably an important subsistence resource to most groups, may not have had an important role in determining rank for all local groups. Ultimately, we argue that human agency, involving the skillful manipulation of social mechanisms such as marriage, trade, and warfare by opportunistic chiefs, was more important than the resource base in determining local group rank in at least one case, that of the Tsimshian.

THE TSIMSHIAN:
LATE EIGHTEENTH TO MID-NINETEENTH CENTURY

At the time of European contact late in the eighteenth century, the Tsimshian were one of three Northwest Coast nations speaking closely related languages. The Tsimshian, the focal group of our study, occupied the lower Skeena drainage as far upriver as Kitselas Canyon and the coastal area north and south of the mouth of the Skeena (Halpin and Seguin 1990). Of the other two nations, the Nisga'a occupied the lower portion of the Nass River valley and the coast north of Port Simpson, while the Gitksan occupied the middle drainage of the Skeena River above Kitselas Canyon.

The Tsimshian nation encompassed three geopolitical regions. Within each region were several local groups (tribes or villages) comprised of matrilineal house groups, the fundamental political and landowning unit in Tsimshian society. The ten local groups that comprised the Northern Tsimshian maintained summer resource territories along the lower Skeena and permanent winter villages in the area of Metlakatla Passage, near Prince Rupert, British Columbia. The latter are generally referred to as the Coast Tsimshian (Halpin and Seguin 1990), or sometimes as the Metlakatla Tsimshian (Garfield 1951). Two local groups, the Kitselas and Kitsumgalum, sometimes called the Canyon Tsimshian (Duff 1964:18), maintained winter villages and year-round residence in their resource territories on the lower Skeena, near Terrace, British Columbia. Three local groups, the Kitkatla, Kitkiata and Kitasoo, sometimes called the Southern Tsimshian (Halpin and Seguin 1990:267), occupied the coastal area south of the mouth of the Skeena from Porcher Island to Swindle Island (Fig. 1).

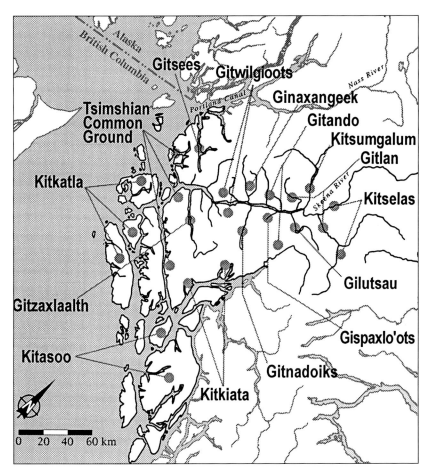

Fig. 1. Local groups of the Tsimshian.

The Tsimshian local groups and their resource territories had long been in existence by 1831 when Fort Simpson, the first permanent EuroCanadian trading post in Tsimshian territory, was established near the mouth of the Nass River. Three years later, the fort was moved south to the present site of Lax Kw'alaams

(Port Simpson), where many Tsimshian subsequently took up residence. In 1857, the Methodist missionary William Duncan arrived at Fort Simpson to begin a ministry among the Tsimshian, eventually moving with many of the people back to Metlakatla. During this period the Tsimshian world was radically transformed by the new colonists, and many of the local groups amalgamated into two main settlements, but the identity and autonomy of the local groups was maintained. In the 1840's, one of the original Metlakatla local groups, the Gitwilksebau, was assimilated by another group, the Gilutsau, reducing the number of local groups in this region from ten to nine (Hodge 1907:709; Barbeau 1917:403; Allaire 1984:92).

Tsimshian society was highly structured. The principle of rank or social precedence was rigidly adhered to, and was used to differentiate people into named positions of status. Lineage-based house groups and local groups were also ranked (Halpin 1973; Garfield 1939). Positions of rank pertaining to individuals, house groups and local groups were established and reaffirmed at elaborate feasting and exchange ceremonies, the famous potlatches. The groups that hosted the most frequent and most elaborate potlatches were, invariably, highest ranked.

Tsimshian local groups derived their names from their traditional resource territories along the lower Skeena and along the coast to the south. Each local group territory was composed of resource areas owned by the house groups (Halpin 1973; Inglis and MacDonald 1979:7). While the Canyon Tsimshian and Southern Tsimshian local groups maintained winter villages in their resource territories, the Coast Tsimshian moved seasonally from their coastal winter villages near Metlakatla to summer villages in their resource territories. Figure 1 shows the lower Skeena and coastal territories of the Tsimshian local groups as they existed early in the nineteenth century (Barbeau and Beynon 1915-1956; Inglis and MacDonald 1979:3; Allaire 1984:88; MacDonald, Coupland and Archer 1987).

TSIMSHIAN LOCAL GROUP RANK

Tsimshian local group rank was not immutable. During the early decades following European contact, local group rank changed often during a relatively brief period. Six accounts, each derived from narratives of the rich Tsimshian oral tradition recorded by Marius Barbeau and William Beynon (compiled by MacDonald and Cove 1987), vividly demonstrate the volatility of Tsimshian local group rank. Each ranking was based on seating arrangements, order of gift presentation, order of speaking, and relative amount of wealth received by local group chiefs at potlatches. Each local group except the Gitwilksebau and the

Kitasoo was mentioned in at least one of the rankings. Four of the rankings actually relate to one nineteenth century potlatch hosted by Ligeex, the highest ranking chief of the Gispaxlo'ots, a Metlakatla Tsimshian local group, who had risen to pre-eminent status among all the Coast Tsimshian local groups several generations before European contact (Boas 1916; Garfield 1939; Marsden 1987; Dean 1994; Miller 1997). One narrative, entitled "The *Xmas* Feast of Ligeex," gives the most complete ranking of local groups:

> He called out in order of rank all the chiefs to receive gifts: 1) Ts'basaa; 2) Wisaiks; 3) Wisaak — these three were from Kitkatla; 4) Wisaiks of Ginaxangik; 5) Saxsaxt of Gitwilgoats; 6) Niswaxs of Ginadoiks; 7) Nishlaranus of Gitlan; 8) Nishot of Gitzaxlahl; 9) Nisyaranat of Gitsis; 10) Nishlkumik of Gilodza; 11) Entewiwalp of Gitgaata; 12) Nistarhoik of Kitselas; 13) Skagwait of Gitando; 14) Nisgitelawp of Kitselas; 15) Guhlrax of Kitsemkalem (MacDonald and Cove 1987:93).

Another narrative describing the same feast, entitled "The Last Feast of Ligeex," provided the following order of rank:

> Each man received his gifts in order of rank, the Kitkatla first, then the Ginxangik, the Gilodza, the Gitlan, the Ginadoiks, the Gitsis, the Gitzaxlahl, the Gitando (MacDonald and Cove 1987:101).

Viola Garfield, a principle ethnographer of the Tsimshian, provided the following ranking, also based on the potlatch hosted by Ligeex:

> The Gitxala ranked above the local tribes so Dzibasa received the largest individual contribution and his subchiefs more than those of the other tribes. The rest of the tribes ranked in the following order, Gitsaxlal, Ginaxangik, Gitsis, Gilutsau, Gitwelgots, Ginadoiks, Gitando, and Gitlan (Garfield 1939:204).

In yet another version of this narrative of Ligeex's potlatch, William Beynon wrote:

> And then each of the headmen of the tribes spoke praising Ligeex and his tribe. The first one to speak was Hlu'um, spokesman for Nisyaganaat, chief of the Gitsiis, and then Niyuks, spokesman for Nishlaganoos, chief of the Gitlaan and then Neegmdaw, spokesman for Nishlgumiik, chief of the Giluts'aaw and then Nisahlnaats who was the spokesman for Seeks, chief of the Ginaxangiik and Satsaan spokesman for Nisweexs, chief of the Gitnadoiks and Gilax'aks spokesman for Saxsa'at, chief of the Gitwilgyoots and Niskiyaa spokesman for Nishoot, chief of the Gitzaxhlaahl. Sgagweet, chief of the Gitando, stood in a different position than the others and his spokesman Gamayaam did not speak for his chief, because his position was one that should assist Ligeex who was his clan brother. (The *Xmas* Feast of Ligeex, Beynon n.d., no. 51)

The discrepancies in the four accounts that described the same potlatch show that rankings of individuals and groups depended partly on who was invited to the feast and partly on who was presenting the oral history. A narrative of a Gitando potlatch provides the following order of precedence:

> When all was counted and properly apportioned for distribution to the guests, the first called was Wisaiks, chief of the Ginaxangik. Then came the Raven chief Nishot and his Gitzaxlahl tribesmen; next, Nisyaranat and Kalksek, chiefs of the Gitsis, and their tribesmen Niswaxs and his Ginadoiks tribesmen [sic]; next Nishlaganos, chief of the Gitlan and Saxsaxt and Ligiyutgwatk, chiefs of the Gitwilgoats, and all their tribes.

> The last to be called as guests were the Giludzo tribal chief . . . Nishlkumik . . . (MacDonald and Cove 1987:57).

The last great *Xmas* ("Eating Red") feast of Ligeex was documented in several adawx (Tsimshian oral histories) recorded by Barbeau and Beynon, in the journals of Arthur Wellington Clah, and in the memory painting of the Tsimshian artist, Fred Alexcee (Miller and Eastman 1984). The Ligeex who gave this feast followed the famous Paul Ligeex who converted to Christianity in 1862 and therefore was not able to complete his feasting obligations as leading chief of the Tsimshian. Paul Ligeex died in 1869. His successor was an older man who did not convert to Christianity and never took an English name. That Ligeex was little known in written history but, as Arthur Wellington Clah, a Gispaxlo'ots chief under Ligeex and one of the first Tsimshian to learn English related, the intent of his feast was to commemorate his two predecessors, "old Ligeex" and Paul Ligeex, and in so doing, return the name of Ligeex to its former status. In his journal for January 23, 1871, Clah described Ligeex's trip to Kitkatla to invite the chiefs there to his feast. On January 28, the Kitkatlas arrived. On February 5, after several days of preliminary ceremonies, Clah records: "Feast in Legaic's house for old Legaic, his death long time ago." On February 10, Clah wrote: "Legaic give away all property to chiefs of Tsimshians for his new name, 710 blankets, elk skins, 60 coppers." The next day Ts'ibasaa "went back to his own place and all his people with him." Thus, the preparations for this great feast were made in 1870, and the feast itself was held in February, 1871.

This last great *Xmas* feast marked a turning point for the Coast Tsimshian, and for this reason it was recorded in their adawx as an event of historical significance. Similarly, the southern Tsimshian have recorded the last great *Xmas* feast of Ts'ibasaa in their adawx.

The feast given by the leading chief of the Gitando was attended by his daughter, Victoria Young, who at the time was a chief in her own right. Victoria Young was born in 1834 and died in 1898. This Gitando feast probably took place around the same time as that of Ligeex between 1870 and 1880. Victoria Young was recorded in the Clah journals as the acknowledged leader of the Gilutsau in 1888.

Years later, William Beynon recorded the Feast of Nisyaganaat, chief of the Gitsees. Beynon, who held the name, Gwisk'aayn, actually attended the feast on behalf of the Gitlan. It probably took place around 1930.

> And the money was set out on the table. Then 'Watida'ax, another leading Gitsiis headman stood up, and he lifted up the wealth and began calling out the names of those to whom the money was to be given: first Ligeex . . . and all the headmen of the Gispaxlo'ots, next Sgagweet . . . and all the Gitando headmen, then 'Wiiseeks, the Ginaxangiik chief . . . and all the Ginaxangiik headmen, next Saxsa'axt, the Gitwilgyoots chief . . . and all the headmen of the Gitwilgyoots, after that Gwisk'aayn [of the Gitlaan], then Nishlgumiik, the Giluts'aaw chief . . . and all the Giluts'aaw headmen, next Nisweexs, the Gitnadoiks chief . . . and all the Gitnadoiks headmen, then Nisho'ot, the Gitzaxhlaahl chief . . . and all the Gitzaxhlaahl headmen. (William Beynon n.d.)

In another example of change in local group rank that probably dates to the 1830's, Garfield provided an account of how the Ginakangeek were shamed by the Kitkatla and their chief, Ts'basaa. "Previous to this episode their [Ginakangeek] chief [Tsa-qaxs] was called second at a feast or in gift giving, and Ts'basaa was third. Now they lost their place to Ts'basaa and have never regained it" (Garfield 1939:266). In fact, following the incident, Wisaiks emerged as the highest ranking chief of the Ginakangeek, while Tsa-qaxs dropped to fifth among his own local group (Dean 1994:50).

The foregoing evidence clearly shows that the order of precedence of Tsimshian local groups was not fixed, but was, in fact, subject to rapid and dramatic changes. Admittedly, the period in question was a turbulent one in Tsimshian history, when their world was transformed by colonial settlement, depopulation, and the influx of European trade goods. Nevertheless, the changes in rank occurred in the absence of any significant changes in salmon productivity in local group territories, which suggests that the two variables, local group rank and salmon abundance, were not strongly correlated.

TSIMSHIAN SALMON FISHING PRACTICES

The salmon fishing season in the Tsimshian area begins in late May or early June with the first runs of Chinook (*O. tshawytscha*) and continues late into the fall or early winter with the last runs of Coho (*O. nerka*). In early summer, the Tsimshian left their winter villages for fish camps or summer villages in their resource territories. Most Coast Tsimshian and Canyon Tsimshian fishing territories centered around one or two main streams or rivers that emptied into the lower Skeena. Ginadoiks territory, for example, included the watershed of the Gitnadoiks River, which drained Alastair Lake and flowed north into the Skeena River (Fig. 1). Salmon productivity of those territories varied considerably. The Gilutsau, for example, who controlled the Lakelse River, received annual escapements of 566,500 salmon, mainly pinks (*O. gorbuscha*) (Table 1). Gispaxlo'ots territory, on the south side of the Skeena around Dasque and Whitebottom Creeks, was impoverished by comparison, with annual escapements of less than 1000 salmon.

The Kitselas, who controlled Kitselas Canyon, were one of the few groups who actually took a significant portion of their salmon catch directly from the Skeena River. Only 2 km long, Kitselas Canyon is the first major constriction of the Skeena, about 150 km upriver from the mouth (Emmons 1912; Inglis and MacDonald 1979; Coupland 1988). Historically, it was an important salmon fishing location providing good access to salmon that ascended the river beyond that point.

The Gitwilgiots and Gitzaklalth controlled large portions of the coast near the mouth of the Skeena, in addition to their lower Skeena territories. The Gitzaklalth owned the Dundas Island group and the Gitwilgiots owned the Stephens Island group which separated the inner coastal waters of Chatham Sound from the outer waters of Dixon Entrance. The Ginakangeek also owned important coastal territories. The remainder of the coastal area between the mouth of the Skeena and Fort Simpson was considered common ground and could be fished by all Coast Tsimshian groups.

The coastal territories south of the mouth of the Skeena belonged to the Kitkatla, Kitkiata and Kitasoo. These territories were not part of the Skeena drainage, but included numerous small coastal streams that received salmon runs.

Table 1. Local group rank, population size, and salmon abundance data for the Tsimshian of the mid-nineteenth century

	Local group rank					Local group population size[1]	Salmon abundance[1]
Gitando potlatch	Gitsees potlatch	Ligeex's feast (Beynon)	Last feast of Ligeex	Garfield's ranking	Xmas feast of Ligeex		
Ginakangeek	Gispaxlo'ots	Gispaxlo'ots	Gispaxlo'ots	Gispaxlo'ots	Gispaxlo'ots	436 (2)	< 1,000 (13)
Gitzaklalth	Gitando	Kitkatla	Kitkatla	Kitkatla	Kitkatla	171 (11)	430,150 (4)
Gitsees	Ginkangeek	Gitsees	Ginakangeek	Gitzaklalth	Ginakangeek	265 (5)	2,950 (12)
Ginadoiks	Gitwilgiots	Gitlan	Gilutsau	Ginakangeek	Gitwilgiots	214 (8)	138,900 (7)
Gitlan	Gitlan	Gilutsau	Gitlan	Gitsees	Ginadoiks	219 (6)	44,750 (10)
Gitwilgiots	Gilutsau	Ginakangeek	Ginadoiks	Gilutsau	Gitlan	414 (3)	54,542 (9)
Gilutsau	Ginadoiks	Gitnadoiks	Gitsees	Gitwilgiots	Gitzaklalth	115 (13)	100,725 (8)
—	Gitzaklalth	Gitwilgiots	Gitzaklalth	Ginadoiks	Gitsees	219 (6)	150,225 (5)
—	—	Gitzaklalth	Gitando	Gitando	Gilutsau	297 (4)	566,448 (2)
—	—	—	—	Gitlan	Kitkiata	698 (1)	589,188 (3)
—	—	—	—	—	Kitselas	189 (10)	c. 1,000,000 (1)
—	—	—	—	—	Gitando	202 (9)	44,267 (11)
—	—	—	—	—	Kitsumkalum	145 (12)	142,400 (6)

[1] Numbers in parentheses represent rank positions.

Data on salmon abundance were derived from the Department of Fisheries and Oceans annual target counts of salmon escapements in 199 streams and rivers in Tsimshian territory for the 45-year period from 1950 to 1994 (Table 1). Escapement figures were provided by the Department of Fisheries and Oceans which conducts annual counts of fish runs on most rivers in Tsimshian territory. The figures quoted are target data, estimates of what the annual run should be based on patterns observed since the 1940's. Salmon runs have declined consistently in the twentieth century, probably due to commercial fishing, and nineteenth century escapement figures would most likely have been higher than current targets. Following the method of Donald and Mitchell, we estimated the total annual run of salmon available to each Tsimshian local group in its territory by identifying with a local group each stream for which escapement data exist. This procedure was complicated, however, by the fact that the territories of the Coast Tsimshian and Canyon Tsimshian provided each local group with potential access to salmon in the same river, the Skeena.

The Skeena River receives runs of over 2,000,000 salmon annually directly from the Pacific Ocean. They can be divided into three categories. One includes salmon, about 30-40 percent of the total run, which ascend the Skeena only a short distance before branching off into spawning streams in Coast Tsimshian local group territories. They are included in the territorial escapement estimates given in Table 1.

A second category includes salmon which ascend the Skeena only a short distance, but do not branch off into tributary streams. During odd calendar years, 165,000 pink salmon spawn in the main channel of the Skeena River (Aro and Shepard 1967). An estimated 25,500 pink salmon spawn in the main channel of the Skeena in even years. The reason for this "odd-year/even-year" difference is that pink salmon which run on the Skeena are on a two-year cycle, with odd years dominant. An unknown number of chum salmon (O. keta) also spawn in the main channel of the lower Skeena. Those "main channel spawners," which represent up to 10 percent of the total run, are not included in the territorial escapement estimates given in Table 1, although it is almost certain that each Coast Tsimshian local group with territories on the lower Skeena below Kitselas Canyon made at least some use of those fish.

Our third category of salmon is the largest and the most difficult to deal with. Over 50 percent of the total Skeena run, including the bulk of the sockeye and pink salmon, ascend the Skeena beyond Kitselas Canyon, the inland frontier of Tsimshian territory, passing through the fishing territories of the Metlakatla local groups on route to spawning streams in the interior of British Columbia. Each local group had *potential* access to those salmon as they migrated through their territories. To illustrate this point, consider again the example of the Ginadoiks. Table 1 assigns Ginadoiks territory an average annual escapement of 44,750 salmon, the escapement in the Gitnadoiks River. But the Ginadoiks also controlled a short section of the Skeena River at the mouth of the Gitnadoiks River, where well over 1,000,000 salmon passed annually without branching off into the Gitnadoiks River. Had the Ginadoiks fished for salmon in this section of the Skeena their territorial escapement figures would be much higher than those given in Table 1. But, like most other Metlakatla Tsimshian, the Ginadoiks underutilized that potential.

Below Kitselas Canyon, local groups fished the tributary streams of the Skeena far more intensively than the Skeena River itself. In general, traditional Tsimshian fishing technology was not well-suited to catching salmon in the Skeena. Before the arrival of Europeans, the main salmon procurement techniques were weirs, other types of traps such as basket traps, and dip nets (Drucker 1965:118; Nolan 1977:135-138). These techniques would have been effective in small, narrow streams or in canyons, but not in the wide, slow-moving lower Skeena. Dip netting, which depends on strong river currents and numerous back eddies, would have been largely ineffective on the lower Skeena except in Kitselas Canyon (see Kew 1992 for a similar argument with respect to the lower Fraser River). We have virtually no information on the use of weirs in the main channel of the Skeena. These mass procurement installations would have been far more effective on the tributary streams.

The most effective salmon-fishing technique in the lower Skeena would have been gill-netting which is commonly used today. But Drucker (1955:169) reports that the gill net and other similar types of nets were unknown to or at least unused by the Tsimshian prior to European contact (see also Rostlund 1952:85). Thus, for most groups the precontact catch from the Skeena River itself was probably quite small compared to the catch from the territorial streams that fed the Skeena. The exception, of course, are the Kitselas who controlled the very productive canyon fishery, and took much of their salmon catch directly from the Skeena using the existing technology.

In odd calendar years, an estimated average of 1,155,000 salmon, mainly sockeye and pink, ascend the Skeena River beyond Kitselas Canyon. In even calendar years, 658,000 salmon run through the canyon. The importance of the canyon for fishing stems not only from the huge numbers of salmon that migrate through it annually, but also from the dense concentration of the fish in one location, "bottlenecked" through this constriction of the Skeena River. This allows human labour to concentrate in one place and exploit the resource more efficiently. By contrast, although the territories of the Kitkatla and Kitkiata also have large salmon escapements, the runs are widely dispersed in the many coastal rivers and streams in each territory. This dispersion would inhibit the concentration of labour in any one place making exploitation of the resource less efficient than in the canyon. For this reason we rank Kitselas territory first in terms of salmon abundance (Table 1). Likewise, we rank the Gilutsau second ahead of the Kitkiata, even though salmon abundance in Kitkiata territory is slightly greater than in Gilutsau territory (Table 1). The reason is because salmon in Gilutsau territory were concentrated in the Lakelse River, whereas salmon in Kitkiata territory were dispersed in many rivers.

The escapement figures in Table 1 represent an average of the odd and even-year runs. The figures probably underestimate the number of salmon available to the Coast Tsimshian below Kitselas Canyon. Undoubtedly, each of local group there exploited pink and chum salmon which spawned in the main channel of the Skeena River. However, since we have no reason to believe that some local groups exploited those fish more than others, the ranks of those territories in terms of salmon escapement should not be affected. Those groups could also have taken salmon from the rivers and creeks that constituted Tsimshian common ground, the total target escapement for which is 168,500 fish.

We suspect that the Gispaxlo'ots and Ginakangeek fished the common ground more intensively than the other groups. Table 1 shows low salmon escapements and high population figures for both groups. The number of salmon spawning annually in Gispaxlo'ots territory was so small that the average yield would have been barely two fish per person. In Ginakangeek territory, the yield would have been only slightly higher; 11 fish per person. In contrast, the next lowest yield would have been for the Ginadoiks at 204 fish per person. The Gispaxlo'ots and Ginakangeek, two of the highest ranked Tsimshian local groups, simply could not have survived on the salmon available to them in their lower Skeena territories.

The escapement figure for the Kitselas given in Table 1, although technically accurate, is somewhat misleading, since obviously many salmon escaped the traps and nets of the canyon only to be taken by Gitksan and Wet'suwet'en fishermen farther upriver. However, our concern here is with escapement sizes, not with catch sizes. No local group exploited all salmon in their territory in a given year.

POPULATION SIZE ESTIMATES

Our local group population size estimates for the Tsimshian were derived from Schoolcraft (1857:487) whose figures are based on a census conducted in 1845 by which time many Tsimshian had moved to Fort Simpson (Table 1). The most populous local group, at 698 men, women, boys and girls (slaves not included), were the Kitkiata who ranked tenth in social precedence in the narrative of "The *Xmas* Feast of Ligeex." Next most populous at 436 individuals were the high ranking Gispaxlo'ots. At 45 individuals, the Gitwilksebau were least populous, but by 1845 this group had been all but assimilated by the Gilutsau. Surprisingly, the Gitlan were the third most populous local group with 414 people, despite the fact that they were not highly ranked in any of the narrative accounts, and in fact ranked low in order of precedence in two of the accounts. Even more surprising are the Kitkatla who ranked high in each narrative in which they are mentioned, but who ranked eleventh in population with 171 people.

RANK, SALMON, AND POPULATION SIZE AMONG THE TSIMSHIAN

Donald and Mitchell (1975:343) found salmon abundance to be a good predictor of population size, and population size a good predictor of local group rank among the Southern Kwakiutl. In the Tsimshian case, however, the results appear quite different.

Rank order correlations of the three variables were calculated for each of the six Tsimshian local group rankings (four versions of Ligeex's feast, the Gitando feast, and the Gitsees feast, Table 2). The six correlations for local group rank with salmon abundance ranged from 0 to -0.61. The correlation for population with salmon abundance was also negative at -0.17. Only local group rank with population size produced positive correlations (four of six), ranging from -0.13 to 0.53. In total, seven of the 12 correlations involving local group rank were negative, one was "zero" (a perfect non-correlation), and the four positive correlations were only weak or moderate. Quite simply, the data revealed that salmon abundance did not predict population size, and population size did not predict local group rank among the Tsimshian during the mid-nineteenth century. Perhaps most surprising of all was the fact that two of the highest ranking Tsimshian local groups, the Gispaxlo'ots and the Ginakangeek, had the least productive salmon territories.

Table 2. Rank order correlations of local group rank with population size and salmon abundance for the mid-nineteenth century Tsimshian[1]

Source of local group rank	Local group rank with salmon abundance	Local group rank with population size
Xmas feast of Ligeex	-0.46	0.26
Last feast of Ligeex	-0.12	0.53
Garfield's ranking	-0.01	-0.09
Ligeex's Feast (Beynon)	0.00	0.53
Gitando Potlatch	-0.61	-0.13
Gitsees Potlatch	-0.49	0.38

[1] Rank order correlations are Spearman's r values.

"SALMONOPIA" AND THE IMPORTANCE OF OTHER RESOURCES

To this point our investigation of the relationship between ranking and resources among the Tsimshian has focused exclusively on salmon. Monks (1987) and Ames (1994), among others, have suggested that some researchers tend to over-emphasize the importance of salmon in modeling Northwest Coast socioeconomic systems, thus obscuring the contributions of other resources. With tongue in cheek, Monks (1987:119) refers to the situation as "salmonopia," "the inability to see all of the food resources because of the salmon." If salmon abundance was not critical to the order of Tsimshian local group rank, could other subsistence resources have played a role?

Next to salmon, eulachon (*Thaleichthys pacificus*) was probably the second most important food resource to the Tsimshian. This anadromous fish was rendered for its oil ("grease"), a highly prized commodity traded over the famous "grease trails" that crisscrossed the region (MacDonald 1979:41; MacDonald, Coupland and Archer 1987). The main eulachon fishery on the northern Northwest Coast, near the mouth of the Nass River in late winter, attracted people from as far away as southeastern Alaska, the Queen Charlotte Islands, and the upper Skeena River. Although Tsimshian local groups actively participated in the Nass River eulachon fishery, and most local groups owned fishing locations near the mouth of the Nass, there was no evidence that any group held an advantage over the others in terms of wealth or status from its access to eulachon. One source of wealth and power, however, may have been the grease trails, which take their name from the long distance trade of eulachon oil. According to MacDonald, some grease trails were controlled by certain families, were marked by clan carvings on trees, and were subject to strict controls and tariffs on the movement of scarce commodities. The movement of eulachon over the trails was generally open to use by all, but movement through a group's territory was always subject to permission (MacDonald 1984:78; Prince 1998).

After anadromous resources, coastal marine food resources were most important to the Tsimshian economy. Most Tsimshian groups had fishing and hunting rights at the coast, and the Ginakangeek, who were highly ranked in all four accounts, may have benefited most from this privilege. Strictly speaking, however, four local groups for whom we have information on rank, the Gitwilgiots, Gitzaklalth, Kitkatla, and Kitkiata, controlled large coastal territories, which gave them greater access to marine resources than the other local groups. However, this does not appear to have translated into higher rank. From the six rankings available to us, only the Kitkatla, mentioned in four rankings, were consistently ranked high This was because their chief, Ts'basaa, was the leading chief of the Southern Tsimshian. The Kitkiata, mentioned only in the narrative of the *Xmas* Feast of Ligeex, were relatively low ranked. The Gitzaklalth were high ranked twice, low ranked three times, and ranked seventh of 13 in the *Xmas* Feast of Ligeex. The Gitwilgiots were relatively high ranked in the *Xmas* Feast of Ligeex, but low ranked in three accounts, and ranked fourth of eight in the Gitsees feast.

HUMAN AGENCY, SOCIAL MECHANISMS, AND TSIMSHIAN LOCAL GROUP RANK

We have seen that local group rank was mutable, capable, in fact, of rapid and dramatic change, and not strongly correlated to resource abundance or population size. How, then, can we account for the differences in rank we have seen? Many examples from the early historic records, both indigenous and European, indicated that certain Tsimshian chiefs made skillful use of social mechanisms, including marriage alliances, trade relations and warfare, to raise the rank of their respective local groups.

One of the best recorded examples of a local group with a "salmon-poor" resource base defending, maintaining, and, ultimately, advancing its rank through the use of social mechanisms was that of the Gispaxlo'ots and their leader, Ligeex. Marsden and Galois (1995) reconstructed the early contact period activities of

Ligeex in detail using Tsimshian oral traditions recorded early in the twentieth century and European documents from the nineteenth century. Late in the eighteenth century, the Gispaxlo'ots were one of the highest ranked Tsimshian local groups due, in part, to Ligeex's ancestral right to trade with the Gitksan of the upper Skeena River. This privilege was the result of a series of wars, peace settlements, and marriage alliances between the House of Niswamak, later to be called the House of Ligeex, and the leading Kitselas House of Nistaxho'ok. The Kitselas, as with all tribes, had the right to restrict travel through their territories, in this case through the canyon at Kitselas. They also originally enjoyed exclusive trading privileges with the "Gitluusek," the Gitksan local group that would later move upriver to become the Kitwanga. As a result of intensive efforts by the House of Niswamak over several generations, access through the canyon and a share in the trade with these Gitksan was granted to the Gispaxlo'ots. Later, after Ligeex became the head chief of this house, he extended the Gispaxlo'ots' privileges to include an exclusive trade alliance with the Gitksan further upriver. As a result of this consolidation of economic privileges by the House of Ligeex, the Gispaxlo'ots rose to prominence among all the Coast Tsimshian (Marsden 1987).

Arthur Wellington Clah's comment on Feb. 8, 1892, offers an indication of the duration of this process of consolidation:

> James Fisher put up village stone for 5 head chiefs named Legaics who die years ago. Some die many years before white man come and one last year, one buried Skeena River 200 years ago, that I not see, an old Legaic die 300 years, one Dr. Kennedy's father in law died Fort Simpson 52 years ago, 4 Legaics buried Fort Simpson, 1 in Metlakatla they mark how many Legaics buried in village stone – one stone to go on the island where Legaic died in water last year.

The rise of the Gispaxlo'ots to pre-eminence among the Coast Tsimshian thus took place over several centuries, beginning with the House of Niswamak, and continuing for at least 300 years with the House of Ligeex.

When European traders arrived in the Tsimshian area beginning in 1787, the first significant exchange commodity was sea otter pelts. Lacking sea otter hunting territories of their own, the Gispaxlo'ots were in danger of losing status to the Kitkatla and Ginakangeek, who benefited directly from their ownership of sea otter hunting grounds and protected anchorages from which European vessels conducted trade. Ligeex could not have anticipated this development, but he responded to the situation by quickly arranging marriages with the leading families of the Gitwilgiots and the Gilutsau, who were also principles in the sea otter trade. The former alliance gave the Gispaxlo'ots access to sea otter pelts through hunting grounds, and the latter granted them access to a principle European anchorage north of Metlakatla. Both alliances also gave Ligeex trading privileges with the Haida. These transactions allowed the Gispaxlo'ots to engage in the sea otter trade and maintain their relatively high status while other Tsimshian groups suffered losses in prestige.

By the first decade of the nineteenth century, sea otter populations were in decline due to overhunting, and trade with the Europeans began to focus on land-based furs such as beaver. Given his ancestral trading relations along the Skeena River with the interior Gitksan, Ligeex was in a favoured position as the interior-coast fur trade increased in importance. He acted decisively to consolidate Gispaxlo'ots trading rights. His Eagle clan relative, Sagawan, already controlled trade to the interior through the Portland Canal. Both Ligeex and Sagawan married into the leading family of the Nisga'a of the Nass River, creating a tripartite alliance which effectively controlled trade to the interior through three of the four major routes (Skeena River, Nass River, and Portland Canal). Only the Stikine River was beyond Ligeex's reach.

Marriage alliances were not the only means by which Ligeex maintained Gispaxlo'ots' rank. The threat of violence, launching raids, and at times engaging in outright warfare were all components of Ligeex's strategy. By 1821 the interior fur trade was in full stride and the Northwest Company began trading furs obtained from the Wet'suwet'en, the eastern neighbors of the Gitksan, east through interior routes. Ligeex and his Gitksan allies responded to this threat to their trade by sending an armed party of 30 men to visit the Wet'suwet'en to encourage them to trade through coastal routes. The threat of violence implicit in the visit seemed to have the desired effect for in the following years Wet'suwet'en furs moved west through the trade routes of the Gispaxlo'ots and their allies.

In a similar series of events, Hlit'ux, a Nisga'a chief from the lower Nass, challenged Ligeex's control of the Nass River trade by embarking on a trade journey directly to the Gitksan villages of Kitwancool, Kispiox, and Gitanmaks. Laden with goods Hlit'ux could not return to the Nass by overland routes and instead canoed down the Skeena. He was stopped at Kitselas by Ligeex's allies, and his goods were seized. In retaliation, Hlit'ux raided his Tsimshian rivals at their eulachon fishing sites on the lower Nass River the following year. The Gispaxlo'ots responded in kind and a simmering conflict of retributive raiding continued for many years. However, the brunt of Ligeex' wrath fell, not on Hlit'ux, but on the Gitksan with whom he traded. A force of Gispaxlo'ots warriors headed into Gitksan territory and attacked all the villages which had traded with Hlit'ux, burning them to the ground and capturing a large number of slaves. This large scale attack did not result in a war, probably because of the strength of the Gispaxlo'ots and their allies. When the attack force finally reached Gitanmaks, word of their arrival had preceded them and they found the village abandoned and the houses stripped of their walls and furnishings.

By the late 1820's, the Gispaxlo'ots enjoyed firm control of the land-based fur trade. The Hudson's Bay Company, recently amalgamated with the Northwest Company, increased its role in Tsimshian trade in 1831 when it constructed Fort Simpson, on the lower Nass River. Ligeex immediately made efforts to gain an upper hand in the fur trade with the fort. In the same year that Fort Simpson was built Ligeex's daughter, Sudaahl, married Dr. Kennedy, the Hudson's Bay Company's clerk and surgeon. This alliance conferred several benefits on the Gispaxlo'ots, including influence over where to relocate the fort. In 1834, the Hudson's Bay Company moved Fort Simpson from its original site to Lax Kw'alaams (McLoughlin's Harbour), territory owned by the Gispaxlo'ots. His marriage alliance with a prominent Fort Simpson employee gave Ligeex preferred access to the largest fur trader on the Northwest Coast, and the relocation of the trading post gave the Gispaxlo'ots rights to obligatory gifts from other Native traders visiting the fort.

In sum, what we know of Ligeex indicates that the fortunes of the Gispaklo'ots' rank correlated with economic factors, but that these factors were primarily a consequence of trade, strategic marriage alliances, and threat or actual use of violence. They had little, if anything, to do with salmon or other food resource production.

Another example of a chief using social mechanisms to advance local group rank was provided by Ts'basaa of the Kitkatla. As mentioned, Kitkatla fortunes rose at the beginning of the fur trade through their ownership of sea otter hunting grounds and favoured anchorages for European trading vessels. With the decline of the trade in sea otter pelts and the increase in trade of inland furs, the Kitkatla were placed at a disadvantage. Ts'basaa responded initially by establishing an alliance with the Kitimat of Douglas Channel and by cultivating trade relations with American traders. However, with the dominance of Ligeex and the rise of the Hudson's Bay Company, Ts'basaa lost ground and by the 1830's the Kitkatla were exploiting a new avenue to wealth and status, that of slave raiding. An account by Mitchell (1984) shows how Ts'basaa translated raiding into wealth and prestige. In 1837, Ts'basaa raided the Nawitti of northern Vancouver Island, returning with 20 slaves. Many of the slaves were traded to the Tlingit for furs which Ts'basaa took in the fall of that year to Fort Simpson where he traded the furs for European manufactured goods. The items were distributed by Ts'basaa at a feast he hosted a few months later. In five months, the Kitkatla had converted a successful slave raid into greater prestige and status.

CONCLUSIONS

The relationship between aspects of social organization and the resource base has been a major issue in Northwest Coast ethnology, and continues to be so in anthropological archaeology. Ecologically-oriented models for the Northwest Coast have strongly emphasized salmon abundance as a resource variable of primary importance in the determination of rank or social precedence. That position has most clearly been taken and most strongly supported by Donald and Mitchell (1975) in their study of Southern Kwakiutl local group rank, but it has also underlain several more general Northwest Coast models, including those of Fladmark (1975), Schalk (1977), and Matson (1983, 1992; Matson and Coupland 1995).

The present study has shown, however, that the results obtained by Donald and Mitchell in their Kwakiutl study do not hold for all Northwest Coast groups. In the case of the Tsimshian, salmon abundance had little effect on the determination of local group rank. The primary factor determining Tsimshian local group rank, at least during the early period of contact and interaction with Europeans, appears to have been human agency, specifically, the strategic use of social mechanisms by opportunistic individuals like Ligeex and Ts'basaa. In the case of Ligeex and the Gispaxlo'ots, high rank was achieved through trade, marriage, and warfare, despite or, perhaps, because of ownership of a salmon-poor territory. So successful was Ligeex in establishing and defending his prerogatives that by the middle of the nineteenth century he had become the "high chief" of the Tsimshian (Miller 1997:168-169). Ts'basaa and the Kitkatla had access to abundant salmon, although the dispersed distribution of salmon in their territory may have worked against large concentrations of labour and large catches of fish at any one location. In any event, Ts'basaa resorted not to intensified salmon fishing, but to slave-raiding in order to maintain a position of high rank for himself and his local group. By the middle of the nineteenth century only Ts'basaa rivaled Ligeex in prestige.

Among the Tsimshian, social ranking was a dynamic process, perhaps, made possible but not determined by resource abundance. Chiefs and their followers gained (and occasionally lost) status through opportunism, manipulation, and use of force, in short, through their own political actions. To paraphrase V. Gordon Childe, chiefs like Ligeex and Ts'basaa made themselves.

REFERENCES CITED

Allaire, L. (1984). A native mental map of Coast Tsimshian villages. In *The Tsimshian: Images of the Past; Views for the Present*, edited by M. Seguin, University of British Columbia Press, Vancouver, pp. 82-98.

Ames, K.M. (1994). The Northwest Coast: Complex hunter-gatherers, ecology, and social evolution. *Annual Review of Anthropology* 23:209-229.

Aro, K.V., and M.P. Shepard (1967). Pacific Salmon in Canada. Part IV, Salmon of the North Pacific Ocean: Spawning Populations of North Pacific Salmon. *International North Pacific Fisheries Commission Bulletin* 23. Vancouver.

Barbeau, M. (1917). Growth and Federation in the Tsimshian Phratries. In *Proceedings of the 19th International Congress of Americanists*, Washington, pp. 402-408.

Barbeau, M.C., and W. Beynon (n.d.). The Marius Barbeau and William Beynon Fieldnotes (1915-1956). Unpublished manuscript, Canadian Centre for Folk Culture Studies, Canadian Museum of Civilization, Hull.

Beynon, W. (n.d.). *The Beynon Manuscript*. Manuscripts from the Columbia University Library. University Microfilms International, Ann Arbor.

Boas, F. (1887). Census and reservations of the Kwakiutl Nation. *Bulletin of the American Geographical Society* 19 (3):225-232.

Boas, F. (1916). Tsimshian mythology. In *Thirty-first Annual Report of the Bureau of American Ethnology, 1909-1910*, U.S. Government Printing Office, Washington, pp. 29-1037.

Boas, F. (1925). *Contributions to the Ethnology of the Kwakiutl*. Columbia University Contributions to Anthropology 3. New York.

Childe, V.G. (1951). *Man Makes Himself*. New American Library, New York.

Clah, A.W. (n.d.). Journal of Arthur Wellington Clah, 1858-1909. Microfilm, Public Archives of Canada, Ottawa.

Codere, H. (1950). Fighting with Property; A Study of Kwakiutl Potlatching and Warfare 1792-1930. University of Washington Press, Seattle and London.

Coupland, G. (1988b). *Prehistoric Cultural Change at Kitselas Canyon*. Archaeological Survey of Canada Mercury Series Paper 138. Canadian Museum of Civilization, Hull.

Dean, J.R. (1994). "These Rascally Spackaloids." The Rise of Gispaxlots Hegemony at Fort Simpson, 1832-40. *BC Studies* 101:41-78.

Donald, L., and D.H. Mitchell (1975). Some Correlates of Local Group Rank Among the Southern Kwakiutl. *Ethnology* 14:325-346.

Drucker, P. (1955). *Indians of the Northwest Coast*. American Museum Science Books. The Natural History Press, New York.

Drucker, P. (1965). *Cultures of the North Pacific Coast*. Chandler Publishing Company, New York.

Drucker, P., and R.F. Heizer (1967). *To Make My Name Good: A Reexamination of the Southern Kwakiutl Potlatch*. University of California Press, Berkeley and Los Angeles.

Duff, W. (1964). *The Indian History of British Columbia, Volume 1: The Impact of the White Man*. Anthropology in British Columbia Memoir 5. Provincial Museum of British Columbia, Victoria.

Emmons, G.T. (1912). The Kitselas of British Columbia. *American Anthropologist* 14:467-471.

Fladmark, K.R. (1975). *A Paleoecological Model for Northwest Coast Prehistory*. Archaeological Survey of Canada Mercury Series Paper 43. Canadian Museum of Civilization, Hull.

Ford, C.S. (1941). *Smoke From Their Fires: The Life of a Kwakiutl Chief*. Yale University Press, New Haven.

Garfield, V.E. (1939). Tsimshian clan and society. *University of Washington Publications in Anthropology* 7 (3):167-340.

Garfield, V.E. (1951). The Tsimshian and their neighbours. In *The Tsimshian Indians and their Arts*, edited by V.E. Garfield and P.S. Wingert, Douglas & McIntyre, Vancouver, pp. 3-70.

Halpin, M.M. (1973). The Tsimshian Crest System: A Study Based on Museum Specimens and the Marius Barbeau and William Beynon Field Notes. Ph.D. Dissertation, Department of Anthropology, University of British Columbia, Vancouver.

Halpin, M.M., and M. Seguin (1990). Tsimshian peoples: Southern Tsimshian, Coast Tsimshian, Nishga, and Gitksan. In *Handbook of North American Indians, Vol. 7, Northwest Coast*, edited by W. Suttles, Smithsonian Institution, Washington, pp. 267-284.

Hodge, F.W. (1907). *Handbook of American Indians North of Mexico*. Bureau of American Ethnology Bulletin 30. Washington.

Inglis, R.I., and G.F. MacDonald (1979). Introduction. In *Skeena River Prehistory*, edited by G.F. MacDonald and R.I. Inglis, Archaeological Survey of Canada Mercury Series Paper 87, Canadian Museum of Civilization, Hull, pp. 1-17.

Kew, M. (1992). Salmon Availability, Technology, and Cultural Adaptation in the Fraser River Watershed. In *A Complex Culture of the British Columbia Plateau*, edited by B. Hayden, University of British Columbia Press, Vancouver, pp. 177-221.

MacDonald, G.F. (1979). Kitwanga Fort National Historic Site, Skeena River, British Columbia: Historical Research and Analysis of Structural Remains. Manuscript Report Series 341. Parks Canada, Calgary.

MacDonald, G.F. (1984). The epic of Nekt: The archaeology of metaphor. In *The Tsimshian: Images of the Past; Views for the Present*, edited by M. Sequin, University of British Columbia Press, Vancouver, pp. 65-81.

MacDonald, G.F., G. Coupland, and D.J.W. Archer (1987). The Coast Tsimshian ca. 1750. In *The Historical Atlas of Canada*, edited by C. Harris, University of Toronto Press, Toronto, pp. 32-33.

MacDonald, G.F., and J. Cove, eds. (1987). *Tsimshian Narratives: Volume 2, Trade and Warfare*. Canadian Museum of Civilization, Hull.

Marsden, S. (1987). An historical and cultural overview of the Gitksan. Delgamuuk v. the Queen, Vol. 1 and 2. *Exhibit*:1051-1053.

Marsden, S., and R. Galois (1995). The Tsimshian, the Hudson's Bay Company, and the geopolitics of the Northwest Coast fur trade, 1787-1840. *The Canadian Geographer* 39:169-183.

Matson, R.G. (1983). Intensification and the development of cultural complexity: the northwest versus the northeast coast. In *The Evolution of Maritime Cultures on the Northeast and Northwest Coasts of America*, edited by R.J. Nash, Simon Fraser University Department of Archaeology Publication 11, Burnaby, pp. 125-148.

Matson, R.G. (1992). The evolution of Northwest Coast subsistence. In *Long Term Subsistence Change in Prehistoric North America*, edited by D.R. Croes, R. Hawkins, and B.L. Isaac, Research in Economic Anthropology, Supplement 6, JAI Press Inc., Greenwich, pp. 367-428.

Matson, R.G., and G. Coupland (1995). *The Prehistory of the Northwest Coast*. Academic Press, San Diego and London.

Miller, J. (1997). *Tsimshian Culture: A Light Through the Ages*. University of Nebraska Press, Lincoln.

Miller, J., and C.M. Eastman, eds. (1984). *The Tsimshian and Their Neighbors of the North Pacific Coast*. University of Washington Press, Seattle and London.

Mitchell, D.H. (1984). Predatory warfare, social status, and the North Pacific slave trade. *Ethnology* 23 (1):39-48.

Monks, G. (1987). Prey as bait: The Deep Bay example. *Canadian Journal of Archaeology* 11:119-142.

Nolan, R. (1977). The Utilization of Fish Resources by the Coast Tsimshian: Predicting Optimal Patterns of Exploitation. M.A. Thesis, Department of Department of Anthropology, Trent University, Peterborough.

Orans, M. (1975). Domesticating the functional dragon: An analysis of Piddocke's potlatch. *American Anthropologist* 77:312-328.

Piddocke, S. (1965). The potlatch system of the Southern Kwakiutl: A new perspective. *Southwestern Journal of Anthropology* 21:244-264.

Prince, P. (1998). Settlement, Trade, and Social Ranking at Kitwanga. Ph.D. Dissertation, Department of Anthropology, McMaster University, Hamilton.

Rosman, A., and P.G. Rubel (1971). *Feasting with Mine Enemy: Rank and Exchange Among Northwest Coast Societies*. Waveland Press Inc., Prospect Heights.

Rostlund, E. (1952). *Freshwater Fish and Fishing in Native North America*. University of California Publications in Geography 9. Berkeley.

Schalk, R. (1977). The structure of an anadromous fish resource. In *For Theory Building in Archaeology*, edited by L. Binford, Academic Press, New York, pp. 207-249.

Schalk, R. (1981). Land use and organizational complexity among foragers of northwestern North America. In *Affluent Foragers*, edited by S. Koyama and D.H. Thomas, Senri Ethnological Studies 9, National Museum of Ethnology, Osaka, pp. 53-75.

Schoolcraft, H.R. (1857). Historical and Statistical Information Respecting the History, Condition and Prospects of the Indian Tribes of the United States. Lippincott, Philadelphia.

Seguin, M. (1984). Introduction. In *The Tsimshian: Images of the Past; Views for the Present*, edited by M. Seguin, University of British Columbia Press, Vancouver, pp. ix-xx.

Sneed, P. (1971). Of salmon and men: An investigation of ecological determinants and aboriginal man in the Canadian Plateau. In *Aboriginal Man and Environments on the Plateau of Northwest America*, edited by A. Stryd and R. Smith, University of Calgary Archaeological Association, Calgary, pp. 229-242.

Suttles, W. (1960). Affinal ties, subsistence, and prestige among the Coast Salish. *American Anthropologist* 62:296-305.

Suttles, W. (1962). Variation in habitat and culture on the Northwest Coast. In *Proceedings of the 34th International Congress of Americanists, 1960*, Vienna, pp. 522-537.

Suttles, W. (1968). Coping with abundance: subsistence on the Northwest Coast. In *Man the Hunter*, edited by R.B. Lee and I. Devore, Aldine, Chicago, pp. 56-68.

Tolmie, W.F. (1963). The Journals of William Fraser Tolmie, Physician and Fur Trader. Mitchell Press Ltd., Vancouver.

Vayda, A.P. (1961). A re-examination of Northwest Coast economic systems. *Transactions of the New York Academy of Sciences* 23:616-624.

Artifact Distributions at the Kitwanga Hill Fort: Protohistoric Competition and Trade on the Upper Skeena

Paul Prince

ABSTRACT

This paper examines the distribution of artifacts at Kitwanga Hill Fort for signs of spatial differentiation related to aboriginal control of trade and social inequity. Excavations by George MacDonald identified two components: an early historic or protohistoric period component (ca. A.D. 1750-1830) with five plank houses, and an earlier component which I interpret here as initial protohistoric. My analysis of the collection found European trade goods to be unequally distributed among the later component houses, with the house having the greatest number of trade goods also having significant within-house differentiation. In the earlier component, indigenous items far outnumber European goods in all parts of the site. I argue here that the Northwest Coast system of social differentiation and control of trade became clearly marked as the volume of trade and competition increased.

RÉSUMÉ

Cet article examine la distribution des objets au fort de Kitwanga Hill en vue de déceler des signes de différenciation spatiale reliée au contrôle aborigène du commerce et de l'inégalité sociale. Les fouilles faites par George McDonald ont identifié deux couches composantes: une composante remontant au début de la période historique ou protohistorique (vers 1750-1830) comportant cinq maisons de planches, et une composante antérieure que j'interprète ici comme le début de la période protohistorique. Mon analyse de la collection

In *Perspectives on Northern Northwest Coast Prehistory*, edited by Jerome S. Cybulski. Hull: Canadian Museum of Civilization, Archaeological Survey of Canada, Mercury Series Paper 160, pp. 249-268, © 2001.

a révélé que les biens de commerce européens étaient inégalement distribués parmi les maisons des composantes plus récentes , alors que les maisons qui avaient le plus grand nombre de biens de commerce comportaient aussi une variation significative de ces objets à l'intérieur. Dans les composantes plus anciennes, les biens indigènes dépassaient de loin le nombre de biens de commerce européens partout dans le site. À mon avis, le système de différenciation sociale et le contrôle du commerce sur le Côte Nord-Ouest se sont imposés avec l'accroissement du volume du commerce et de la compétition.

INTRODUCTION

The Kitwanga Hill Fort figures prominently in aboriginal oral traditions of trade, warfare and social competition during the period of indirect contact with Europeans (MacDonald and Cove 1987). Based on these traditions and architectural characteristics of the fort revealed by his excavations, George MacDonald (1984, 1989) constructed a model of intense intergroup competition in the Skeena River region for access to European trade during the protohistoric period with disruptions in ethnic boundaries and the balance of power and wealth. Other researchers have credited competition for European trade in the protohistoric period with contributing to the spread or elaboration of the Coast Tsimshian system of managing wealth and resources up the Skeena to the Carrier (Steward 1955; Kobrinsky 1977; Bishop 1983, 1987) and Gitksan (Ames 1979a). In this paper, I outline the spatial implications of the competition models for the development of the Northwest Coast system of displaying and restricting access to exotic items and present original analysis of the Kitwanga artifact distributions in this context.

THE DEVELOPMENT OF NORTHWEST COAST CULTURE ON THE SKEENA

REGIONAL AND CULTURAL CONTEXT

The Kitwanga Hill Fort is situated on the Kitwanga River, 5 km from its confluence with the Skeena River. This is the territory of the Gitwangak division of the Gitksan. The Gitksan are a Tsimshian group whose historic territory includes the upper Skeena River valley (above Kitselas Canyon) and much of its tributary drainage system along with a large portion of the upper Nass River system (Fig. 1). Ethnographically, the Gitksan followed a river oriented version of the Northwest Coast culture pattern (Halpin and Seguin 1990). The Northwest Coast culture pattern is typified by a high degree of sedentism with multiple family households, split plank dwellings and permanent villages; a hunting-fishing-gathering economy with an emphasis on stored salmon; hereditary positions of status with resource ownership and marked differences in wealth; ritualized exchange and elaborate crest art and mythology (Matson and Coupland 1995:6). The origins of this culture pattern, particularly the social inequities in power, privilege and wealth between ranked classes, is of fundamental importance to northern Northwest Coast and Skeena River prehistory (MacDonald and Inglis 1981:37; Coupland 1988a:211, 1993; Maschner 1991). However, its prehistoric roots on the upper Skeena remain poorly known.

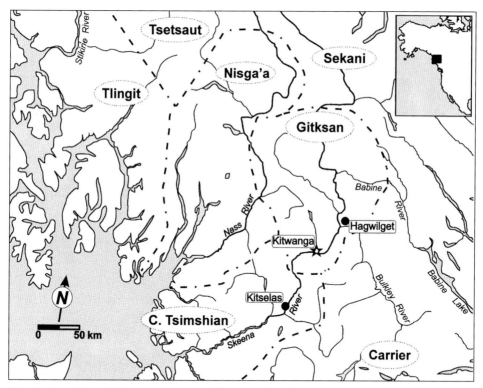

Fig. 1. *Location of Kitwanga Fort and historic Tsimshian territories (adapted from MacDonald and Cove 1987).*

Down river at Kitselas Canyon, excavations have indicated occupation as early as 3000 B.C. (Coupland 1988a, 1988b). Coupland argues that Kitselas Canyon was used seasonally by people who wintered on the coast until 1200 B.C., when a permanent village was established as indicated by two rows of rectangular house depressions at the Paul Mason site, GdTc-16. Sedentism at Kitselas is hypothesized by Coupland (1988a:237) to have been made possible by the development of intensive salmon procurement and storage technologies, motivated by a desire for emergent corporate groups to ensure access to nearby salmon resources. In his model, social differentiation then evolved in situ between 500 B.C. and A.D. 500 (the Kleanza Phase) as a consequence of the differential productivity of corporate group territories, and competition, in the form of trade and warfare between aspiring elites over labour and resources, which increased their prestige, wealth and following, and validated and created further inequities (Coupland 1988a:239). An earlier model put forth by Allaire (1979) suggests that cultural complexity was introduced to Kitselas Canyon through acculturation of an interior population by the Coast Tsimshian. Neither Allaire nor Coupland presents direct evidence for prehistoric ranked society at Kitselas. Instead, social inequity is argued for the Kleanza Phase based on the presence of items such as labrets, slate mirrors and daggers which, by ethnographic analogy, may have signified personal status, and by broad similarities to the contemporaneous phases at Prince Rupert Harbour (Coupland 1988a:225-229).

After A.D. 500 there is a gap in known occupations at Kitselas until the eighteenth and nineteenth centuries when a fortress (Gitlaxdzawk, GdTc-1) and village (Gitsaex, GdTc-3) were situated at the canyon (Coupland 1988b:241). These two communities are more convincingly demonstrated, based on substantial differences in house floor size and associated storage capacity, to have had ranked social organization (Coupland 1988a:232-233; Maschner 1991:929). The Northwest Coast pattern of social differentiation is thus clearly in evidence at Kitselas 300 years ago and, probably, as early as 1500 years ago.

In the upper portion of the Skeena drainage, the most substantial excavated prehistoric site is GhSv-2 at Hagwilget Canyon on the Bulkley River near its confluence with the Skeena. Excavations by Ames (1979b) identified three components: Zone A, a multi-purpose occupation layer with an imprecisely provenienced radiocarbon date of 1500 B.C.; Zone B, which represents a long period of limited use as a fishing site; and Zone C, which represents the post A.D. 1820 Wet'suweten occupation of the site. Ames (1979b) and Allaire (1979) noted similarities in the assemblage of Hagwilget Zone A and the Skeena Phase (1600-1200 B.C.) at Kitselas, and suggested an interior population may have migrated down river to Kitselas at this time. Coupland (1988b:125-126), however, interprets the Skeena phase at both sites as representing summer-fall "base camps," although he does not indicate why they would leave either canyon in winter, or where the Hagwilget population would go. Zone A at GhSv-2 did include storage pits, hearths, fish and animal remains, and a diverse lithic assemblage (Ames 1979b) and could just as easily be interpreted as a year round occupation. In the absence of detailed faunal analysis, any interpretation of seasonality at Hagwilget remains equivocal.

Other excavated prehistoric components on the upper Skeena have not been as well defined but do not seem to represent major settlements. A cache of war clubs collected from Hagwilget Canyon in the nineteenth century has been loosely dated to A.D. 1 based on stylistic similarity to excavated examples from Prince Rupert Harbour, and has been taken as evidence for the existence of the North Coast pattern of warfare and exchange between chieftains on the upper Skeena (Coupland 1989:208; MacDonald 1987:viii; Duff 1963). However, this assertion cannot be supported by reference to firm evidence of other aspects of the developed Northwest Coast pattern.

PROTOHISTORIC COMPETITION AND RANKING

Various models account for the development of social ranking in the Skeena drainage above Kitselas Canyon as a factor of intertribal borrowing, including intermarriage and incorporation, and (or) population movement and territorial expansion, either initiated or accelerated by participation in trade in European goods originating along the peripheries of the region in the eighteenth and nineteenth centuries. Russians explored the coast of Alaska at least as early as the 1740's and had established a fur trade with native links to the south by the 1760's (MacDonald 1989:24). Western Europeans and Americans were trading from ships all along the Northwest Coast from the 1770's to 1820's (Fisher 1977). Several land based posts were established in the hinterland of the Skeena headwaters between 1806 and 1826 including Fort St. James, Fort Kilmaurs, and Fort Connelly, while Fort Simpson was established on the coast in 1831 (MacDonald 1989:21-26; Halpin and Seguin 1990:281). In the early stages of the fur trade, and even after interior posts were established, the coast operated as the main source of exotic new European goods, and the interior as a source of furs, with coastal Native middlemen trading between the two (Ray n.d.). This phase of indirect contact on the Skeena defines the protohistoric period from A.D. 1700-1830.

According to MacDonald (1989:17, 1987:vii), trade between the interior and coast along the Skeena corridor extends back some 5000 years as indicated by Mt. Edziza obsidian at Prince Rupert Harbour, and an elaborate network of trade corridors (eulachon grease trails) was well established 2000 years ago. The advent of trade in European goods for furs along these corridors in the protohistoric period has been argued to have heightened interaction between coastal chiefs and interior Athapaskan big men, bringing new wealth and prestige to the interior, and stimulating the adoption of the Northwest Coast system of managing resource territories and wealth by means of formalized hereditary statuses (Steward 1955; Kobrinsky 1979; Rubel and Rosman 1983; Bishop 1983, 1987).

Adams (1973) and Ames (1979b) have suggested that a process of intertribal acculturation also influenced the development of ranked society in Gitksan territory. In this model, population and resource pressure caused groups of Tsimshian to expand upriver into new territories, incorporating some small local groups into their lineages to maintain optimal sizes and rubbing off onto others through borrowing. According to Ames (1979b:236), this process of "Tsimshianization" was not complete before being accelerated by competition for European trade goods in the eighteenth and nineteenth centuries, which provided upriver populations with the wealth to adopt the Northwest Coast system directly.

MacDonald (1984, 1989) has argued that this competition during the protohistoric period caused wide scale change in terms of ethnic boundaries and warfare over control of trade but he does not go so far as to suggest it introduced cultural complexity to the Skeena. In MacDonald's view, a complex network of intertribal trade, warfare and ranked societies was in place on the North Coast and Skeena more than 2000 years ago and remained "relatively stable" until the early 1700's (MacDonald 1984:79; 1987:viii). MacDonald (1984) feels that the new and rare European items introduced, especially guns, quickly disrupted indigenous patterns of power and exchange. In particular, trade routes that connected the upper Skeena and interior to the upper Nass and thence to Alaska and Russian trade became highly prized. MacDonald (1984:78) feels that this led to efforts to control access to trade routes and exacted tribute on the part of emerging warrior chiefs with the most important routes becoming controlled by Native fortresses such as Kitwanga, the base of an ambitious chief named Nekt. MacDonald also proposes that territorial expansion and population movement occurred in the early 1700's, with the Coast Tsimshian displacing the Tlingit from the mouths of the Nass and Skeena and the Gitksan displacing Athapaskans from the upper Nass and Skeena to attain greater access to Alaskan trade routes (MacDonald 1984:79-80).

MacDonald's model thus describes an increase in the fortunes and power of interior chiefs and a geographic spread of territories, and implies an increase in societal complexity.

SETTLEMENT PATTERN CORRELATES OF COMPETITION MODEL

The above models of a social ranking system gradually spreading up the Skeena until being accelerated or heightened by European trade have been constructed mainly from oral traditions (MacDonald 1984:78), sketchy historical documentation (Steward 1955; Bishop 1987), the distribution of ethnographic traits (Rubel and Rosman 1983; Kobrinsky 1977), ecological modeling (Ames 1979a), and by analogy with the archaeology of Prince Rupert Harbour (Bishop 1987; MacDonald 1987). Yet, each reconstruction implies a significant re-ordering of social and settlement systems over time which I felt should be reflected in the regional and community settlement pattern.

Much of the upper Skeena valley and many of its tributaries have been surveyed by cultural resource management and research projects (e.g., Ames 1971, Acheson 1977, Montgomery 1981, Carlson and Bussey 1990, Albright 1987). Attempts at synthesis and interpretation of the resultant data are just beginning (Prince 1995). Distribution analysis of archaeological sites registered with the British Columbia Archaeology Branch in the Skeena and Nass River drainages indicates a significant scarcity of prehistoric villages above Kitselas Canyon (n=2), while the post-contact settlement pattern shows a dramatic increase in the number of villages (n=12), many with defensive features, and a tendency to be situated near the junctions of trade routes (Prince 1995). I conducted a survey of the Kitwanga River valley (a major trade artery) to test the apparent shift in settlement and its association with European trade (Prince 1996). Only one new habitation site was found, a group of four circular pit houses, GiTa-2, one of which was radiocarbon dated to 220 ± 90 B.P., with a two sigma calibrated range of A.D. 1470-1950 (Beta-88442). This site could thus fall within a very broad range of time, but is clearly of a different architectural tradition than the historic Gitksan plank houses and may have a different ethnic affiliation. Oral traditions of the Gitksan recount conflicts in the fur trade era with the Athapaskan Tsetsaut who had semi-subterranean houses (MacDonald and Cove 1987:25; Barbeau 1929:60-63). I contend that these data indicate a relatively recent expression of the Northwest Coast traits of permanent plank house villages, conflict, and control of trade in the upper Skeena region.

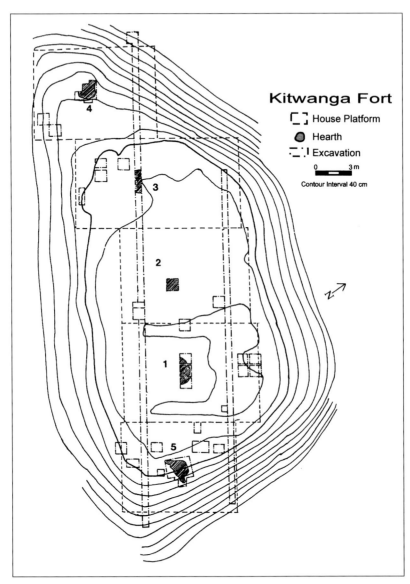

Fig. 2. Plan of Kitwanga Fort and excavations (after MacDonald 1989).

Artifact distributions at the Kitwanga Hill Fort are examined here for evidence of protohistoric social competition at a local level in terms of inequities in wealth and access to exotics between and within households. Although MacDonald presents his argument for protohistoric competition in two publications which describe his excavations at the Kitwanga Hill Fort (MacDonald 1984, 1989), he leaves his ethnohistoric model and the archaeological record largely unarticulated. My rationale for conducting spatial analysis at Kitwanga is that the ethnographic Gitksan organized space in their houses and villages according to social rank, and the fort is situated at a critical location on the trade routes and may be expected to preserve a material record of the processes operating in protohistory.

The basic social-economic unit of the ethnographic Gitksan was a matrilineal household ("house") whose members ideally occupied a multiple family dwelling (Cove 1982:6; Halpin and Sequin 1990:274). Within a village, houses were often of differing rank and situated relative to one another accordingly (Duff 1959:13). Space within houses was also allocated according to rank with the chief's family at the rear of the house and the lowest ranking family at the front (Duff 1959:37).

Trade in both prehistoric and historic contexts has been interpreted as an important source of exotic items used by elites to validate and display their status (Ferguson 1983; Bishop 1987; Coupland 1988). Further, the wealth and potential military advantage of European trade goods is argued by MacDonald (1984:80) to be the main impetus for competition between emerging elites in the protohistoric period. Both the ethnographic pattern and the protohistoric competition model have spatial implications that are testable archaeologically. If control of trade was a prerogative of the elite, and space within villages and houses was arranged along the lines described in the ethnographies, then the distribution of European trade goods within and between houses at Kitwanga may be a fair measure of social inequity and competition. Further, it might be expected that differentiation would become more marked over time.

KITWANGA EXCAVATIONS AND COMPONENTS

Kitwanga Fort is situated atop an isolated, steep sided hill on the lower Kitwanga River. In 1979, George MacDonald conducted excavations on behalf of Parks Canada to aid in interpretation and management of the site. Surface contours indicated three rectangular house platforms on top of the hill (Fig. 2). Trenching revealed two additional houses, one at either end of the hill, which were likely partially supported on stilts (MacDonald 1989:743). Construction of these two houses (Houses 4 and 5) probably occurred after the other three and had to accommodate constraints of limited space (MacDonald 1989:67).

Table 1. *Frequencies of artifacts per house*

	House 1		House 2		House 3		House 4		House 5	
Category	Levels 1-4	Levels 5-14	Levels 1-4	Levels 5-12	Levels 1-4	Levels 5-9	Levels 1-4	Levels 5-12	Levels 1-4	Level 5
Manufactured European Items:										
Beads	95	10	5	5	16	2	3	2	1	—
Pistol barrel	—	—	—	—	—	—	—	—	1	—
Gunflints	1	1	—	—	—	1	2	—	—	—
Brass key	1	—	—	—	—	—	—	—	—	—
Adze	—	—	1	—	—	—	—	—	—	—
Mirror glass	1	—	—	—	—	—	—	—	—	—
Undiagnostic G1	3	2	—	—	—	—	—	—	1	—
Iron pot	—	—	—	1	—	—	—	—	—	—
Subtotal	*101*	*13*	*6*	*6*	*16*	*3*	*5*	*2*	*3*	*0*
Modified European Items:										
Knife blade	—	—	—	—	2	—	—	—	—	—
Dagger	—	—	—	—	—	—	—	—	1	—
Leister prong	—	—	1	—	—	—	—	—	—	—
Perforated thimble	—	—	1	—	—	—	—	—	—	—
Nose ring	—	1	—	—	—	—	—	—	—	—
Copper tubes	3	1	—	1	—	—	—	—	—	—
Copper band	—	—	—	—	1	—	—	—	—	—
Copper wires	2	—	—	—	—	—	—	—	—	—
Copper rivet	1	—	—	—	—	—	—	—	—	—
Iron wires	3	1	1	—	1	—	—	—	—	—
Folded iron	—	2	—	—	—	—	—	—	—	—
Unidentified iron	2	1	—	—	—	—	—	—	—	—
Subtotal	*11*	*6*	*3*	*1*	*4*	*0*	*0*	*0*	*1*	*0*
Native Items:										
Abraders	8	1	2	—	1	4	—	—	—	—
Hammerstones	2	1	—	—	—	2	—	1	—	—
Cobble choppers	1	—	1	—	—	—	—	—	—	—
Cobble cores	—	2	—	1	—	—	—	—	—	—
Cobble spalls	5	6	3	3	6	5	4	—	1	—
Projectile points	—	3	—	—	—	—	—	—	—	—
Retouched flakes	—	—	1	—	—	—	1	—	—	—
Flakes	6	61	3	17	10	15	8	1	1	1
Bone harpoon	1	—	—	—	—	—	—	—	—	—
Rib spatulate	—	—	—	—	—	1	—	—	—	—
Unidentified bone	—	—	—	—	—	1	—	—	—	—
Ground shell	1	—	1	—	—	1	—	—	—	—
Ochre nodules	7	3	1	1	5	—	1	—	—	—
Subtotal	*31*	*77*	*12*	*22*	*22*	*29*	*14*	*2*	*2*	*1*
Grand total	*143*	*96*	*21*	*29*	*42*	*32*	*19*	*4*	*6*	*1*

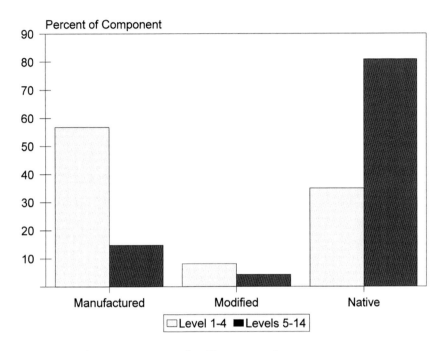

Fig. 3. Percentage of artifact categories per component.

In addition to the trenches, test units were placed within each of the houses to define their internal structure. The houses were not evenly sampled. The area of excavation in House 1 was 17.25 m²; in House 2, 12 m²; in House 3, 10.25 m²; in House 4, 11 m²; and in House 5, 18.25 m². Nor was the depth of excavation equal in all units. Excavations were conducted in 5 cm arbitrary levels. The trenches were excavated to sterile glacial soil deposits at a fairly uniform depth of 1 m below surface; while most test units were limited in depth to artifact bearing levels. The lowest artifact bearing level excavated in each house was as follows: House 1, level 14; House 2, level 12; House 3, level 9; House 4, level 12; and House 5, level 5. Because the area and volume of excavation varies between excavation units and houses, artifact frequencies have been converted to percentages for most of the spatial comparisons presented below and statistical tests were run to determine the strength of observed patterns.

Architectural features, including hearths, occur about 20 cm below surface, indicating that the house floors belong with levels 1-4. Site stratigraphy does not provide any clear indications of substantial architecture earlier than level 4. The artifact assemblage from levels 1-4 is comprised mainly of items of European manufacture, followed by indigenous stone and bone artifacts and reworked trade metals (Table 1, Fig. 3). Diagnostic trade goods range in date of manufacture from 1750-1850. These dates and the proportions of European, modified European, and indigenous artifacts are characteristic of the protohistoric or early historic period.

Artifacts occurring below level 4 include European items and modified European materials, although indigenous materials are the majority. The relatively small quantities of European materials suggests this represents the initial phase of the protohistoric period.

MacDonald (1984:73, 1989:67) cautioned that many of the features associated with the houses intrude into lower levels and that landscaping may have occurred during construction, such that the early component may be a mixture of late prehistoric and contact period material. In his view the stone tool industry, particularly in the vicinity of House 1 below a charcoal lens, represents a prehistoric occupation dating A.D. 1550-1650 (MacDonald 1984:73, 1989:68-70). However, it has been demonstrated in several cultural contexts that the introduction of metals does not lead immediately to the extinguishment of stone tool technology (Bradley 1987; Rogers 1990; Prince 1992) and none of the lithics at Kitwanga are very temporally sensitive. In addition, a chi square test of the proportions of European, modified European, and Native artifacts in levels 1-4 and level 5 and below indicates the pattern shown in Figure 3 is non-random (X^2=81.7, phi=0.21, $p < 0.001$). Further, the distribution between the two components of small artifacts (flakes and beads) which could be expected to be affected equally by admixture is even more non-random (X^2=107.4, $p < 0.001$, phi=0.4). Therefore, for the purposes of the following analysis, I treated levels 1-4 and levels 5-14 as separate components of the protohistoric period and then examined the horizontal distribution of artifacts within each component.

LATE COMPONENT INTER-HOUSE COMPARISONS

The proportions of European trade goods (a combined category of modified and unmodified items) to indigenous artifacts in levels 1-4 of each house were compared to determine if there were inequities in their spatial and, by extension, social distribution. The House 5 assemblage is extremely small and statistically random. Although the sample sizes are uneven, the artifact distributions in Houses 1-4 are statistically non-random, with a high overall probability of significance (X^2 =33.7, $p < 0.001$, phi=0.15). House 1 stands out with a high ratio of European to Native artifacts, while Houses 2 and 3 have slight majorities of Native artifacts, and House 4 has a predominance of Native material (Fig. 4).

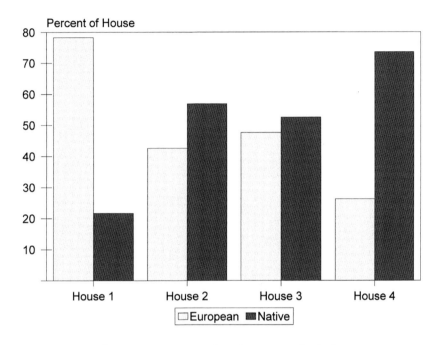

Fig. 4. Inter-house comparisons of artifact categories in late component.

My impression is that House 1 had greater access to trade goods than the other houses and was, perhaps, of highest rank, while House 4 had limited access and low status. The high status of House 1 is also suggested by its architecture, which includes a central depression and raised area around two sides and the rear (Fig. 2). These features in historic Tsimshian contexts are associated with the houses of lineage heads (Halpin and Seguin 1990:271). This house was interpreted by MacDonald (1989:75), with the aid of Gitwangak informants, to be the home of Chief Nekt.

LATE COMPONENT INTRA-HOUSE COMPARISONS

MacDonald's excavation also tested various portions of the house interiors (Fig. 2). In the present study excavation units were grouped into front, middle and rear for each house, and within house comparisons of artifact distributions were made for evidence of differentiation that may be related to household inequities. The distributions of European and Native artifacts within Houses 2, 4 and 5 have high probabilities of statistical randomness, probably due to the extremely small sample sizes produced when these house assemblages were divided by area. The distributions in Houses 1 and 3 have low probabilities of randomness, although less confidence can be placed in House 3 (Fig. 5). The within-house artifact distributions of House 1 has a X^2 of 24.7, probability of randomness of < 0.001, and phi of 0.17; while House 3's distribution has a X^2 of 4.9, p=0.08, and phi =0.12. House 1 shows a predominance of European over Native goods in its middle and rear, and the reverse trend in the front. In House 3, the middle area has a predominance of European over indigenous artifacts, while the front and rear show the reverse trend. The trend in the rear of House 3 may be exaggerated by the relatively small amount of excavation in that area.

In both Houses 1 and 3, some degree of control of trade items and social inequity between house members may have been in operation. This is much more strongly suggested with greater statistical confidence for House 1 which closely approximates the ethnographic model of chiefs, in this case Nekt, occupying the house rear.

EARLY COMPONENT HORIZONTAL DISTRIBUTIONS

In the earlier component, there are no clear indications of substantial architecture. For purposes of horizontal comparisons in this component, I treated the later house locations as arbitrary spatial units. The distribution of artifacts indicates that activity was concentrated in the areas occupied later by Houses 1, 2 and 3 (Table 1). In each of these three areas, Native artifacts are by far the majority (Fig. 6). No strong differentiation is evident, but the distribution of artifact categories between the three house platforms has a 28 percent chance of randomness (X^2=2.5, phi=0.016, p=0.28). While this statistical association is weak, I would argue that the pattern shown in Figure 6 is strong enough to indicate that there was no area of concentration for exotic materials during the early phase of occupation, and that such a homogenous distribution is unlikely to simply result from later disturbance.

Given that substantial architecture is not clearly defined and was, perhaps, not present in the early component, within-house comparisons are not possible.

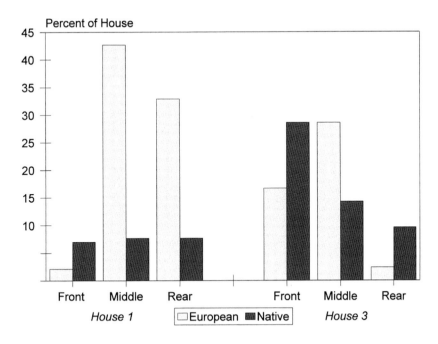

Fig. 5. Distribution of artifact categories within Houses 1 and 3.

DISCUSSION

Based on the above distribution analyses, I argue there are strong indications of unequal access to European trade goods between houses in the late component. The house identified as belonging to Chief Nekt (House 1) has the highest proportion of trade goods, perhaps reflecting his control of this resource and high status for his house. This and one other house (House 3), also have significant within-house differences in the distribution of trade goods, suggesting unequal access to exotics between household members. These patterns conform to both ethnographic expectations of spatial organization and models of competition between elites for control of European goods during the protohistoric period.

In the early component, the spatial distribution of European and indigenous goods across the site is undifferentiated. While sample sizes in this component are small and the pattern of distribution is not statistically strong, the homogenous distribution of European goods stands in dramatic contrast to the late component and is not likely the result of random disturbance. What European goods were brought to the site during this phase of occupation may have been evenly distributed between community members, although unequivocal evidence for the locations of social groups (houses) is lacking. What can be said with confidence is that the strict restrictions on access to European goods operating in the late protohistoric period are not in evidence in the initial protohistoric period. A comparison of artifact distributions between the two components shows a marked increase in spatial differentiation over time which may have been related to an increase in social differentiation.

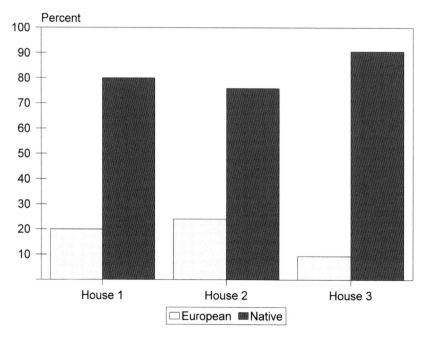

Fig. 6. Horizontal distribution of artifact categories in early component.

The greatest difference between the components is in intensity of occupation. The late component consists of five relatively large multiple family dwellings with abundant storage features, squeezed into a small, probably palisaded area. The early component has refuse and storage features, but was much less intense. The attraction of the hill in both phases of occupation was probably defense and trade but these seem to have been much more important in the late component. The sudden shift in the importance of the fort, accompanied by the appearance of marked spatial differentiation in the distribution of trade goods within the settlement, and an increase in the number of villages in the upper Skeena region at about the same time, all conform to the model of European trade contributing to the expansion of social competition.

CONCLUSION

As is proposed for the prehistoric north coast and lower Skeena (Coupland 1988a; MacDonald 1987), warfare, extensive trade and social ranking on the upper Skeena are surely related during the protohistoric period; but there is no evidence that they gradually evolved as a consequence of the prior development of resource control and multiple family corporate groups. Admittedly, the prehistory of the upper Skeena is sketchy. Salmon fishing and intensive settlement are in evidence 3500 years ago at Hagwilget Canyon, with warfare perhaps 2000 years ago. But it is not until 1700 years later that the whole suite of Northwest Coast traits appears suddenly and widespread throughout the upper Skeena as a seeming result of historical regional and extra-regional factors.

REFERENCES CITED

Acheson, S. (1977). Heritage Resource Impact Statement: Test Excavations at GgSw 5, Kitseguecla/Skeena Crossing. Unpublished manuscript, Resource Information Centre, Heritage Conservation Branch, Government of British Columbia, Victoria.

Adams, J.W. (1973). *The Gitksan Potlatch: Population Flux, Resource Ownership and Reciprocity*. Holt, Rinehart and Winston, Toronto.

Albright, S. (1987). Report on 1985 Archaeological Investigations of Gitksan-Wet'suweten Villages. Unpublished manuscript, Git-Wet Tribal Council, Hazelton.

Allaire, L. (1979). The cultural sequence at Gitaus: A case of prehistoric acculturation. In *Skeena River Prehistory*, edited by G.F. MacDonald and R.I. Inglis, Archaeological Survey of Canada Mercury Series Paper 87, Canadian Museum of Civilization, Hull, pp. 18-52.

Ames, K.M. (1971). Site Survey of the Middle Skeena Valley. Unpublished manuscript, Resource Information Centre, Heritage Conservation Branch, Government of British Columbia, Victoria.

Ames, K.M. (1979a). Stable and resilient systems along the Skeena River: The Gitksan Carrier boundary. In *Skeena River Prehistory*, edited by G.F. MacDonald and R.I. Inglis, Archaeological Survey of Canada Mercury Series Paper 87, Canadian Museum of Civilization, Hull, pp. 219-243.

Ames, K.M. (1979b). Report of Excavations at GhSv 2, Hagwilget Canyon. In *Skeena River Prehistory*, edited by G.F. MacDonald and R.I. Inglis, Archaeological Survey of Canada Mercury Series Paper 87, Canadian Museum of Civilization, Hull, pp. 181-218.

Barbeau, M. (1929). Totem Poles of the Gitksan, Upper Skeena River, British Columbia. *National Museum of Canada Bulletin* 61.

Bishop, C. (1983). Limiting access to limited goods: The origins of stratification in interior British Columbia. In *The Development of Political Organization in Native North America*, edited by E. Tooker, Proceedings of the American Ethnological Society, 1979, Washington, pp. 148-164.

Bishop, C. (1987). Coast-Interior exchange: The origins of stratification in northwestern North America. *Arctic Anthropology* 24:72-83.

Bradley, J. (1987). *The Evolution of the Onondaga Iroquois; Accommodating Change 1500-1655*. Syracuse University Press, Syracuse.

Carlson, A., and J. Bussey (1990). Archaeological Inventory and Impact Assessment, Bulkley River Lower Hagwilget Canyon. Unpublished manuscript (Permit 1989-102), Resource Information Centre, Heritage Conservation Branch, Government of British Columbia, Victoria.

Coupland, G. (1988a). Prehistoric economic and social change in the Tsimshian area. In *Prehistoric Economies of the Pacific Northwest Coast*, edited by B.J. Isaac, Research in Economic Anthropology, Supplement 3, JAI Press, Greenwich, pp. 211-243.

Coupland, G. (1988b). *Prehistoric Cultural Change at Kitselas Canyon*. Archaeological Survey of Canada Mercury Series Paper 138. Canadian Museum of Civilization, Hull.

Coupland, G. (1989). Warfare and social complexity on the Northwest Coast. In *Cultures in Conflict: Current Archaeological Perspectives*, edited by D.C. Tkaczuk and B.C. Vivian, The University of Calgary Archaeological Association, Calgary, pp. 205-214.

Coupland, G. (1993). Recent archaeological research on the northern coast. *BC Studies* 99:53-76.

Cove, J. (1982). The Gitksan traditional concept of land ownership. *Anthropologica* 24:3-17.

Duff, W. (1959). *Histories, Territories and Laws of the Kitwancool.* Anthropology in British Columbia Memoir 4. Royal British Columbia Museum, Victoria.

Duff, W. (1963). Stone clubs of the Skeena River area. In *Provincial Museum Annual Report for 1962*, edited by W. Duff, Royal British Columbia Museum, Victoria, pp. 2-12.

Ferguson, B. (1983). Warfare and redistributive exchange on the Northwest Coast. In *The Development of Political Organization in Native North America*, edited by E. Tooker, Proceedings of the American Ethnological Society, 1979, Washington, pp. 133-147.

Fisher, R. (1977). *Contact and Conflict: Indian-European Relations in British Columbia, 1774-1890.* University of British Columbia Press, Vancouver.

Halpin, M.M., and M. Seguin (1990). Tsimshian peoples: Southern Tsimshian, Coast Tsimshian, Nishga, and Gitksan. In *Handbook of North American Indians, Vol. 7, Northwest Coast*, edited by W. Suttles, Smithsonian Institution, Washington, pp. 267-284.

Kobrinsky, V. (1977). The Tsimshianization of the Carrier Indians. In *Problems in the Prehistory of the North American Subarctic: The Athapascan Question*, edited by J. Helmer, University of Calgary Archaeological Association, Calgary, pp. 201-210.

MacDonald, G.F. (1984). The epic of Nekt: The archaeology of metaphor. In *The Tsimshian: Images of the Past; Views for the Present*, edited by M. Sequin, University of British Columbia Press, Vancouver, pp. 65-81.

MacDonald, G.F. (1987). Introduction. In *Tsimshian Narratives: Volume 2, Trade and Warfare*, edited by G. MacDonald and J. Cove, Directorate Mercury Series Paper 3, Canadian Museum of Civilization, Hull, pp. vii-xxv.

MacDonald, G.F. (1989). *Kitwanga Fort Report.* Canadian Museum of Civilization, Hull.

MacDonald, G.F., and J. Cove, eds. (1987). *Tsimshian Narratives: Volume 2, Trade and Warfare.* Canadian Museum of Civilization, Hull.

MacDonald, G.F., and R.I. Inglis (1981). An overview of the North Coast Prehistory Project (1966-1980). *BC Studies* 48:37-63.

Maschner, H.D.G. (1991). The emergence of cultural complexity on the northern Northwest Coast. *Antiquity* 65:924-934.

Matson, R.G., and G. Coupland (1995). *The Prehistory of the Northwest Coast.* Academic Press, San Diego and London.

Montgomery, P. (1981). Terrace-Cedarvale Impact Assessment Survey. Unpublished manuscript, Resource Information Centre, Heritage Conservation Branch, Government of British Columbia, Victoria.

Prince, P. (1992). A People with History: Acculturation and Resistance in Kimsquit. M.A. Thesis, Department of Archaeology, Simon Fraser University, Burnaby.

Prince, P. (1995). Holding Down the Fort: Sedentism and Trade Routes in the Middle and Upper Skeena Valley. Paper read at Annual Meeting of the Canadian Archaeological Association, Kelowna.

Prince, P. (1996). Report on the 1995 Archaeological Survey in the Kitwanga Valley. Unpublished manuscript (Permit 95-147), Resource Information Centre, Heritage Conservation Branch, Government of British Columbia, Victoria.

Ray, A. (n.d.). The Early Economic History of the Gitksan and Wet´suweten Territory. Unpublished manuscript, Git-wet Tribal Council, Hazelton.

Rogers, D. (1990). *Objects of Change: The Archaeology and History of Arikara Contact With Europeans.* Smithsonian Institution Press, Washington.

Rubel, P.G., and A. Rosman (1983). The evolution of exchange structures and ranking: Some Northwest Coast and Athapaskan examples. *Journal of Anthropological Research* 39:1-25.

Steward, J. (1955). *A Theory of Culture Change: The Methodology of Multilinear Evolution.* University of Illinois Press, Chicago.

Prospects and Opportunities for Archaeological Site Management in the Prince Rupert Harbour Area

Bjorn O. Simonsen

ABSTRACT

The Prince Rupert Harbour area has been the scene of numerous archaeological investigations over the past three decades, with the work of George MacDonald, Richard Inglis, David Archer, and Gary Coupland among the most notable. Despite all this attention, there is still no long-term archaeological resource management plan for this important part of the Northwest Coast culture area. The paper examines the reasons for that absence in the context of confusing and often conflicting jurisdictional factors which have tended to discourage planning efforts. This has condemned archaeological resources within the harbour area to an uncertain future, very much like the "demolition by neglect" syndrome affecting the preservation of more recent heritage structures. The paper examines the future roles of provincial and federal government agencies in developing long-term management and site protection plans, and contrasts this with the prospects and viability of local government and First Nations efforts, for both the Prince Rupert Harbour area and other locations throughout British Columbia and Canada.

RÉSUMÉ

La région du Prince Rupert Harbour a constitué, au cours des trois dernières décennies, la scène de nombreuses fouilles archéologiques, dont les plus connues sont celles de George McDonald, de Richard Inglis, de David Archer, et de Gary Coupland. En dépit de toute cette attention, il n'existe pas encore un plan de gestion à long terme des ressources archéologiques

In *Perspectives on Northern Northwest Coast Prehistory*, edited by Jerome S. Cybulski. Hull: Canadian Museum of Civilization, Archaeological Survey of Canada, Mercury Series Paper 160, pp. 269-281, © 2001.

pour cette importante partie de cette région culturelle de la Côte Nord-Ouest. Cet article examine les raisons qui expliquent cette absence dans le cadre de facteurs souvent confus et conflictuels de juridiction qui ont eu tendance à décourager les efforts de planification. Cette situation a condamné les ressources archéologiques dans la région du port à un avenir incertain, à l'image du syndrome de la «démolition par négligence» qui affecte la préservation du patrimoine bâti plus récent. Cet article examine le rôle futur des agences gouvernementales, provinciales et fédérales, à développer des plans de gestion et de protection des sites à long terme, et en fait la critique compte tenu des perspectives et de la viabilité des efforts déployés par le gouvernement local et celui des Autochtones, à la fois pour la région de Prince Rupert Harbour et d'autres endroits en Colombie-Britannique et au Canada.

INTRODUCTION AND BACKGROUND

This paper is modified from a version originally prepared for presentation in a symposium organized for the 29th Annual Meeting of the Canadian Archaeological Association entitled "Perspectives on Northern Northwest Coast Prehistory, 1966-1996." The symposium marked the inception of the 30th anniversary of the North Coast Prehistory Project which was conceived and directed by Dr. George F. MacDonald of the Canadian Museum of Civilization. Archaeological work at Prince Rupert Harbour formed a major component of the project, resulting in an initial inventory of archaeological sites in the Prince Rupert area and establishing the first archaeological sequence for the north coast of British Columbia based on excavation of a number of shell midden sites (MacDonald and Inglis 1981). Several archaeology students who worked under George MacDonald's general direction have continued with site inventory and excavation work in the Prince Rupert region, among them David Archer, Richard Inglis and Gary Coupland (e.g., Inglis 1976; Coupland, Bissell and King 1993; Archer, this volume). The author was also one of the students who continued an involvement with north coast archaeology during the subsequent three decades, mainly in the form of archaeological impact assessment and salvage projects (Simonsen 1988).

Since the initiation of the Prince Rupert Harbour project in 1966, the archaeological landscape of the area has seen much change. Although a number of both large and small-scale archaeological salvage projects have taken place in response to the pressures of urban development, with the early 1970's archaeological salvage project at the Lachane site (GbTo 33) directed by Richard Inglis being the largest, many of the harbour's archaeological resources are still relatively intact. This is despite the affects of major port developments over the past 20 years, which destroyed all of the Lachane site, and the combined effects of numerous smaller development projects associated with the growth of Prince Rupert and its harbour facilities. It is probably fair to say that the extant archaeological resources in the Prince Rupert region have remained in a relatively undisturbed state as a result of their isolation (from active development areas) and by the fact that many such sites are situated within unoccupied Indian Reserve lands. The latter category of land tenure within the harbour area is significant in both size and numbers and most of the reserves remain undeveloped except for late nineteenth and early twentieth century uses as garden plots by Metlakatla based First Nations families.

The active role played by the Museum of Northern British Columbia must also be mentioned in the context of archaeological preservation and public awareness within the north coast area. This institution has always had a keen interest in Prince Rupert's archaeological past and this interest increased in response to George MacDonald's mid-1960's Prince Rupert program. The museum has not only played a major role in the protection of archaeological resources and in the interpretation of the area's archaeological history to residents and visitors alike, but has worked closely with the Metlakatla Indian Band in the preservation and management of local archaeological resources.

There is a growing trend in British Columbia, as well as in other parts of North America and the world, for indigenous (or First Nations) groups to begin to take control of the protection and management of their own cultural heritage resources from existing government agencies. This movement has taken on special significance in British Columbia in the context of current treaty negotiations between First Nations and the two senior levels of government, federal and provincial. The Treaty Process, which involves roughly half of all Indian Bands in British Columbia, is moving at a very slow pace, possibly due to a lack of government will to proceed rapidly with the resolution of settlements which would not only see the transfer of considerable amounts of Crown Lands (both Federal and Provincial) to various First Nations groups but also include substantial compensation packages, mostly in the form of cash settlements. The latter form of compensation will be particularly significant in treaty settlements for urban areas where remaining Crown Land is almost non-existent.

British Columbia First Nations are particularly interested in assuming a greater role in the management and protection of archaeological resources, as compared to so-called "traditional use areas" and other types of heritage resources, since there is a well established process (including a legislative base) for this, but which is presently managed by the province. Traditional use areas such as hunting territory, fishing places, plant gathering areas, etc. are not given the same focus and most are not being protected by existing legislation. B.C. First Nations are, therefore, targeting archaeological resources in their efforts to become masters of their own heritage.

THE ARCHAEOLOGICAL RESOURCE MANAGEMENT CONTEXT

Even though archaeological resource management (ARM) programs exist in some form within all provincial and territorial jurisdictions in Canada and are minimally present within the federal government system, their effectiveness tends to be poor. All provincial jurisdictions currently have legislation in place which professes to protect archaeological resources and which makes provision for a process to manage the exploitation of archaeological resources. The latter is done almost exclusively through permit systems which attempt to regulate how and by whom archaeological resources can be exploited. Existing permit systems, therefore, focus on the regulation of archaeologists and the archaeological discipline in general through often cumbersome bureaucratic processes rather than on the protection of the actual archaeological resource. Where a regulatory body exists (and not every province in Canada has one), they tend to be centralized in provincial capitals rather than being de-centralized through a regional network of offices and staff resources. Only Quebec and Ontario maintain minimal decentralized administrations for archaeological protection and management purposes. British Columbia has a totally centralized administration for ARM and the shortfalls of this will be made clear in a later section of the paper.

Of particular significance to the subject matter of this paper is the fact that local government administrations within British Columbia (i.e. Regional Districts and Municipal Governments) have no role in the protection or long term management of archaeological resources that are associated with First Nations heritage. If one were to ask a local government politician or administrator why this is the case, they would probably say that archaeology falls within the exclusive jurisdiction of the province. Yet this is not necessarily so. Although perusal of the *B.C. Heritage Conservation Act* (Government of British Columbia 1994) certainly gives the impression that archaeology is entirely within the realm of provincial government responsibility and control, nothing in the Act forbids a local government to set up its own archaeological resource management program (under a Heritage Commission) or to designate an archaeological site as an added protection measure.

Unfortunately, municipalities have been given the impression that archaeology is something that is better left to the province and to professional archaeologists. The often self-imposed mysticism of the discipline, coupled with a fiercely protective government bureaucracy and the interests of an academic establishment focused on protecting its turf has conspired against the localization of archaeological resource management not only in British Columbia but throughout Canada.

Canada also stands out as one of the few nations in the world that has not enacted comprehensive federal antiquities legislation to protect archaeological resources and empower the creation and maintenance of a national ARM administration. This is the case despite being a signatory to every international convention calling for all states to enact such legislation. The most commonly heard reason for this state of affairs is that archaeological resources in Canada are primarily a provincial or territorial responsibility and that these jurisdictions already have adequate legislation and management programs in place. This is similar to the argument used by local governments, as outlined above, as a reason to not manage archaeological resources within their own jurisdictions. In the case of the federal government, there is not even legislation on the books which protects archaeological resources on lands under their own exclusive jurisdiction. Such lands include Indian Reserves, National Harbours, and lands related to National Defense, to mention a only a few.

Before totally condemning the Government of Canada for failing in its duty to protect and manage archaeological resources, it must be noted that archaeological sites and features located within the boundaries of National Parks are given a measure of protection under the terms of the National Parks Act. The Parks Canada division of the Department of Canadian Heritage maintains an active archaeological management, research, and interpretive program with decentralized offices and staff in many regions of the country. However, a brief attempt in the early 1990's by the Government of Canada to enact antiquities legislation and a national office to administer an ARM program fell by the wayside. We are told that opposition to the proposed legislative package by some First Nations organizations who could not support the notion of Crown ownership of archaeological resources sounded its death knell. In the end, the short-lived federal ARM office fell victim to government budget cuts.

COMPONENTS OF A SUCCESSFUL ARM PROGRAM

The most successful archaeological resources management programs are those which have the following components:

1) strong political will to maintain a comprehensive and well resourced program;

2) strong antiquities legislation or regulations that provide:
   a) clear guidelines and penalties for infractions,
   b) adequate court back-up services (i.e. prosecution and enforcement); and
   c) adequate penalties to deter infractions

3) a strong, ongoing archaeological site inventory program;

4) a site assessment and evaluation program tied to a long-term site management and preservation program; and

5) a decentralized administration that provides for regional offices and staff.

The Province of Ontario has probably come closest to establishing ARM programs which include most of these components. Ontario was, at one time, the only jurisdiction in Canada with a truly regional network of ARM offices. Also in the past, Alberta maintained a system of regional archaeologists from an administrative base in Edmonton. Although Ontario still maintains a small decentralized system, Alberta has seen most of its former ARM program decimated as a result of government budgetary cuts and program restructuring.

An apparent general lack of political will for the establishment and (or) maintenance of strong ARM programs in Canada seems to be tied to our collective governments' peculiar habit of passing (often) strong legislation which boldly declares "thou shalt not disturb archaeological resources," and then ignoring the enforcement and administration of such legislation. Our own peculiar form of parliamentary democracy seems incapable of ensuring that governments be held accountable for the enforcement and proper administration of their own laws. Do governments and government administrations not have a fiduciary responsibility to uphold the laws and regulations that they have assumed the responsibility of enforcing? In Canada, it appears that the answer is no.

Compare this to the situation in the United States of America. There, legislation is not passed unless the government responsible, whether at the Federal or State level, commits adequate funding and staff resources to ensure that the law being proposed can be enforced and adequately administered. These become fiduciary responsibilities and both government agencies and their administrations are often taken to court (by private citizens or special interest groups) for not carrying out these responsibilities. This comparison makes one wonder if any level of government in Canada should even attempt to legislate for the protection and management of archaeological resources if it is not their intention to follow-through by providing adequate resources for enforcement and administration.

PROSPECTS FOR LOCALLY-BASED ARM PROGRAMS

As illustrated above, there are no existing provincial or federal government ARM programs in Canada that are even close to being considered adequate, apparently due to a lack of political will and the lack of fiduciary accountability on the part of governments and their administrations. This situation is not expected to improve and, in fact, most established ARM programs have been severely reduced over the past few years as a result of government cut-backs and restructuring. The present situation in British Columbia has followed the national trend with no change to the ongoing lack of interest at the political level towards supporting adequate ARM programs. Is the time right for local government at either the municipal or regional district level to become involved in the protection and management of archaeological resources? Are there other possibilities that would allow more regionally-based organizations, such as museums and heritage organizations, to become involved? And what about the role of First Nations in all of this? Is it not their heritage that we are talking about here?

Given the present situation in the province of British Columbia, as well as in most other Canadian provinces, in order for local or regionally-based ARM programs to work and be cost effective, they would have to be a part of a province-wide network that had direct support from the provincial level of government and which operated under the authority of provincial legislation. However, as already pointed out there is neither the political will nor the resource allocations and fiduciary accountability in the present system for such a program to work, even though it would be a great improvement over what now exists.

Beyond the faint possibilities of a senior-level government supported ARM program, could a municipality or a regional district support such a program on its own? Certainly at the Regional District level in B.C. this would be possible, especially if combined with an overall program of Cultural Resource Management (CRM) that included all aspects of cultural heritage (i.e. archaeology, historic sites and buildings, a regional museums network, Heritage Commissions, etc.). Such a program could be supported by various levels of government, as well as by fee for service charges to developers and others using the services of the regional CRM administration. Under such a scheme, archaeological resources would be given overall protection under provincial legislation (similar to the current *Heritage Conservation Act*), but the responsibility for protection and management would be divested in each of about thirty Regional Districts through a Heritage Commission or similar umbrella organization.

The above scenario implies the creation of thirty Heritage Commissions - one for each Regional District in the province - and therein lies a major problem. The possibility for the creation and funding of thirty separate heritage management units throughout British Columbia, given the present fiscal and political climate, is almost inconceivable. Is there another option? The following section of the paper explores the possibility of a First Nations organized and run ARM program and looks at opportunities for such a program to be a model for other First Nations-run Archaeological Resources Management agencies throughout Canada.

A FIRST NATIONS ARM PROGRAM FOR BRITISH COLUMBIA

A First Nations oriented program for the management and protection of archaeological resources for any area of British Columbia could be set up under the auspices of either an individual Indian Band, or, for a much larger territory, a Tribal Council. It may also be possible to create a completely new First Nations organization dedicated to the specific tasks of operating a combined ARM and CRM program. If the area to be included in such a program were limited, an individual Band might be the most appropriate base for such a program. However, since a successful program would require a minimum of one full-time staff person - preferably someone with archaeological/ARM training and experience - as well as an office and additional resources to support a site inventory and assessment program, it would be difficult to support financially under a single Band administration. This scenario also assumes that the archaeological resources of any particular area can be directly associated with the present constituents of the local Indian Band and that there are no overlapping claims to territory or cultural resources such as archaeological sites.

A number of B.C. First Nations have initiated their own process for managing cultural heritage resources within their territories. These include the Kamloops Indian Band, the Skeetchesten Indian Band, the Sto:lo Nation, the Heiltsuk Nation, the Ktunaxa-Kinbasket Tribal Council and the Tsilhqot'in National Government, to name a few. As implied by the foregoing organization's names, some programs are at the local Band level of organization while others are administered at the Tribal Council level. For the purposes of this paper, and to elaborate on the author's own vision for a regionalized approach to the management of First Nations cultural heritage resources, I will use the Tsimshian Tribal Council (TTC) of British Columbia's north coast region as an example of how a First Nations oriented and administered ARM/CRM program might work.

In my view, the most workable scenario from both political and administrative standpoints would be for the Tsimshian Tribal Council, based in Prince Rupert and representing the interests of seven separate Bands who constitute all groups who traditionally occupied or utilized the north coast area of British Columbia, to administer a comprehensive ARM program. For this program to be cost effective and in keeping with the overall mandate of the Tsimshian Tribal Council, it would include all of the traditional territories of the various nations who are members of the TTC.

From an archaeological resources management point of view, it makes sense to administer the archaeological resources of this vast coastal area from a regional perspective. Prince Rupert would be the most practical administrative centre for a Tsimshian Nation ARM/CRM program since this centre is well positioned geographically to all of the other parts, contains the head office of the TTC, is the center of various government offices and related infrastructure, and is where there is most pressure on archaeological resources from development activity. First Nations individuals from this region of B.C. can also obtain college and university level education in anthropology or archaeology, as well as specific resource management oriented training (such as GIS mapping), through the Community College system or the University of Northern British Columbia.

A regional First Nations based ARM program at Prince Rupert would be ultimately responsible to the Tsimshian Tribal Council but would have its own Board of Directors (or Steering Committee) to set policy, review program proposals and applications for archaeological investigations and to provide advice and direction to staff. The composition of the Board or Committee would be representative of the various Tsimshian groups having an interest in the ARM/CRM program and willing to support its aims. The Tsimshian ARM/CRM unit would employ or contract professional and technical staff headed by a qualified archaeologist with previous experience in CRM work. The ARM/CRM unit would be responsible for running an ongoing site inventory and assessment program as well as ongoing archaeological research and interpretive programs, and would administer a permit program related to archaeological research projects by professional archaeologists, and impact assessments sponsored by land development proponents.

The creation of a First Nations based ARM/CRM program as outlined above, could act as a catalyst for attracting First Nations individuals to participate directly in archaeological research and resource management activities including field survey and excavation work, laboratory analysis, artifact conservation tasks, and basic administrative positions. Although there are more and more First Nations students enrolling in university and college based archaeological programs, the number of graduates from these programs remains low. In my view, this is directly tied to the lack of opportunities for First Nations graduates to obtain meaningful employment in the archaeological research and ARM fields. The proposed ARM/CRM program would create more educational and training opportunities in these fields for First Nations individuals and the program could easily be tied into one or more university and college based cultural resource management programs through a co-op type arrangement that could benefit all parties.. Unfortunately, these programs do not currently exist, in part because the province's universities and colleges have been slow in identifying job-oriented training as a priority, opting instead for traditional academically based offerings.

LAYING THE FOUNDATIONS FOR THE ARM/CRM PROGRAM

As already alluded to in an earlier section of this paper, the protection and management of archaeological resources within British Columbia is presently within the exclusive jurisdiction of the provincial government, administered through the Archaeology Branch of the Ministry of Small Business, Tourism and Culture. The Archaeology Branch administers the archaeology components of the *Heritage Conservation Act* from a centralized office in Victoria, the provincial capital, and may not be fully capable of carrying out its mandate due to a number of factors. These include deficiencies in resources (staff and money), lack of a presence outside of Victoria, an unclear mandate, lack of interest and support at the political level, and inconsistent priorities.

From a First Nations perspective, there are growing concerns that despite the existence of provincial legislation to protect archaeological resources, sites continue to be destroyed and First Nations do not have much say in the protection and management of their own heritage resources. The archaeological component of the *Heritage Conservation Act* is often seen as working against the wishes of First Nations to preserve the past by the issuance of "Investigation Permits" that authorize archaeological investigations of a site or "Alteration Permits" which allow developers to destroy archaeological remains during the process of development. Many First Nations see the archaeological permit process simply as a means to resolve development pressures through systematic archaeological investigation projects. These are, in turn, often perceived simply as a means of legitimizing the exploitation of archaeological resources by a privileged few, namely those in the archaeological community. The *Act* presently vests all legal authority for the management of archaeological resources in the hands of the province (notwithstanding the comments made earlier in this paper concerning potential involvement by Municipalities and Regional Districts). Could a First Nations based ARM program, as proposed above, gain the legal power to administer the archaeological components of the present *Heritage Conservation Act*?

Following from the model presented earlier, an obvious long-term option is for an existing First Nation organization such as the Tsimshian Tribal Council, acting on behalf of its member groups, to negotiate the devolvement of provincial responsibility for archaeological resources management to themselves, either through direct negotiations with the government of British Columbia or through the current treaty process or other avenues.

To be effective, the devolvement of ARM/CRM responsibilities from the province to the TTC must include all known and potential Tsimshian archaeological resources, whether situated on "Tsimshian Land", "Crown Land", or "Private Lands." In other words, Tsimshian archaeological resources would be managed based on cultural affiliation criteria rather that along legal land status lines.

A short term solution for the devolvement of provincial archaeological resources management responsibilities to the TTC would be for the TTC to negotiate an Interim Agreement with the Province of British Columbia by invoking a yet to be used section of the *Heritage Conservation Act* which allows the Minister responsible for its administration to enter into such agreements with First Nations. This section of the Heritage Conservation Act (Section 4) states that:

> The Province may enter into a formal agreement with a first nation with respect to the conservation and protection of heritage sites and heritage objects that represent the cultural heritage of the aboriginal people that are represented by that first nation.

Section 4 also empowers the Minister to transfer several key responsibilities related to the administration of the *Act*, including the issuance of Permits for archaeological investigations, to a First Nation (Government of British Columbia 1994: Section 4.1 (4) (e)). Presumably, any interim agreement such as that suggested above would be replaced by the terms of a Treaty that may eventually come into force between the Tsimshian Nation on the one hand and British Columbia and Canada on the other. The terms of the treaty might also include measures for direct Tsimshian responsibility for the management of archaeological resources within Federal Crown lands, since, to my knowledge, no Federal mechanism similar to Section 4.1 of the provincial *Heritage Conservation Act* exists at the present time.

CONCLUSIONS

The foregoing sections of this paper have provided evidence to show that archaeological resource management in Canada is still in its infancy with no serious activity at the federal government level. Within British Columbia the situation is somewhat better with strong legislation in place. However, there is a lack of political will and government resources for the enforcement of legislation and for an effective archaeological resource management program. In particular, the lack of a decentralized, regional approach to ARM has been detrimental to site conservation efforts and in providing for local input to the resource management process. Although it is possible for local governments to become active in the ARM process, this has not happened, mostly due to a perception that archaeology is the sole responsibility of the province through its Archaeology Branch.

The apparent present state of senior government neglect and malaise can be attributed in part to shrinking resources and changing priorities within government. However, the real culprit appears to be a lack of political will coupled with ineffective efforts on the part of the archaeological community to convince governments that archaeological resources are important and should be preserved and properly managed. Efforts by some archaeological interest groups (e.g., the Canadian Archaeological Association; see Nicholson, Pokotylo and Williamson 1996) to enlist the support of First Nations have not been very successful and there is a perception among the latter that archaeologists are an elitist group who exploit First Nations' archaeological resources for their own ends.

This paper has argued that archaeological resources could be better managed at the local or regional level either by Municipal governments or by Regional Districts. A case has also been made for the direct management of archaeological resources by local First Nations who have a direct cultural link with the archaeological resources of their traditional territory, through a dedicated Cultural Heritage Resources Management Unit, created in the short term through an interim agreement between First Nations organizations and the Province of British Columbia, and which could in the long term be an important feature of an eventual Treaty Agreement between First Nations and the Provincial and Federal governments.

REFERENCES CITED

Coupland, G., C. Bissell, and S. King (1993). Prehistoric subsistence and seasonality at Prince Rupert Harbour: Evidence from the McNichol Creek site. *Canadian Journal of Archaeology* 17:59-73.

Government of British Columbia (1994). *The Heritage Conservation Act (Chapter 165)*. The Queen's Printer, Victoria.

Inglis, R.I. (1976). 'Wet' site distribution – the northern case, GbTo-33 – the Lachane site. In *The Excavation of Water-Saturated Archaeological Sites (Wet Sites) on the Northwest Coast of North America*, edited by D.R. Croes, Archaeological Survey of Canada Mercury Series Paper 50, Canadian Museum of Civilization, Hull, pp. 158-185.

MacDonald, G.F., and R.I. Inglis (1981). An overview of the North Coast Prehistory Project (1966-1980). *BC Studies* 48:37-63.

Nicholson, B., D. Pokotylo, and R. Williamson, eds. (1996). *CAA/AAC Statement of Principles for Ethical Conduct Pertaining to Aboriginal Peoples: A Report from the Aboriginal Heritage Committee*. Canadian Archaeological Association and Department of Communications, Ottawa.

Simonsen, B.O. (1988). Final Report on Archaeological Salvage Excavations and Construction Monitoring at the Lachane Site (GbTo-33) Prince Rupert, B.C. Unpublished manuscript (Ms. No. 3033), Information Management Services (Archaeological Records), Canadian Museum of Civilization, Hull.